CONTEMPORARY POETRY

CONTEMPORARY POETRY

EDITED BY

MARGUERITE WILKINSON

Granger Index Reprint Series

BOOKS FOR LIBRARIES PRESS
PLAINVIEW, NEW YORK

First Published 1923
Reprinted 1975

REF
PR 1224
.W5
1973
Cop.1

Library of Congress Cataloging in Publication Data

Wilkinson, Marguerite Ogden Bigelow, 1883-1928, comp.
    Contemporary poetry.

    (Granger index reprint series)
    Reprint of the 1923 ed., issued in series: Modern
readers' series.
    1. English poetry--19th century. 2. English
poetry--20th century. 3. American poetry--19th
century. 4. American poetry--20th century. I. Title.
II. Series: Modern readers' series.
PR1224.W5 1973   821'.008   73-2833
ISBN 0-8369-6416-0

To My Lifelong Friend
Julia L. Sheffield

PREFACE

The poetry presented and discussed in this book has been written and published within a period of about fifty years. The American section begins with the work of James Whitcomb Riley, who was born in 1849, and the British section with that of William Ernest Henley, born the same year. I believe that no work by poets born before 1849 is offered for consideration in these pages.

This temporal line of demarcation for the beginning of the period may seem to be arbitrary, but it serves a practical purpose. It releases me from the impossible task of dealing fairly with the great Victorians, and with giants like Thomas Hardy and Walt Whitman, in a book devoted chiefly to their successors. To be sure, it makes it necessary to pass over the matchless lyrics of Christina Rossetti, the greatest of the singing women of England, who was born on December 5, 1830, and to disregard, also, the distinguished achievement of our American lyrist, Emily Dickinson, born just five days later. But like the great men who were their contemporaries, these two poets are sure of their laurels, and they deserve consideration at length and in a place apart. Readers of good literature are certain to find them sooner or later.

At the other end of the period I am setting the year 1915. In general it is true that poets are not represented in this volume unless part of their work was introduced to the public before 1915. But this is a rough boundary line and, in a few instances, I am going a little beyond it. These exceptions are made by request of my publishers and not because I wish to break my own rules. Whenever an exception is made it is because the poems included or the poets represented, although not known for so long a time as the others, are now as well known and have, moreover, a decided value in this book. Several poems of the war published after 1915 are already as well known as popular poems of the period published before that year and have already made their makers famous. Aline Kilmer and Jean Starr Untermeyer were well known in literary circles before their books were published and their poetry is as interesting to the public as the poetry of their husbands, Joyce Kilmer and Louis Untermeyer.

Most of the poems in this collection have been tested by what little time has elapsed since their publication and have won not only the approval of critics, but also the interest of the public that reads poetry. I have not used poems that are mere technical experiments, poems that have value only for critics, poems that are too sophisticated and subtle to be interesting to normal young people. Much of what is being written nowadays appeals only to mature intellectuals, to people who have studied poetry deeply and long. To such readers we might commend the work of T. S. Eliot, D. H. Lawrence, Maxwell Bodenheim, Ezra Pound, Conrad Aiken, and others who have challenged the serious attention of our reviewers. But this book is not for mature intellectuals. It is not for specialists. It is for the young sons and daughters of ordinary intelligent Americans. For that reason the poems included in it can all, in one way or another, reach into the common life. It is a conservative collection of familiar poems by contemporary poets. And while I regret that I was unable to secure permission to use Mr. Aiken's "Morning Song of Senlin" and Mr. Pound's "Ballad of The Goodly Fere," I am comforted by the hope that students more than ordinarily interested in poetry will find these poems later. Their authors, certainly, will be better understood in college days (or later) than in the high school period.

The treatment accorded William Vaughn Moody can hardly be explained in this way. I have done my best to persuade his publishers to permit me to represent him to better advantage. It has been impossible.

Let me say, also, that no attempt has been made to "represent all the poets." I have tried to put as few burdens as possible on the minds of students and have preferred to represent poets by one thoroughly good poem — a long poem if that seemed most appropriate — rather than to fill up the book with numerous odds and ends of a negligible sort by poets relatively unimportant to young people. I have used long narratives whenever I have been able to find them, rather than brief and bizarre "objects of art." The number of poets represented is not great, but the quality of the poems used is, I believe, excellent.

This book has been planned for use as a text in schools that offer courses in contemporary poetry. Nevertheless, I have made it with the hope that it will be enjoyed even more than it is studied. For without enjoyment the study of an art is fruitless. I hope that readers will find here a happy introduction to contemporary poetry. I hope that they will find, also, an incentive to go on reading more contemporary poetry, to go on reading about it. Perhaps it will not be amiss to set down the names of books suitable for supplementary reading.

First of all I should suggest the use of *The Little Book of Modern Verse* and *The Second Book of Modern Verse* by Jessie B. Rittenhouse (Houghton Mifflin). They are the best of all American anthologies. No other American anthologist has ever shown such excellent taste, such imperturbability before changing literary fashions, such catholicity and freedom from unfair prejudice.

For a general understanding of the meaning and value of poetry the reader should seek Max Eastman's admirably written book on *The Enjoyment of Poetry* (Scribner's). Louis Untermeyer's *New Era in American Poetry* (Holt) is good reading, and the latest volume of Ward's *English Poets* (Macmillan) will be helpful. A fuller explanation of my own thought about contemporary poetry is to be found in *New Voices* (Macmillan).

MARGUERITE WILKINSON.

INDEX OF POETS

INDEX OF POETS

INDEX OF POETS

INDEX OF POEMS

INDEX OF POEMS

INDEX OF POEMS

INDEX OF POEMS

CONTENTS

CONTENTS

CONTENTS

CONTENTS

CONTENTS

ENGLISH, IRISH AND CANADIAN POETS

CONTENTS

CONTENTS

CONTENTS

CONTEMPORARY POETRY

AN INTRODUCTION

We know that poetry is not a mere pastime for scholars, although the study of it is a subtle and delightful occupation for mature minds. It is not a more or less difficult intellectual game played by refined people in their leisure hours. It does not exist in order that it may be studied. On the contrary, it is a natural and powerful art concerned with feelings shared by all mankind. Poets mean it to give pleasure, or that deeper and more solemn satisfaction called **Poetry** joy. Poetry is the sharing of life in patterns of rhythmical words.

For this reason poetry should not be analyzed until it has been enjoyed. Like religion, it should come to people first of all as an experience. Later, because of the value of that experience, they will be willing, perhaps eager, to learn what can be learned about it by analysis; they will show an intelligent interest in design, rhythm, images, symbols, and diction.

Any attempt to reverse this natural order of procedure can do little good and may do much harm. The person who has never enjoyed a poem does not care how poems are made, does not know, in his own mind, why they should ever be made. If circumstances make it necessary for him to begin his knowledge of poetry by learning to dissect poems, he may learn a good deal about poetry without ever knowing poetry at all. And because of the association of irksomeness with his initiation he may acquire a distaste for an art which might have enriched his life. But if he is introduced to poetry in a happier and more human way, if he finds in it a beautiful experience, something to be enjoyed and shared, he will have, from the beginning, a far keener interest in it, and, eventually, a fuller understanding of the rudiments of the art.

Suppose a boy reads Mr. Chesterton's magnificent "Lepanto" simply with a view to finding out how many spondees are in its martial lines. Is it not likely that he will miss the details of the story, the flash and glow of the picturing, the heroic emotion, the superb energy of the music in which those spondees have their part? But the boy who knows the historical facts on which the poem is founded; who reads it aloud, as well as silently, with heart and mind in the story; who can, once and forever, "get into the swing of it," as the saying goes—that boy will miss none of the good things which a poem ought to give, and, furthermore, he may discover for himself that certain kinds of syllables in juxtaposition produce a certain musical effect that stirs people in a certain real and definite way. When that has happened, his ears are open to the music of poetry and the study of scansion becomes less difficult and much more interesting.

Or suppose that a young girl reads Walter de la Mare's exquisite little nocturne, "Silver," with a mind conscientiously bent on discovering the figures of speech in it. Is it not probable that she will miss the lovely peace of the picture, the calm melody of the language, the concentrated quietness of the mood? But if she reads "Silver" simply with the hope of sharing a fine spiritual experience, she is likely to find these good things, and may discover for herself, sooner or later, what happy miracles can be wrought through the use of personification, metaphor, simile, and adroit repetition. She will have gained an incentive to the study of all literary devices used to achieve such altogether lovable results.

No matter how much we may know about poetry, our approach to a poem should always be as simple and natural as possible, the result of a willingness to share an experience with the poet. Even the sophisticated critic must *taste the flavor* of a poem before he can pronounce upon it justly or describe its composition. And this is true because, in all poetry worthy of the name, music and meaning, image and emotion, form and substance, are so closely united that they cannot be separated without great loss. Nothing in a poem should ever be considered except in relation to the rest of the poem. What the poem as a whole has to give, what it sings, what it is — that is what concerns the reader. If it does not concern him, we need not bother about it at all, for our time will surely be wasted.

Sara Teasdale, our eminent woman lyrist, who has just made an admirable anthology for young children called *Rainbow Gold* (Macmillan), is most emphatic in what she has to say about presenting poetry to them.

"I do not think a child should have to analyze poetry at all. It is likely to turn him against it forever. A love of poetry is too valuable a possession to jeopardize it by turning poetry into a task."

And again she says: "A child should enjoy a poem just as he enjoys going out in an automobile, without understanding the mechanism of it, and without needing to know what was in the inventor's mind when he made it."

These statements, of course, need some qualification. Sara Teasdale would not wish the adult to remain forever in ignorance of the history of poetry, of the laws of the art, of the qualities that mean excellence. But in common with all

true poets she regrets the fact that the scientific approach is
often the first and only approach made to poetry. In
common with all good poets she desires an artistic approach,
which is, in reality, simpler, easier, and more direct. Such
an approach lets discernment and discrimination and
analysis follow receptivity, as they should. It lets us look
at the flower for a while before attempting to dissect its parts.
It does not begin by making receptivity and interest im-
possible. And it gives the strongest possible incentive to
study by making people wish to understand an experience
which they have made their own.

The first thing to do with any poem is to read it, once
silently, and then aloud. It should be well read the first
time it is heard by any group so that the music of it will be
evident. A discussion of the mood, meaning, and manner
of the poem may follow, in which as many people as possible
are encouraged to take part. And it may happen that the
most suggestive and inspiring remarks will be made by the
simplest, not by the cleverest, of the listeners. For like
religion again, poetry is sometimes hidden from the wise
that it may be revealed to babes. After the discussion the
poem should be read again by another reader, and the
chances are that the group will hear much more in it than
was heard at first, provided that the discussion was free and
not forced or formal. When a taste for poetry and an
interest in it have been cultivated in this way, perhaps it will
be safe to begin the analytical study necessary for educa-
tional purposes, letting the beginning be gradual and adven-
turous, so that all who study may feel a part of the pleasure
of making artistic discoveries.

A few of the poems in this book could be well read by a
class in unison. Richard Hovey's famous "Stein Song,"

Reading Poetry

Rudyard Kipling's "Recessional," and "America the Beautiful," by Katharine Lee Bates are poems of this character. "The Santa Fé Trail" by Vachel Lindsay and "A Chant Out of Doors" by Marguerite Wilkinson, might be read antiphonally, one person taking the interpolated lines like the song of the "Rachel Jane" in "The Santa Fé Trail" or the stanzas in "A Chant Out of Doors" and the others in the group taking the main narrative or the choral parts. Just as people with poor voices enjoy singing hymns in church though they would never sing solos, so people who do not enjoy reading alone can get a certain pleasure from reading poems in this way if the reading is well managed. It is an excellent training in rhythm.

The danger of merely noisy reading must be avoided, however, for that would spoil any poem, although, in poems like "The Santa Fé Trail," a certain exuberance is essential. And certain kinds of poetry should never be read in unison. It would be unendurable to hear a group of imperfectly trained readers jogging along together through the perfect lines of "The Wild Swans at Coole" by William Butler Yeats, or through the delicate verbal music of "Tears" by Lizette Woodworth Reese. Reading in unison should be a practice reserved for poems in which a certain choral feeling is implicit, for hymns, maxims, or jolly ballads like "The Glory Trail" by Badger Clark.

The reading of poetry is an art in itself, and few there be that find out how it should be done. Although many critics will disagree, it is my opinion that poets, in general, read lyrics better than trained "readers" and "elocutionists," because they are mindful of the music and realize that a certain quietness of mind and heart are essential to the reception of a lyric. The trained "reader" is usually a "dramatic reader," accustomed to a conversational style, and makes the lyric sound conversational. But the best lyric is most clearly not conversation, but song. The reader must subordinate his own personality to the music of the lines, therefore, so that in quietness, and without distraction, the song may be heard.

Here again the simple and sincere approach to poetry is of great assistance. Even the reader should simply receive and share the poem. If he can, he will escape self-consciousness, and he will not need to worry about "expression." That will take care of itself. For if we read clearly and rather slowly, following the poet's music, and if we are at one with the poems we read, trusting them to create their own atmosphere, it is difficult not to get a sense of their meaning into our voices. Therefore, it is desirable that the reader, and all of the others in the group, whether they read aloud or not, should come to poetry with the hope of sharing an experience.

The poems in this book offer an exceedingly wide range of poetic experience. They are of many kinds. It is a far cry from the delicate whimsy of John Drinkwater's "Feckenham Men" to the vigorous masculine adventure of Rudyard Kipling's "Ballad of East and West," or from the social passion of Edwin Markham's "Man With a Hoe" to the suggestive picturing in miniatures like Alfred Kreymborg's "Idealists" and "Old Manuscript." Naturally, our response to poetic experience should be varied, according to kind.

We should not be solemn when we read "In the Poppy Field" by James Stephens, and we should take up "The Glory Trail" by Badger Clark with humor and the glorious zest of play. When we read John Hall Wheelock's "Earth" we may be thoughtful, and we should be serious with Francis Thompson. In this matter again the simplicity of our approach will save us from difficulty. For if we expect to share an experience, we shall not be trying to make the poet's lines accommodate themselves to our moods, but, far more courteously, we shall be trying to share what the poet has to give.

Sometimes that sharing is impossible for us. What then? Shall we blame the poet? Shall we blame ourselves? In justice we should not blame anybody. No sane person can possibly like all of the poems in any collection. The chances are that even the maker of the collection does not like everything in it, but has included a number of selections that have found favor with other critics. It is quite possible for a tolerant person to realize that there may be certain aesthetic values in a poem which has no meaning for him and gives him no pleasure. It is quite possible for such a person to realize that the particular poem which means nothing to him Likes may mean more than any other in the book to some other and
Dislikes human being whose taste is neither better nor worse than his own, but simply of another kind. Many people whose lives might otherwise be enriched by the enjoyment of poetry are led to suppose that they do not like it by other well-meaning people who have offered the wrong poem at the wrong time in the wrong way. To pretend that we should all like all of these poems is to encourage hypocrisy. The mere fact that a reader does not enjoy James Whitcomb Riley's "When the Frost Is on the Punkin" — a most popular poem — does not prove that he does not enjoy poetry, or that he cannot. We might as well say that the man who will not eat oatmeal does not like food!

Therefore a book of this kind should be used with great

freedom. The reader should be allowed to enjoy as fully as possible the poems which make the strongest appeal to him, and he should be permitted to pass lightly over at least a few of the poems — those that he does not like. His taste will be improved by his cultivation of his own enthusiasms, his frank acknowledgment of his own preferences, and his willingness to give respect to the dissimilar preferences of others. There is almost no hope for the reader who thinks that he must like everything offered simply because it is in a book, or because somebody else likes it. There is little hope for that other reader who thinks that a poem is poor or unimportant simply because he finds no pleasure in it himself. He is not to blame, perhaps. It may be that life has not yet furnished him with a clue to that particular poetic experience. But the poet is not necessarily to blame either. If the reader does not enjoy "When the Frost Is on the Punkin," he may find delight in John Masefield's "Night Is on the Downland." If he does not care for oatmeal, let him have the staff of life!

As I have already said, the poems in this book offer a wide range of poetic experience. This period — the past fifty years — has been characterized by productivity and variety. It has been the period of the Irish Renascence, of the Abbey Theater, of the plays of John Synge and Lady Gregory, of the lyrics and dramas of William Butler Yeats, of the prose and verse of James Stephens, of the fiery protests of the Irish Revolutionary Brotherhood. This period has given John **Period Covered** Masefield and A. E. Housman to English literature, a master of poetic narrative and a master of the lyric. And they are but two stars of the first magnitude in a galaxy of distinguished singers. The latter part of this period has given us the American Renascence with all of its poetry magazines and little theaters, with the supreme achievements of Edwin Arlington Robinson and Robert Frost and Sara Teasdale, and with the admirable achievements of many others.

If the poets are many, and if they are exceedingly productive, and if their work is of many kinds, be it remembered that the literary influences have been countless. As the broad stream of literature rolls from age to age, more and more tributaries are poured into it. Only a large and complete literary history could trace out the lines of influence that have been drawn through this period, making it what it has been. Many pages would be required for an adequate discussion of spiritual ancestries here in America alone. It is most interesting to follow the progress of our emancipation from a too single-hearted obedience to English taste and English ideas, to see the sudden overflow of that Titanic vigor which is characteristically American, in Walt Whitman and in his admirers a generation later, to catch a glimpse of French and Oriental influences in the work of Amy Lowell and Eunice Tietjens, to find Robert Frost sustained by a background of Emerson, and Edgar Lee Masters rising up out of the Greek Anthology. Walt Whitman, in particular, has had his numerous disciples, but his influence and importance are overestimated to-day, I believe, just as they were underestimated in his own time. Not a few American poets of our period have been inspired by the melodious clarity of Edgar Allan Poe and by the sweet spontaneity of Sidney Lanier, whose *Science of English Verse* (Scribner's) is a masterly book on rhythm and should be in the hands of all serious students of poetry. But it is chiefly important to remember that the American poet of to-day is a blood-brother of the world, if he wishes to be, touched by a thousand impulses and interests unknown to his predecessors, moving spiritually with long, deep, and circuitous currents of thought that reach from the rising to the setting sun.

These manifold influences account in part for the rich variety of the poetry of the period. It is not that the great eternal laws of art have changed. It is simply that modern poets have learned more ways of using them so that, with the unceasing evolution of human personality there is to be found an unceasing evolution in the expression of personality. The new poetry is never absolutely new when it is absolutely poetry. It is simply a growth out of the old which has all the slight variations that go with heredity. The poets of to-day are true to the memory of their great predecessors, not when they imitate them in thought and feeling and manner, halting beside the past that is gone and making graven images of it, but when, living fully in their own times, mindful of the past, dreaming a superb future, they make their craftsmanship conform to the living spirit which is the significance of their work, carrying the noble traditions of our thought and speech as far forward as they can, and producing work remarkable for a new dignity, originality, and power. Old laws always afford new opportunities to genius, for genius is always new.

Perhaps we may rightly devote a little time and thought to the new ways of making poems that have caused much discussion in the later years of the period, to the new ways of making patterns for poems, the new or "organic" rhythms, the new uses of images, symbols, and diction. Let us consider first of all the new ways of making patterns — the new designs.

In all that human beings make for use, beauty, and enduring life, we find the design or pattern. And in all good patterns we find that the law of symmetry and the law of variety must be remembered. The penalty of forgetting either law is failure. When a tree grows with all of its branches on one side, it is in peril because it lacks symmetry. A great wind may blow it down. If a tree could grow with every branch on one side exactly like every other branch on every side, it would offend us, for it would lack the somewhat irregular grace of living things and would seem to be as dead as if it had been manufactured, for it would lack variety. Trees that we love have branches on all sides, but the branches differ one from another. Symmetry and variety are pulling against each other in the design and creating the equilibrium that means beauty. Now a true poem is not a manufactured thing, but a living expression of a living heart and mind. Therefore, like the tree, it must have grown up in that heart and mind in obedience to the laws of symmetry and variety, it must be the result of a tension between these two forces, it must have found an equilibrium between them that is satisfactory to people who care for poetry.

Patterns

In all times when poems have been well made, poets have been making patterns for them. These patterns have been of many kinds. The Psalms in our Bibles were made in accordance with the Hebrew idea of design, a parallelism or balancing of words and phrases, emotions and ideas, one against another. Take, for example, the first two verses of Psalm XXIX:

> Give unto the Lord, O ye mighty, give unto the Lord
>   glory and strength.
> Give unto the Lord the glory due unto his name; worship
>   the Lord in the beauty of Holiness.

Both verses begin with the same phrase and offer the same idea. Both verses are divided logically into two sections.

It is the "mighty" who are to give the "glory due" and the "beauty of Holiness" in the second verse is balanced against the "glory and strength" of the first. This parallelism provides the symmetry of the pattern. The variety is subtly secured in symbol, cadence, and diction. If we turn to Alfred Kreymborg's deft little poem, "Idealists," we shall find symmetry of design secured in exactly the same way, through a sort of parallelism, and variety of design also secured through the adroit use of symbol, cadence, and diction. The same method of making a pattern for a poem is to be seen in Carl Sandburg's "Cool Tombs."

The Japanese, who think that we have too many words in our poems, have made symbolism, of which we shall have more to say later on, the basic principle in the patterns of their little poems in seventeen and thirty-one syllables. Several attempts to do this have been made in English. Perhaps it can be done if the poetic idea is simple and if the poet is willing to be brief. Carl Sandburg's "Fog" would not be a poem at all if it were not for the vitality of the symbol used for the fog — the quietness of the cat — and if it were not for the clever use of it in a small pattern of short sounds. Perhaps some of my readers will not admit that it is a poem. They will demand a more strongly marked symmetry; and they may be right in demanding it. But it is worth while for us to remember that rhyme and meter have not been fundamentally important always and everywhere in the making of patterns for poems. We should be willing to let poets create beauty as they wish, provided that they do create it.

A very large part of the world's poetry has found its symmetry of design in rhythm, and in much of the poetry written in our language we find rhyme used as a secondary

symmetry, marking off and defining rhythm. The variety
in much of our poetry has been secured by the use of
small changes in the cadence of the typical rhythm of the
pattern (the insertion of an extra syllable in a line of blank
verse for the sake of avoiding monotony is an illustration of
what I mean here), by image, symbol, and story, by the use
of contrasted meanings, by sound echoes and a varied
arrangement of rhymes, and in countless other ways that the
cunning of craftsmen has provided for the pleasure of readers.
In poems like "Path Flower" by Olive Tilford Dargan the
rhythmical pattern is very symmetrical, one stanza being
very much like another in its rhythmical effect. Yet slight
changes that make for the essential variety are to be found;
otherwise we could not call "Path Flower" an excellent
poem. In Ralph Hodgson's "Song of Honour" the sym-
metry of the pattern still depends on the balancing of
cadences in the rhythm, but there is much more variety,
for it enters into the main stream of the rhythm which
changes somewhat from line to line; and, although the main
stream of the rhythm is of one quality and kind, the lines
vary even as to their length. But perhaps this relation of
rhythm to the pattern of a poem can be understood only
after a long and careful consideration of rhythm.

   "Rhythm" is a kinder, larger, and more poetic word than
"meter." "Meter" suggests measurement — a mathe-
matical process — but "rhythm" suggests movement and
life, for it comes from an old Greek word that means "to
flow." We may think of rhythm, therefore, as the wave-like **Rhythm**
flowing of sequences of sound in poetry. And in thinking of
it in this way we shall be thinking of something far more
fundamentally important than any rules of prosody given in
our rhetorics. We shall be thinking of the force that is

behind and beyond those rules, of a force most intimately related to the very life of our bodies. For we live and have our being rhythmically. A flaw in the rhythm of the blood may mean a disease of the heart. A break in the rhythm may mean death. And our emotions change the rhythms of our bodies, quickening or retarding, accentuating or interrupting. Now perhaps the personal quality in rhythm, which is likely to be much better understood soon in the light of modern psychology, is a quality which belongs to certain habitual or frequent moods and emotions which poets "recollect in tranquillity" and get into the movement of the lines of their poems.

However this may be, it is quite certain that this personal quality in rhythm is a real thing. Nobody has to be a poet to feel it. The rhythms of Rudyard Kipling are quite unlike the rhythms of Walter de la Mare, and yet both men sound new notes and make new tunes in our language, tunes that are unmistakably individual and personal. The same thing is true of Conrad Aiken and Vachel Lindsay in our own country. It would be ridiculous to expect John Drinkwater's quiet emotions to flourish in the rhythms of G. K. Chesterton. It would be absurd to ask Edith M. Thomas to romp across the prairies of thought to the tune of Vachel Lindsay's "Santa Fé Trail." The poetry of Edgar Lee Masters would be valueless if set to the delicate verbal melodies of Edna St. Vincent Millay. The precision of meter in Edwin Arlington Robinson's exquisitely wrought stanzas is the natural accompaniment of the keenness and subtlety of his thought. It is significant that the rhythmical tunes of Dr. Drummond, Thomas Augustine Daly, and James Whitcomb Riley are all admirably suited to the homeliness of the themes with which they are united and to the gentle colloquialisms of the poems. Perhaps the personal quality in rhythm has never been more apparent than in the poetry of the past fifty years. Modern rhythms are personal because they are "organic"; which is to say that they are related to the nature of the poets who produce them.

Modern poets sometimes mean even more than that when they speak of "organic rhythm"; they sometimes mean a rhythm that bears direct and constant relation to the feeling and thought expressed in a poem, changing as thought and feeling change more or less from line to line. When sense and sound grow together in the mind of the poet, his music and the poetic lift of his emotion have an organic unity that stirs the reader. We find such organic rhythm in G. K. Chesterton's "Lepanto," which would sound martial from beginning to end even if we did not know the language, in "The Highwayman" by Alfred Noyes, which has all the haste and fluency of exciting adventure, in "Monotone" by Carl Sandburg, which is as quiet musically as the calm beauty it celebrates, in "Everyone Sang" by Siegfried Sassoon, which is as spontaneous in language as it is in thought, full of the actuality of the feeling described, and finally, in Louise Imogen Guiney's noble lyric of passing life, "The Wild Ride." *Organic Rhythm*

What has been called the *"vers libre* movement" has been valuable chiefly because it has been a way of making experiments with organic rhythm. In the making of free verse the thought or theory of the value of organic rhythm has been carried to extremes, for often it has not been modified by any other thought or theory about rhythm. The mnemonic value of regularly recurrent stresses, their value in subduing the practical man in us and releasing the imaginative man by their music, the part that rhythm usually plays as a contribution to structural symmetry in the pattern of a poem — these things have been forgotten or disregarded by most of the makers of free verse. That is why their work Vers
Libre is more valuable as instructive experiment, teaching flexibility in the use of rhythm, than as definite and certain achievement. For no one theory of life or of art can be carried to such extremes, can go unmodified by other theories without danger of serious loss.

Only a few poets have used free verse, or unrhymed cadence (which may be a better name for it), creditably, not to say beautifully. And numerous poetasters, ignorant of the ancient symmetrical patterns of English verse, persons who could not write a quatrain smoothly and successfully, seized the opportunity afforded by the vogue of free verse to place themselves before the public in the guise of poets. Yet it was only a disguise; for such poetasters simply cut up long level lines of prose into random lengths and set them down chaotically on pages that would have been better clean. Such chopped up prose lines had no true poetic cadence because no lift of authentic poetic emotion produced them. Therefore they had no power over readers. And when the novelty of it had worn off the public was bored rather than amused by the shrieking, grimacing, headline quality of much that was called free verse. And many of the most ardent advocates of free verse, many of the poets who learned to use it to the best advantage, have already returned to the use of more symmetrical patterns and more regularly stressed rhythms.

Nevertheless the best and most musical free verse has a charm and distinction of its own. "The Most Sacred Mountain" by Eunice Tietjens is full of rapture and exultation in sound as in sense. "Sea Gods" by H. D. has a

stately grace and passionate fluency that give keen pleasure
to anybody who is sensitive to verbal music.

And now that I have mentioned H. D. I must say a word
or two of the group of Imagist Poets to which she belongs, for
their thought of rhythm is interesting and they have written
free verse as well as any poets who have been experimenting   Imagism
with it.   They came before the public in 1914-15 with their
work and their manifesto.   Probably the most important
members of the school were H. D. (Mrs. Richard Aldington),
Richard Aldington, John Gould Fletcher, and Amy Lowell.
Here is their theory of rhythm as it was set down briefly in
Some Imagist Poets, 1915 (Houghton Mifflin).   They say
that a poet ought

To create new rhythms — as the expression of new moods — and
not to copy old rhythms which merely echo old moods.   We do not
insist upon "free verse" as the only method of writing poetry.
We fight for it as a principle of liberty.   We believe that the indi-
viduality of the poet may often be better expressed in free verse
than in conventional forms.   In poetry, a new cadence means a
new idea.

This idea raised a hullabaloo among critics.   Therefore, in
their next anthology, the Imagists explained their theory of
rhythm more fully in a preface which should be read by all
who wish to understand it perfectly and in detail (see
Some Imagist Poets, 1916).   Since the publication of that
anthology individual members of the group have gone on
explaining their theories of rhythm to the public in interesting
and individual ways.   John Gould Fletcher has much to say
of rhythm in the preface to *Goblins and Pagodas* (Houghton
Mifflin, 1916).   Amy Lowell has written much on the
subject for periodicals and in her several books.   F. S. Flint
introduces his *Otherworld* (The Poetry Bookshop, 1920)

with an exceedingly thoughtful discussion of unrhymed cadence. D. H. Lawrence goes over the ground again in the preface to *New Poems* (Huebsch, 1920). If anybody has said the last word on free verse, the Imagists have said it, but the gist of it all is to be found in the brief paragraph quoted from their first manifesto, and especially in the sentence, "In poetry, a new cadence means a new idea."

Before going on to a discussion of the other tenets of Imagism, let me say a few words about polyphonic prose, a **Polyphonic Prose** hybrid form midway between verse and prose, introduced into our language by Amy Lowell and used most admirably in the long narratives in her book *Can Grande's Castle*. In her preface Miss Lowell has this to say of polyphonic prose:

In the preface to *Sword Blades and Poppy Seeds* I stated that I had found the idea of the form in the works of the French poet, M. Paul Fort. But in adapting it for use in English I was obliged to make so many changes that it may now be considered as practically a new form. The greatest of these changes was in the matter of rhythm. M. Fort's practice consists, almost entirely, of regular verse passages interspersed with regular prose passages. But a hint in one of his poems led me to believe that a closer blending of the two types was desirable, * * * .

The first thing to be remembered about polyphonic prose is that the rhythms are irregular, like the rhythms of prose in the main, but that the use of rhymes and sound echoes and the clever manipulation of the lines give polyphonic prose a greater fluency and zest than can be found in ordinary prose. Like verse, polyphonic prose makes constant use of rhyme and balances sounds one against another. It is, in verity, many-sounding. But like prose it does not permit these rhymes and sound echoes to come always at equal intervals, and many of them are subtly disguised so that they are not noticeable in and of themselves, but are merely a part of the texture of the poem.

This can be understood better by the use of a quotation from John Gould Fletcher's "Clipper Ships," a splendidly vigorous bit of modern literature:

Beautiful as a tiered cloud, skysails set and shrouds twanging, she emerges from the surges that keep running away before day on the low Pacific shore. With the roar of the wind blowing half a gale after, she heels and lunges, and buries her bows in the smother, lifting them swiftly, and scattering the glistening spray-drops from her jibsails with laughter.

If the rhymes and sound echoes are underlined here, it will be noticed that they are many — perhaps more than are usually found in regular verse — but that they recur at irregular intervals. For example, the third word after "shore" rhymes with it, but the rhyme for "after" is separated from it by twenty-three words.

This book offers another poem in polyphonic prose for consideration. It is "The Paper Windmill" by Amy Lowell. No poets except the Imagists seem to have been greatly interested in the use of this new form, which cannot be used without a considerable amount of technical skill.

Because the Imagists typify certain tendencies of poetic development to-day, it may be interesting to quote other articles from the artistic creed which they gave to the public in 1915. They maintained that poets ought

To use the language of the common speech, but to employ always the *exact* word, not the nearly exact, nor the merely decorative word.

To allow absolute freedom in the choice of subject. It is not good art to write badly about aeroplanes and automobiles; nor is it necessarily bad art to write well about the past. We believe passionately in the artistic values of modern life, but we wish to point out that there is nothing so uninspiring nor so old-fashioned as an aeroplane of the year 1911.

To present an image (hence the name: "Imagist"). We are not a school of painters, but we believe that poetry should render particulars exactly and not deal in vague generalities, however magnificent and sonorous. It is for this reason that we oppose the cosmic poet, who seems to us to shirk the real difficulties of his art.

To produce poetry that is hard and clear, never blurred nor indefinite.

Finally, most of us believe that concentration is the very essence of poetry.

Most of the principles laid down for us in these articles of the Imagists are very old indeed and have always been good principles of the art of poetry. No good poet who ever wrote would deny that "concentration is the very essence of poetry." And no school less modern and radical than the Imagist School would have dared the trite preachment on the use of the "exact" word! If Noah made poems on dull days in the Ark, he must have made them with images. The Imagists were on absolutely solid ground when they made most of these early pronouncements. And we can only find cause for argument when we perceive that often their fear of being like the "cosmic poets" led them to shun the common human experiences as material for poems and brought about an over-emphasis on sense impressionism, when we discover that a poetry made "hard and clear" after their manner is sometimes a poetry without suggestive overtones and inspirational content, a poetry as cold as it is hard. But perhaps enough has been said of the Imagists, who are now developing not as a school, but as individuals. I have discussed *vers libre*, polyphonic prose, and Imagism at length because new things are sometimes more difficult to understand than old things, not because I consider this work more important than other work that is being done to-day. Perhaps it would be well to ask how other poets of the period have felt with regard to such important matters as diction, images, symbols, and the choice of themes for poetry.

A good poet must know words in families as other men and women know people. He must know that, like people, words do not always live together in harmony. They have their preferred associations. He must know their meanings — the minds in them; he must know the emotions that Words they excite— the hearts in them; and he must understand their sounds, long and short, soft and resistant, rough and smooth, bright and sombre — the beauty of words. He must make his poems out of living words that are in living relationship to what he wants to say.

The use of the words of common speech in poetry is no new thing. The masters have always used them. But the theory of their importance received new emphasis from Wordsworth and from Walt Whitman. And about twenty-five years ago William Butler Yeats began preaching the use of the best contemporary speech as the language of poetry. The result is that the poets of the period have refrained from the use of a pedantic, top-loftical language in poetry. They believe that the words that belong to love and marriage, to friendship and death, are good enough words for art.

That is why we seldom find the archaic forms of the pronouns "ye" and "thou" used in the verse of the period. "Thou" is still used in religious poetry, in addressing Deity, but is seldom used in modern love poetry, or as a general vocative. The forms of the verbs that belong with these pronominal forms are less used, also. "Has" is used instead of "hath" in the poetry of our time, and "does" instead of "doth."

The best poets of the period do not use such old-fashioned words as "adown," "mayhap," "methinks," nor such awkward little phrases as "did swoon" at the end of a line because the meter needs an extra syllable. "Beautiful" and "bountiful" are considered as poetic as "beauteous" and "bounteous." The sky does not need to be "azure." It may be as blue as larkspur. The poets of to-day believe that the "exact" word must be a living word that exactly tells what it is meant to tell. If their words are too far away from life the poem will seem to be too far away from mankind. Those who are interested in the study of the natural use of words in poetry should give good heed to the poetry of John Masefield, Wilfred Wilson Gibson, and Robert Frost.

We must remember, of course, in studying diction, that the problem of the use of words in short, singing lyrics differs greatly from the problem of the use of words in narratives. A. E. Housman, Sara Teasdale, and William H. Davies must make their brief lyrics out of simple, melodious words. But in "The Horse Thief," a narrative, William Rose Benét is quite justified in letting his thief speak of "the bandana I bought at Bowie." When Vachel Lindsay tells of the automobiles on the Santa Fé Trail drinking "gasoline from big red flagons," he is adding to the verisimilitude of his presentation of the scene. The presentation of personality by the use of dialect adds a new liberty. We must not scold James Whitcomb Riley because his vocabulary is not like that of Francis Thompson. It is chiefly important to remember that it is always the living words that must be used to offer mankind the living word.

The study of words passes gradually into the study of images and symbols. The image is simply the word or group of words chosen to give us a sense impression of the thing the poet has in mind. In his famous "Recessional," Rudyard Kipling speaks of a "far-flung battle line." That gives a more vivid impression than would be possible if one spoke prosily of the English soldiers encamped in all parts of the world, for it appeals to our motor sense. In "Wanderers" Walter de la Mare says that the stars are "attired in silver," which gives us a mental image appealing to our visual sense. Padraic Colum's "Old Woman of the Roads" is made up almost entirely of images of things that would give pleasure to a lonely old woman, and it is these images that make the poem a concrete and powerful bit of writing. Images and Symbols

The important thing to remember about images is that they should be fresh-minted for us in every poem. They should be the natural and inevitable result of the poet's deep and sincere realization of the facts of experience and of what he wants to say about them. And it is noteworthy that by the mere quality of the images used it is often possible to judge of a poet's sincerity. The true poet no longer writes of a "stately lily," a "modest violet," "red passion growths," "lust of power," "endless aeons," "perilous peaks," or "pomp and pageant of the fall," because these old and trite images cannot possibly tell the reality of what he has felt. He turns from them with an instinctive disgust. They are the rubber-stamp makeshifts of the manufacturers of easy verse. The true poet, writing of nature, says nothing at all, perhaps, of his "vision far but fair" and of the "ardour of the soul," but he makes them live for us by the use of concrete imagery like that which Robert Louis Stevenson uses freshly and vividly in his "Romance":

> I will make you brooches and toys for your delight
> Of bird-song at morning and star-shine at night.

The good poet can truly work such miracles. He can make brooches out of bird-song!

The beauty of symbolism leads the human spirit farther than the beauty of imagery. Many of the best poets of our period have written poems that are remarkable for their symbolism, poems that are, in reality, large, compound, and subtly amplified metaphors. One of the most notable of these is "The Falconer of God" by William Rose Benét. I have pointed out the character of the symbolism in it in the notes given before the poem. In Edwin Markham's "Lincoln," the hero of America is likened to a tree, a "kingly cedar." Mr. Markham says:

> And when he fell in whirlwind, he went down
> As when a kingly cedar green with boughs
> Goes down with a great shout upon the hills;
> And leaves a lonesome place against the sky.

This is one of the best of the poems about Lincoln. And it is a fine study for those interested in symbolism. For in it the qualities of natural objects, of rocks and rain and red earth are used as symbols of spiritual qualities in the hero. Poems like "The Falconer of God" and "Lincoln" help us to realize what symbolism is and tell us far more about it than a definition could. But we may say for convenience that an image becomes a symbol when the poet would make us realize, through his imagery, something that is far more important than the thing for which the image stands, since it has a spiritual, not a merely physical existence.

The symbol that Mr. Markham has used to describe Lincoln, the symbol of the tree, is a very old one. In the history of literature the tree is used again and again as the symbol of the race, the family, the strong man. The truth seems to be that the best symbols are all old and have been used often. Wherever men and women have been led by life to feel certain things in a certain way, they have used certain symbols as the inevitable way of expressing themselves. In hot countries everlasting heat used to be the symbol of eternal damnation; in cold countries, everlasting cold. Again and again the seasons, spring, summer, autumn, and winter are made to mean birth, growth, maturity, and death. A winding river is life. The seed of the man is the child. The banner is the nation. The summit is success. The Cross is Christianity.

If such symbols are old, how is it that they can retain their force and freshness? The answer to that question is one word — realization. The poet who has realized their meaning for himself in relation to facts of his own experience which he wishes to express is likely to use them freshly and forcefully. He will find a new form of words for the use of them, and that form of words will be his own. The general symbol of the tree became specific for Edwin Markham in the "kingly cedar." The same general symbol became specific for John Gould Fletcher in the "gaunt scraggly pine" in his poem on Lincoln. The two poems about the same hero used the same symbol, but they are not at all alike. It is all a matter of sincere realization. To be insincere in the world of action is to be less than ethical. To be insincere in the world of poetry is to be less than a poet.

This belief in artistic sincerity is closely associated with the modern poet's attitude toward his theme. There is no such thing as a "poetic subject." A good poet may be able to make poetry about the worn-out boots on the feet of a tramp. A poor poet cannot make his lines dance in time with the slippers of Cinderella. The poetry is in the poet, not in his theme. Good poets of our period, like good poets of all periods, begin their work of creation where they touch life most closely. They take from life anything that interests them and make it into poetry. They know that they can never write well about anything which does not interest them. Therefore, no matter how vitally important a theme may be, if they cannot react toward it with fresh and vitalizing emotion, they will have none of it. They know that their own lives and personalities determine their choices of themes and are revealed through their work. But they know, also, that in spite of changing literary fashions, they can never write good poetry without feeling it first, and the theme must be the spark that kindles the warmth of their emotion.

The themes for poems, then, are unnumbered. And it will be quite evident to any reader of this book that the poets represented in it have divers and diverse enthusiasms. John Masefield, Wilfred Wilson Gibson, Edwin Markham, Florence Wilkinson Evans, William Vaughn Moody, and Vachel Lindsay have been fired by the spirit of democracy forever growing stronger in our modern world and have written poems remarkable for their deep and generous social passion. Francis Thompson's poetry is emphatically religious in its constant adherence to the thought of God. Edwin Arlington Robinson and Edgar Lee Masters are chiefly interested in people as personalities. They tell stories. Amy Lowell has a passionate love for the beauty of the

Themes for Poetry

external world, which is shared by most of the Imagists. John Drinkwater finds his inspiration in the country scenes of England as it was and is and may continue to be. Walter de la Mare has a shadowy world of his own out of which he sends his poems like shy messengers who would enjoy telling us about it. And forever and forever, in this period as in all others, the ancient themes of love and death and nature persist and are brought forward clad in new raiment of words wrought by the new poetic personalities of modern times.

Let me hark back to the definition of poetry with which I began and say that the poet is always the great sharer of life. He breaks the bread of life with us when he shares the things in life that are most dear to him, his thought of the social love of mankind, of the personal love of man and woman, of the joy felt in the evanescent glory of a sunset, of the hopes and passions of our evolving race. The poet is not a direct preacher. His lessons are taught only obliquely, through this sharing of experience. But through this sharing he disciplines our imaginations — always a pioneer force in civilization, ennobles our sympathies, and gives us one of the dearest and finest of all pleasures, a pleasure that is never costly, that is always democratic, and that can last for us as long as life lasts. *The Poet*

Perhaps some of you who read this book will become poets. Perhaps you will be greater than any whose names are set down in these pages, though even if that should come to pass you might never have the joy of knowing it, here, for the world could not find it out until many, many years after death had claimed you. The value of poetry can never be finally tested save by time. But many poems have value for readers who are contemporaries of the poets who make them, even if they are not destined for immortality. And it is the lovers of poetry, always, who make ready for the coming of the great poet who can carry history in a sack across his shoulder while he climbs higher and higher into the Heavens with prophecy for his staff, never forgetful of the sorrows of mankind, never unmindful of the stars that burn above the world. Therefore let me offer this book with the wish that it may bring my readers a little nearer to the love and understanding of poetry.

AMERICAN POETS

JAMES WHITCOMB RILEY

James Whitcomb Riley was born in Greenfield, Indiana, in 1849, the son of a well-to-do lawyer. He read law himself in his youth and it was expected that he would follow his father's profession, but his lively genius asserted itself early in his life and made him one of a troupe of strolling players. He seems to have been a versatile utility man, beating a drum, making up songs, or taking part in performances as occasion required.

He apparently began his work without manifesting either the tense devotion of the genius to his art, or the sentimental conceit of the poetaster. He had humor. He played tricks on the public. His poem *Leonainie*, published over the initials E. A. P., was thought to be a newly discovered poem by Poe! It was simply a literary hoax. He wrote a series of dialect poems and claimed that they were the work of an unlettered Hoosi farmer. A collection of these verses was published in 1883 under the title *The Ole Swimmin' Hole* and immediately made Riley popular. This was reprehensible, but Riley lived it down.

His other books were *Afterwhiles* (1887), *Old-Fashioned Roses* (1888), *Pipes o' Pan at Zekesbury* (1889), and *Rhymes o. 'hildhood* (1890). They all made places for themselves in the hearts of his countrymen, and most American children are familiar with "Little Orphant Annie," "The Raggedy Man," and others, at an early age.

Riley has sometimes been called an American Burns. But Burns was a peasant and his work grew out of the soil without any transplanting. Moreover, Burns found a rich and ancient folklore through which he might work — ballads and tales already familiar to his people. Riley was not a farmer, but he was close to the soil by sympathy; and he found it necessary to give literary form, meaning, and music to a dialect that had not yet been used in literature. Perhaps it would be true to say that Burns was a poet *of* the folk and Riley a poet *for* them. If he was never as great a poet as Burns,. it may still be said that he was a true poet, at best, in spite of his popularity, and that he gave the American people a gift that is valid and valuable, although it is homely and unpretentious. He has been copied, of course, by numerous poetasters who get his meters and his mannerisms into their work, but not his spirit and his art. They can not put the swishing echo of the music of cornfields into their lines as he did:

> The husky, rusty russel of the tossels of the corn,
> And the raspin' of the tangled leaves as golden as the morn;

Riley died in Indianapolis in 1916

A PARTING GUEST

What delightful hosts are they—
    Life and Love!
Lingeringly I turn away,
    This late hour, yet glad enough
They have not withheld from me
    Their high hospitality.
So, with face lit with delight
    And all gratitude, I stay
    Yet to press their hands and say,
"Thanks.—So fine a time! Good night."

—James Whitcomb Riley

From the Biographical Edition of the *Complete Works of James Whitcomb Riley.*

"WHEN THE FROST IS ON THE PUNKIN"

When the frost is on the punkin and the fodder's in the shock,
And you hear the kyouck and gobble of the struttin' turkey-
    cock,
And the clackin' of the guineys, and the cluckin' of the hens,
And the rooster's hallylooyer as he tiptoes on the fence;
O, it's then the time a feller is a-feelin' at his best,
With the risin' sun to greet him from a night of peaceful rest,
As he leaves the house, bareheaded, and goes out to feed the
    stock,
When the frost is on the punkin and the fodder's in the shock.

They's something kindo' harty-like about the atmusfere
When the heat of summer's over and the coolin' fall is here—
Of course we miss the flowers, and the blossoms on the trees,
And the mumble of the hummin'-birds and buzzin' of the
    bees;
But the air's so appetizin'; and the landscape through the
    haze
Of a crisp and sunny morning of the airly autumn days
Is a pictur' that no painter has the colorin' to mock—
When the frost is on the punkin and the fodder's in the shock.

The husky, rusty russel of the tossels of the corn,
And the raspin' of the tangled leaves as golden as the morn;
The stubble in the furries—kindo' lonesome-like, but still
A-preachin' sermuns to us of the barns they growed to fill;
The strawstack in the medder, and the reaper in the shed;
The hosses in theyr stalls below—the clover overhead!—
O, it sets my hart a-clickin' like the tickin' of a clock,
When the frost is on the punkin and the fodder's in the shock.

Then your apples all is gethered, and the ones a feller keeps
Is poured around the cellar-floor in red and yaller heaps;
And your cider-makin's over, and your wimmern-folks is
    through
With theyr mince and apple-butter, and theyr souse and
    sausage too! . . .
I don't know how to tell it—but ef such a thing could be
As the angels wantin' boardin', and they'd call around on
    me—
I'd want to 'commodate 'em—all the whole-indurin' flock—
When the frost is on the punkin and the fodder's in the shock.

               —*James Whitcomb Riley*

From the Biographical Edition of the *Complete Works of James Whitcomb Riley*.

EUGENE FIELD

Eugene Field was born in St. Louis, Missouri, in 1850. He was educated there and in New England. When he was twenty-three he became a reporter on the St. Louis *Evening Journal* and remained a journalist for the rest of his life. His poems were not written for book publication, nor for literary magazines, but for the newspapers on which he worked. He was probably the best of our "newspaper poets," and made his columns in the Denver *Tribune* (1881–1883) and in the Chicago *Daily News* (1883–1895) worth reading and worth remembering. His best work holds humor and sentiment in pleasing equilibrium, and is thus typically American.

His books are *A Little Book of Western Verse* (1889), *With Trumpet and Drum* (1892), *A Second Book of Verse* (1893), and, in collaboration with his brother Roswell M. Field, *Echoes From a Sabine Farm* (1893). A complete edition of his verse was published in 1910. The wit and wisdom of "Our Two Opinions" and the tenderness of "Little Boy Blue" (quoted below) need no explanation. Field died in Chicago in 1895.

OUR TWO OPINIONS

Us two wuz boys when we fell out, —
    Nigh to the age uv my youngest now;
Don't rec'lect what 'twuz about,
    Some small deeff'rence, I'll allow.
Lived next neighbors twenty years,
    A-hatin' each other, me 'nd Jim, —
He having *his* opinyin uv *me*,
    'Nd *I* havin' *my* opinyin uv *him*.

Grew up together 'nd wouldn't speak,
    Courted sisters, 'nd marr'd 'em, too;
'Tended same meetin'-house oncet a week,
    A-hatin' each other through 'nd through!
But when Abe Linkern asked the West
    F'r soldiers, we answered, — me 'nd Jim, —
He havin' *his* opinyin uv *me*,
    'Nd *I* havin' *my* opinyin uv *him*.

But down in Tennessee one night
    Ther' wuz sound uv firin' fur away,
'Nd the sergeant allowed ther'd be a fight
    With the Johnnie Rebs some time nex' day;
'Nd as I wuz thinkin' uv Lizzie 'nd home
    Jim stood afore me, long 'nd slim, —
He havin' *his* opinyin uv *me*,
    'Nd *I* havin' *my* opinyin uv *him*.

Seemed like we knew there wuz goin' to be
    Serious trouble f'r me 'nd him;
Us two shuck hands, did Jim 'nd me,
    But never a word from me or Jim!
He went *his* way 'nd *I* went *mine*,
    'Nd into the battle's roar went we, —
I havin' *my* opinyin of Jim,
    'Nd *he* havin' *his* opinyin uv *me*.

Jim never came back from the war again,
    But I hain't forgot that last, last night
When, waitin' f'r orders, us two men
    Made up 'nd shuck hands, afore the fight.

'Nd after it all, it's soothin' to know
  That here I be 'nd younder's Jim,—
He havin' *his* opinyin uv *me*,
  'Nd *I* havin' *my* opinyin uv *him*.

— Eugene Field

Reprinted from *The Complete Work of Eugene Field*

LITTLE BOY BLUE

The little toy dog is covered with dust,
  But sturdy and staunch he stands;
The little toy soldier is red with rust,
  And his musket moulds in his hands.
Time was when the little toy dog was new,
  And the soldier was passing fair;
And that was the time when our Little Boy Blue
  Kissed them and put them there.

"Now don't you go till I come," he said,
  "And don't you make any noise!"
So, toddling off to his trundle bed,
  He dreamt of the pretty toys;
And, as he was dreaming, an angel song
  Awakened our Little Boy Blue —
Oh! the years are many, the years are long,
  But the little toy friends are true!

Ay, faithful to Little Boy Blue they stand,
    Each in the same old place,
Awaiting the touch of a little hand,
    The smile of a little face;
And they wonder, as waiting the long years through
    In the dust of that little chair,
What has become of our Little Boy Blue,
    Since he kissed them and put them there.

— Eugene Field

Reprinted from *The Complete Works of Eugene Field*

INA COOLBRITH

Ina (Donna) Coolbrith was born in Illinois of New England parentage and went in early childhood across the great overland trail to California, where she was educated in the public schools of Los Angeles. She has won honors not often accorded to women. She is the only woman member of the famous Bohemian Club of San Francisco. She is the first poet laureate chosen for any state in the Union. Her appointment to the poet-laureateship of California by the governor was ratified by the legislature. She was crowned with laurel symbolizing her office at the meeting of the Congress of Authors and Journalists of the Panama-Pacific Exposition in 1915. Her books of verse are *A Perfect Day and Other Poems*, 1884, and *The Singer of the Sea; Songs from the Golden Gate*, 1895.

Her work is all instinct with gracious personality. Perhaps the best of her musical lyrics is the one quoted here, which presents with adequate sincerity a mood and emotion well known to everybody.

WHEN THE GRASS SHALL COVER ME

When the grass shall cover me,
Head to foot where I am lying, —
When not any wind that blows,
Summer-blooms nor winter-snows,
Shall awake me to your sighing:
Close above me as you pass,
You will say, "How kind she was,"
You will say, "How true she was,"
When the grass grows over me.

When the grass shall cover me,
Holden close to earth's warm bosom, —
    While I laugh, or weep, or sing,
    Nevermore for anything,
You will find in blade and blossom,
    Sweet, small voices odorous,
    Tender pleaders in my cause,
    That shall speak me as I was —
    When the grass grows over me.

    When the grass shall cover me!
Ah, beloved, in my sorrow
    Very patient, I can wait,
    Knowing that, or soon or late,
There will dawn a clearer morrow:
    When your heart will moan, "Alas!
    Now I know how true she was;
    Now I know how dear she was" —
    When the grass grows over me!

              — *Ina Coolbrith*

EDWIN MARKHAM

Edwin Markham was born in Oregon City, Oregon, in 1852 and moved to California when he was five years old. As a boy he did many kinds of outdoor work, farming, blacksmithing, and herding. He was educated at the San Jose Normal School and at two western colleges, specializing in ancient and modern literature and in Christian sociology. He lived and worked in California as an educator until 1899, when "The Man With the Hoe" was published in a newspaper. This poem, which used the French peasant in Millet's famous painting as the symbol of oppressed humanity, challenged the interest and sympathy of a world that had begun to realize that there was much wrong in modern industrialism. It was hailed as "the battle-cry of the next thousand years." It was so extravagantly praised in the press that later a natural, but unfortunate reaction set in against it. Yet it still stands and will stand for some time to come as one of the memorable poems of this period, nobly conceived in the love of liberty and justice, and finely executed with all the skill acquired in the years when Mr. Markham was writing lesser poetry on smaller themes.

Mr. Markham's books are *The Man With the Hoe and Other Poems* (1899), *Lincoln and Other Poems* (1901), *The Shoes of Happiness and Other Poems* and *California the Wonderful* (1914), *Gates of Paradise* (1920). In 1922 he was chosen and crowned as poet-laureate of Oregon, the state of his birth. His poem on Abraham Lincoln, quoted here, is as fine in its own way as "The Man With the Hoe," remarkable alike for dignity and restraint, and for the justice and beauty of the strong, old, natural symbols used to describe the character of the hero-president.

> The color of the ground was in him, the red earth;
> The smack and tang of elemental things;
> The rectitude and patience of the cliff;

THE MAN WITH THE HOE

"God created man in his own image, in the image of God created He him."

Bowed by the weight of centuries, he leans
Upon his hoe and gazes on the ground,
The emptiness of ages in his face
And on his back the burden of the world.
Who made him dead to rapture and despair,
A thing that grieves not and that never hopes,
Stolid and stunned, a brother to the ox?
Who loosened and let down this brutal jaw?
Whose was the hand that slanted back this brow?
Whose breath blew out the light within this brain?

Is this the thing the Lord God made and gave
To have dominion over sea and land;
To trace the stars and search the heavens for power;
To feel the passion of eternity?
Is this the dream He dreamed who shaped the suns
And marked their ways upon the ancient deep?
Down all the caverns of Hell to their last gulf
There is no shape more terrible than this —
More tongued with censure of the world's blind greed —
More filled with signs and portents for the soul —
More packt with danger to the universe.

What gulfs between him and the seraphim!
Slave of the wheel of labor, what to him
Are Plato and the swing of Pleiades?
What the long reaches of the peaks of song,
The rift of dawn, the reddening of the rose?

Through this dread shape the suffering ages look;
Time's tragedy is in that aching stoop;
Through this dread shape humanity betrayed,
Plundered, profaned and disinherited,
Cries protest to the Judges of the World,
A protest that is also prophecy.

O masters, lords and rulers in all lands,
Is this the handiwork you give to God,
This monstrous thing, distorted and soul-quenched?
How will you ever straighten up this shape;
Touch it again with immortality;
Give back the upward looking and the light;
Rebuild in it the music and the dream;
Make right the immemorial infamies,
Perfidious wrongs, immedicable woes?

O masters, lords and rulers in all lands,
How will the future reckon with this man?
How answer his brute question in that hour
When whirlwinds of rebellion shake the world?
How will it be with kingdoms and with kings —
With those who shaped him to the thing he is —
When this dumb terror shall appeal to God,
After the silence of the centuries?

— Edwin Markham

THE DEDICATION POEM

Read by Edwin Markham at the dedication of the Lincoln
Memorial at Washington, May 30, 1922. Before reading, he said:
"No oration, no poem, can rise to the high level of this historic
hour. Nevertheless, I venture to inscribe this revised version of
my Lincoln poem to this stupendous Lincoln Memorial, to this far-

shining monument of remembrance, erected in immortal marble to
the honor of our deathless martyr — the consecrated statesman, the
ideal American, the ever-beloved friend of humanity."

LINCOLN, THE MAN OF THE PEOPLE

When the Norn Mother saw the Whirlwind Hour
Greatening and darkening as it hurried on,
She left the Heaven of Heroes and came down
To make a man to meet the mortal need.
She took the tried clay of the common road —
Clay warm yet with the genial heat of Earth,
Dasht through it all a strain of prophecy,
Tempered the heap with thrill of human tears;
Then mixt a laughter with the serious stuff.
Into the shape she breathed a flame to light
That tender, tragic, ever-changing face;
And laid on him a sense of the Mystic Powers,
Moving — all husht — behind the mortal veil.
Here was a man to hold against the world,
A man to match the mountains and the sea.

The color of the ground was in him, the red earth;
The smack and tang of elemental things;
The rectitude and patience of the cliff;
The good-will of the rain that loves all leaves;
The friendly welcome of the wayside well;
The courage of the bird that dares the sea;
The gladness of the wind that shakes the corn;
The pity of the snow that hides all scars;
The secrecy of streams that make their way
Under the mountain to the rifted rock;
The tolerance and equity of light

That gives as freely to the shrinking flower
As to the great oak flaring to the wind —
To the grave's low hill as to the Matterhorn
That shoulders out the sky. Sprung from the West,
He drank the valorous youth of a new world.
The strength of virgin forests braced his mind,
The hush of spacious prairies stilled his soul.
His words were oaks in acorns; and his thoughts
Were roots that firmly gript the granite truth.

Up from log cabin to the Capitol,
One fire was on his spirit, one resolve —
To send the keen axe to the root of wrong,
Clearing a free way for the feet of God,
The eyes of conscience testing every stroke,
To make his deed the measure of a man.
He built the rail-pile as he built the State,
Pouring his splendid strength through every blow;
The grip that swung the axe in Illinois
Was on the pen that set a people free.

So came the Captain with the mighty heart;
And when the judgment thunders split the house,
Wrenching the rafters from their ancient rest,
He held the ridgepole up, and spikt again
The rafters of the Home. He held his place —
Held the long purpose like a growing tree —
Held on through blame and faltered not at praise.
And when he fell in whirlwind, he went down
As when a lordly cedar, green with boughs,
Goes down with a great shout upon the hills,
And leaves a lonesome place against the sky.

                 — Edwin Markham

EDITH M. THOMAS

Edith M. Thomas was born at Chatham, Ohio, in 1854, and educated at the Normal Institute of Geneva, Ohio. She has lived in New York since 1888, and is a notable poet of the period.

Her books are, *A New Year's Masque and Other Poems* (1885), *Lyrics and Sonnets* (1887), *The Inverted Torch* (1890), *A Winter Swallow with Other Verse* (1896), *The Dancers* (1903), *The Flower from the Ashes* (1915).

"Frost To-night" is a perfect lyric of its kind. The rhythm is at once sedate and graceful, the symbolism clear and adequate. By the harvest of flowers we are reminded of the spiritual harvest that we must gather before life's ending.

"FROST TO-NIGHT"

Apple-green west and an orange bar;
And the crystal eye of a lone, one star   .   .   .
And, "Child, take the shears and cut what you will,
Frost to-night — so clear and dead-still."

Then I sally forth, half sad, half proud,
And I come to the velvet, imperial crowd,
The wine-red, the gold, the crimson, the pied, —
The dahlias that reign by the garden-side.

The dahlias I might not touch till to-night!
A gleam of shears in the fading light,
And I gathered them all, — the splendid throng,
And in one great sheaf I bore them along.

In my garden of Life with its all late flowers
I heed a Voice in the shrinking hours:
"Frost to-night — so clear and dead-still"   .   .   .
Half sad, half proud, my arms I fill.

— Edith M. Thomas

KATHARINE LEE BATES

Katharine Lee Bates was born at Falmouth, Massachusetts, in 1859, and was educated at Wellesley College, at Middlebury College, and at Oberlin College. She has been a teacher most of her life and Professor of English Literature at Wellesley College for twenty years. She is the author of many excellent books of prose and verse.

Perhaps the best known and most important of her volumes of verse are *America the Beautiful and Other Poems* (1911), *The Retinue and Other Poems* (1918) and *Yellow Clover* (1922). Not a few of Miss Bates's lyrics have found a well-deserved place in the hearts of hundreds of people. Among the best are "Yellow Warblers" and "Around the Sun." "America the Beautiful," chosen for this book, is both a stately hymn and a warm-hearted prayer. It has been adopted as the official hymn of the American Federation of Women's Clubs.

AMERICA THE BEAUTIFUL

O beautiful for spacious skies,
    For amber waves of grain,
For purple mountain majesties
    Above the fruited plain!
      America! America!
    God shed His grace on thee
And crown thy good with brotherhood
    From sea to shining sea!

O beautiful for pilgrim feet,
   Whose stern, impassioned stress
A thoroughfare for freedom beat
   Across the wilderness!
      America! America!
   God mend thine every flaw,
Confirm thy soul in self-control,
   Thy liberty in law!

O beautiful for heroes proved
   In liberating strife,
Who more than self their country loved,
   And mercy more than life!
      America! America!
   May God thy gold refine,
Till all success be nobleness,
   And every gain divine!

O beautiful for patriot dream
   That sees beyond the years
Thine alabaster cities gleam
   Undimmed by human tears!
      America! America!
   God shed His grace on thee
And crown thy good with brotherhood
   From sea to shining sea!

                — *Katharine Lee Bates*

WILLIAM HERBERT CARRUTH

William Herbert Carruth was born in Osawatomie, Kansas, in 1859, and was educated at the University of Kansas and at Harvard University. He is head of the English department at Leland Stanford University.

He is the author of *Each in His Own Tongue and Other Poems* (1909) from which the title poem is taken for quotation here.

EACH IN HIS OWN TONGUE

A fire-mist and a planet,
    A crystal and a cell,
A jelly-fish and a saurian,
    And the caves where the cavemen dwell;
Then a sense of law and beauty,
    And a face turned from the clod —
Some call it Evolution,
    And others call it God.

A haze on the far horizon,
    The infinite, tender sky,
The ripe, rich tint of the cornfields,
    And the wild geese sailing high;
And all over upland and lowland,
    The charm of the goldenrod —
Some of us call it Autumn,
    And others call it God.

Like tides on a crescent sea-beach,
    When the moon is new and thin,
Into our hearts high yearnings
    Come welling and surging in:
Come from the mystic ocean
    Whose rim no foot has trod —
Some of us call it Longing,
    And others call it God.

A picket frozen on duty,
    A mother starved for her brood,
Socrates drinking the hemlock,
    And Jesus on the rood;
And millions, who, humble and nameless,
    The straight, hard pathway plod —
Some call it Consecration,
    And others call it God.

— *William Herbert Carruth*

LIZETTE WOODWORTH REESE

Lizette Woodworth Reese was born in Baltimore County, Maryland, and educated in private and public schools.   For many years she has been a teacher of English in the Western High School of Baltimore, but she retired in 1921.

Her books are *A Branch of May* (1887), *A Handful of Lavender* (1891), *A Quiet Road* (1896), *Wayside Lute* (1909), and *Spicewood* (1920).   Her work has an exquisite and serene distinction that is rare in her period.   It has never been exploited or noisily praised by those who set literary fashions, but it has been quietly and deeply loved by poets and true lovers of poetry.   Her feminine tenderness is a pervading power in all of her best work, and particularly in "A Christmas Folk Song" and in her famous sonnet, "Tears."

TEARS

When I consider Life and its few years —
A wisp of fog betwixt us and the sun;
A call to battle, and the battle done
Ere the last echo dies within our ears·
A rose choked in the grass; an hour of fears;
The gusts that past a darkening shore do beat;
The burst of music down an unlistening street, —
I wonder at the idleness of tears.
Ye old, old dead, and ye of yesternight,
Chieftains, and bards, and keepers of the sheep,
By every cup of sorrow that you had,
Loose me from tears, and make me see aright
How each has back what once he stayed to weep:
Homer his sight, David his little lad!

— Lizette Woodworth Reese

Clinton Scollard was born at Clinton, New York, in 1860. He was educated at Hamilton College, at Harvard University, and at Cambridge in England. He is a member of the National Institute of Arts and Letters.

He is the author of many books of verse, all written with a meticulously smooth technique. His *Poems—Selected* appeared in 1914. "A Day for Wandering" is gracefully and sincerely written and needs no explanation.

A DAY FOR WANDERING

I set apart a day for wandering;
I heard the woodlands ring,
The hidden white-throat sing,
And the harmonic West,
Beyond a far hill-crest,
Touch its Aeolian string.
Remote from all the brawl and bruit of men,
The iron tongue of Trade,
I followed the clear calling of a wren
Deep to the bosom of a sheltered glade,
Where interwoven branches spread a shade
Of soft cool beryl like the evening seas
Unruffled by the breeze.
And there — and there —
I watched the maiden-hair,
The pale blue iris-grass,
The water-spider in its pause and pass
Upon a pool that like a mirror was.

I took for confidant
The diligent ant
Threading the clover and the sorrel aisles;
For me were all the smiles
Of the sequestered blossoms there abloom —
Chalice and crown and plume;
I drank the ripe rich attars blurred and blent,
And won — Content!

— *Clinton Scollard*

LOUISE IMOGEN GUINEY

Louise Imogen Guiney was born at Boston, Massachusetts, in 1861, and educated in Elmhurst Academy in Providence and by private tutors. In 1901 she went to live in England and died there in 1920.

Her books are *The White Sail and Other Poems* (1887), *A Roadside Harp* (1893), and *Patrins* (1897). *Happy Ending* (1909) contained old and new work, as the author said, "the less faulty half" of all that she had written. Her poetry is remarkable for vigorous thought and clean, deep emotion. "The Wild Ride" is a poem of triumphant faith. Over against the dangers and the transitory delights of this life the poet sets faith in God as the leader of our wild ride through eternity. The rhythm of the poem is exceptionally appropriate and beautiful. "The Wild Ride" deserves a place beside Browning's "Prospice." "A Talisman" is an excellent bit of wisdom in poetic form.

THE WILD RIDE

I hear in my heart, I hear in its ominous pulses
All day, on the road, the hoofs of invisible horses,
All night, from their stalls, the importunate pawing and
neighing.

Let cowards and laggards fall back! but alert to the saddle
Weather-worn and abreast, go men of our galloping legion,
With a stirrup-cup each to the lily of women that loves him.

The trail is through dolour and dread, over crags and
morasses;
There are shapes by the way, there are things that appal or
entice us:
What odds? We are Knights of the Grail, we are vowed to
the riding.

Thought's self is a vanishing wing, and joy is a cobweb,
And friendship a flower in the dust, and glory a sunbeam:
Not here is our prize, nor, alas! after these our pursuing.

A dipping of plumes, a tear, a shake of the bridle,
A passing salute to this world and her pitiful beauty:
We hurry with never a word in the track of our fathers.

(I hear in my heart, I hear in its ominous pulses
All day, on the road, the hoofs of invisible horses,
All night, from their stalls, the importunate pawing and
    neighing.)

We spur to a land of no name, out-racing the storm-wind;
We leap to the infinite dark like sparks from the anvil.
Thou leadest, O God! All's well with Thy troopers that
    follow.

— *Louise Imogen Guiney*

A TALISMAN

Take Temperance to thy breast,
While yet is the hour of choosing,
As arbitress exquisite
Of all that shall thee betide;
For better than fortune's best
Is mastery in the using,
And sweeter than anything sweet
The art to lay it aside!

— *Louise Imogen Guiney*

Richard Hovey was born at Normal, Illinois, in 1864. He was graduated from Dartmouth in 1885. After graduation theology, the stage, journalism, and the rostrum all tempted him in turn, but he turned to literature, finally, and made his place as a dramatist and poet.

He is the author of *The Laurel: An Ode* (1889), *Songs from Vagabondia* (with Bliss Carman) (1894), *More Songs from Vagabondia* (with Bliss Carman) (1896), *Along the Trail* (1898), *Last Songs from Vagabondia* (1900).

He is primarily the poet of good fellowship, believing, as he once said in the *Dartmouth Magazine*, that it is the privilege of the poet to "lay open to the world the heart of man — all its heights and depths, all its glooms and glories." He has written much friendly and healthy poetry that carries in its vigorous music and meaning the energy of a strong and vital personality. It is not strange that "A Stein Song" has become a favorite with young men everywhere. He has written poetry that goes deeper into life and has greater subtlety and power than this famous song. But it is good to find such robust and hearty cheer in verse of this period and we may well be grateful for it and for the spirit that says manfully, at the end of "At the Crossroads,"

> *Here's luck!*
> In the teeth of all winds blowing.

AT THE CROSSROADS

You to the left and I to the right,
For the ways of men must sever —
And it well may be for a day and a night,
And it well may be forever.
But whether we meet or whether we part

(For our ways are past our knowing),
A pledge from the heart to its fellow heart
On the ways we all are going!
Here's luck!
For we know not where we are going.

Whether we win or whether we lose
With the hands that life is dealing,
It is not we nor the ways we choose
But the fall of the cards that's sealing.
There's a fate in love and a fate in fight,
And the best of us all go under —
And whether we're wrong or whether we're right,
We win, sometimes, to our wonder.
Here's luck!
That we may not yet go under!

With a steady swing and an open brow
We have tramped the ways together,
But we're clasping hands at the crossroads now
In the Fiend's own night for weather;
And whether we bleed or whether we smile
In the leagues that lie before us
The ways of life are many a mile
And the dark of Fate is o'er us.
Here's luck!
And a cheer for the dark before us!

You to the left and I to the right,
For the ways of men must sever,
And it well may be for a day and a night
And it well may be forever!

But whether we live or whether we die
(For the end is past our knowing),
Here's two frank hearts and the open sky,
Be a fair or an ill wind blowing!
Here's luck!
In the teeth of all winds blowing.

— *Richard Hovey*

A STEIN SONG

(From *Spring*)

Give a rouse, then, in the Maytime
   For a life that knows no fear!
Turn night-time into daytime
   With the sunlight of good cheer!
      For it's always fair weather
      When good fellows get together,
With a stein on the table and a good song ringing clear.

When the wind comes up from Cuba,
   And the birds are on the wing,
And our hearts are patting juba
   To the banjo of the spring,
      Then it's no wonder whether
      The boys will get together,
With a stein on the table and a cheer for everything.

For we're all frank-and-twenty
   When the spring is in the air;
And we've faith and hope a-plenty,
   And we've life and love to spare;
      And it's birds of a feather
      When we all get together,
With a stein on the table and a heart without a care.

For we know the world is glorious,
  And the goal a golden thing,
And that God is not censorious
  When his children have their fling;
      And life slips its tether
      When the boys get together,
With a stein on the table in the fellowship of spring.

— *Richard Hovey*

MADISON CAWEIN

Madison (Julius) Cawein was born at Louisville, Kentucky, in 1865, and spent his life in that state. He died in 1914.

He wrote many volumes of pleasant, polite, and correct verse, chiefly about nature. Among his books are *Lyrics and Idyls* (1890), and *Vale of Tempe* (1905). His *Collected Poems* appeared in 1911.

"Penetralia," in its own way, says some of the things that John Hall Wheelock says in "Earth."

PENETRALIA

I am a part of all you see
In Nature; part of all you feel:
I am the impact of the bee
Upon the blossom; in the tree
I am the sap, — that shall reveal
The leaf, the bloom, — that flows and flutes
Up from the darkness through its roots.

I am the vermeil of the rose,
The perfume breathing in its veins;
The gold within the mist that glows
Along the west and overflows
With light the heaven; the dew that rains
Its freshness down and strings with spheres
Of wet the webs and oaten ears.

I am the egg that folds the bird;
The song that beaks and breaks its shell;
The laughter and the wandering word
The water says; and, dimly heard,

The music of the blossom's bell
When soft winds swing it; and the sound
Of grass slow-creeping o'er the ground.

I am the warmth, the honey-scent
That throats with spice each lily-bud
That opens, white with wonderment,
Beneath the moon; or, downward bent,
Sleeps with a moth beneath its hood:
I am the dream that haunts it too,
That crystallizes into dew.

I am the seed within the pod;
The worm within its closed cocoon:
The wings within the circling clod,
The germ that gropes through soil and sod
To beauty, radiant in the noon:
I am all these, behold! and more —
I am the love at the world-heart's core.

— *Madison Cawein*

THE WINDS

Those hewers of the clouds, the Winds, — that lair
At the four compass-points, — are out to-night;
I hear their sandals trample on the height,
I hear their voices trumpet through the air:
Builders of storm, God's workmen, now they bear.
Up the steep stair of sky, on backs of might,
Huge tempest bulks, while, — sweat that blinds their sight
The rain is shaken from tumultuous hair:
Now, sweepers of the firmament, they broom
Like gathered dust, the rolling mists along
Heaven's floors of sapphire; all the beautiful blue
Of skyey corridor and celestial room
Preparing, with large laughter and loud song,
For the white moon and stars to wander through.

— *Madison Cawein*

GEORGE STERLING

George Sterling was born at Sag Harbor, New York, in 1869. He was educated in private and public schools and at St. Charles College, Ellicott City, Maryland. For many years he has made California his home and Californians are exceedingly proud of his work.

His books are *The Testimony of the Suns and Other Poems* (1903), *A Wine of Wizardry and Other Poems* (1908), *The House of Orchids and Other Poems* (1911), *Beyond the Breakers and Other Poems* (1915), *The Caged Eagle and Other Poems* (1915), *The Binding of the Beast and Other Poems* (1917), and *Sails and Mirage and Other Poems* (1921).

"The Last Days," which has been chosen to represent his work here, has a sober beauty of rhythm and phrasing that is in accord with the quiet and wistful mood of the lyric. This poem simply tells how one person feels about the coming of the autumn.

THE LAST DAYS

The russet leaves of the sycamore
Lie at last on the valley floor —
By the autumn wind swept to and fro
Like ghosts in a tale of long ago.
Shallow and clear the Carmel glides
Where the willows droop on its vine-walled sides.

The bracken-rust is red on the hill;
The pines stand brooding, somber and still;
Gray are the cliffs, and the waters gray,
Where the seagulls dip to the sea-born spray.
Sad November, lady of rain,
Sends the goose-wedge over again.

Wilder now, for the verdure's birth,
Falls the sunlight over the earth;
Kildees call from the fields where now
The banding blackbirds follow the plow;
Rustling poplar and brittle weed
Whisper low to the river-reed.

Days departing linger and sigh:
Stars come soon to the quiet sky;
Buried voices, intimate, strange,
Cry to body and soul of change;
Beauty, eternal, fugitive,
Seeks the home that we cannot give.

— *George Sterling*

EDWIN ARLINGTON ROBINSON

Edwin Arlington Robinson was born at Head Tide, Maine, in 1869. He was educated at Gardiner, Maine, and at Harvard University. He is a member of the National Institute of Arts and Letters.

He is the author of *The Children of the Night* (1897), *Captain Craig* (1902), *The Town Down the River* (1910), *The Man Against the Sky* (1916), *Merlin* (1917), *Lancelot* (1920), *The Three Taverns* (1920), *Avon's Harvest* (1921), and *Collected Poems* (1921).

In shrewd understanding of mankind and as a brilliant analyst of character, Mr. Robinson has no superior among American poets. He defines personality with unerring precision and his sympathy is exquisite, his humor urbane, his irony wise. By virtue of sure intellectual insight he is sometimes a great poet. His technique, too, is always admirable. The reader may be sure of finding in his work the faultless meter, the vivid phrase, and the essential nobleness of gesture which is part of being a gentleman. Any student who has time and inclination to read more poetry than is given here, would do well to read more of Mr. Robinson's poetry, — say, such poems as "The Master," "The Valley of the Shadow," and "Lazarus."

"The False Gods" is a poem of well-founded idealism — not the easy, sentimental idealism of the soul that has never fought a battle in life, but the idealism of the soul that sees through shams. The keynote of the poem, I believe, is to be found in the line,

For the False Gods are mortal, and are made for you to kill.

"Neighbors" is simply the story of the woman who can never afford to dress well, and it is inimitably told. "The Dark Hills" is a lovely song of everlasting changefulness. "The Gift of God" is a story of human love and faith clothing a man's imperfection with beauty.

67

THE FALSE GODS

"We are false and evanescent, and aware of our deceit,
From the straw that is our vitals to the clay that is our feet.
You may serve us if you must, and you shall have your
    wage of ashes, —
Though arrears due thereafter may be hard for you to meet.

"You may swear that we are solid, you may say that we are
    strong,
But we know that we are neither and we say that you are
    wrong;
You may find an easy worship in acclaiming our indulgence,
But your large admiration of us now is not for long.

"If your doom is to adore us with a doubt that's never still,
And you pray to see our faces — pray in earnest, and you
    will.
You may gaze at us and live, and live assured of our con-
    fusion:
For the False Gods are mortal, and are made for you to kill.

"And you may as well observe, while apprehensively at ease
With an Art that's inorganic and is anything you please,
That anon your newest ruin may lie crumbling unregarded,
Like an old shrine forgotten in a forest of new trees.

"Howsoever like no other be the mode you may employ,
There's an order in the ages for the ages to enjoy;
Though the temples you are shaping and the passions you
    are singing.
Are a long way from Athens and a longer way from Troy.

"When we promise more than ever of what never shall
    arrive,
And you seem a little more than ordinarily alive,
Make a note that you are sure you understand our obliga-
    tions —
For there's grief always auditing where two and two are
    five.

"There was this for us to say and there was this for you to
    know,
Though it humbles and it hurts us when we have to tell
    you so.
If you doubt the only truth in all our perjured composition,
May the True Gods attend you and forget us when we go."

                    — *Edwin Arlington Robinson*

NEIGHBORS

As often as we thought of her,
    We thought of a grey life
That made a quaint economist
    Of a wolf-haunted wife;
We made the best of all she bore
    That was not ours to bear,
And honored her for wearing things
    That were not things to wear.

There was a distance in her look
    That made us look again;
And if she smiled, we might believe
    That we had looked in vain.

Rarely she came inside our doors
    And had not long to stay;
And when she left, it seemed somehow
    That she was far away.

At last, when we had all forgot
    That all is here to change,
A shadow on the commonplace
    Was for a moment strange.
Yet there was nothing for surprise
    Nor much that need be told;
Love with his gift of pain had given
    More than one heart could hold.

              — *Edwin Arlington Robinson*

THE GIFT OF GOD

Blessed with a joy that only she
Of all alive shall ever know,
She wears a proud humility
For what it was that willed it so, —
That her degree should be so great
Among the favored of the Lord
That she may scarcely bear the weight
Of her bewildering reward.

As one apart, immune, alone,
Or featured for the shining ones,
And like to none that she has known
Of other women's other sons, —
The firm fruition of her need,
He shines anointed; and he blurs
Her vision, till it seems indeed
A sacrilege to call him hers.

She fears a little for so much
Of what is best, and hardly dares
To think of him as one to touch
With aches, indignities, and cares;
She sees him rather at the goal,
Still shining; and her dream foretells
The proper shining of a soul
Where nothing ordinary dwells.

Perchance a canvass of the town
Would find him far from flags and shouts,
And leave him only the renown
Of many smiles and many doubts;
Perchance the crude and common tongue
Would havoc strangely with his worth;
But she, with innocence unwrung,
Would read his name around the earth.

And others, knowing how this youth
Would shine, if love could make him great,
When caught and tortured for the truth
Would only writhe and hesitate;
While she, arranging for his days
What centuries could not fulfill,
Transmutes him with her faith and praise,
And has him shining where she will.

She crowns him with her gratefulness,
And says again that life is good;
And should the gift of God be less
In him than in her motherhood,

His fame, though vague, will not be small,
As upward through her dream he fares,
Half clouded with a crimson fall
Of roses thrown on marble stairs.

— *Edwin Arlington Robinson*

THE DARK HILLS

Dark hills at evening in the west,
Where sunset hovers like a sound
Of golden horns that sang to rest
Old bones of warriors under ground,
Far now from all the bannered ways
Where flash the legions of the sun,
You fade — as if the last of days
Were fading, and all wars were done.

— *Edwin Arlington Robinson*

EDGAR LEE MASTERS

Edgar Lee Masters was born at Garnett, Kansas, in 1869, and was educated at the high school and at Knox College, Illinois. He studied law in his father's office, was admitted to the bar in 1891, and became a successful attorney. He is a member of the National Institute of Arts and Letters.

He wrote several plays and several books of verse of a derivative type before he became famous in 1915 with the publication of *Spoon River Anthology*. The *Greek Anthology* is the prototype of this famous collection of self-descriptive epitaphs. The citizens of Spoon River are permitted to startle the world by telling, in an exceedingly vivid way, and with the fewest possible words, the absolute truth about themselves and about the chief crises in their lives. It is a book of post-mortem revelation. None of the later books take rank with this one either in popular success or critical appraisal. But good poems are to be found in *Songs and Satires* (1916), *The Great Valley* (1916), *Toward the Gulf* (1918), and *Starved Rock* (1919). In particular, I might recommend "Silence," "At Sagamore Hill," "My Light with Yours," and "Johnny Appleseed," which is given below. Mr. Masters is a realist and quite unafraid of the ugliness of life either for himself or for his readers. But if he leads his readers through the mud of ugliness and sin, it is true that he is not dully unmindful of the stars overhead . It is only as an idealist that he is a masterly poet, for it is the starlight and not the mud that inspires the moving rhythm and the profound thinking in the best of his work. It is truer of him than of most other poets that, when his thoughts are unlovely the measures of his verse halt and stumble, when his thoughts are beautiful his measures are of one sort with them.

"Lucinda Matlock" and "Anne Rutledge" are two of the best epitaphs from *Spoon River Anthology*. "Johnny Appleseed" is founded on the life story of a quaint American personality. His real name was John Chapman and he was born in 1775 and traveled West ahead of the white man through Ohio and Eastern Indiana, planting apple orchards.   He planted about a hundred thousand acres of apple trees, chiefly in clearings in the woods, "for children to come, who will gather and eat hereafter."   An account of his life is given in *Harper's Monthly* for November, 1871.   Vachel Lindsay, also, has written a poem called "Johnny Appleseed," but it is too long for inclusion in this book.

LUCINDA MATLOCK

I went to dances at Chandlerville,
And played snap-out at Winchester.
One time we changed partners,
Driving home in the moonlight of middle June,
And then I found Davis.
We were married and lived together for seventy years,
Enjoying, working, raising the twelve children,
Eight of whom we lost
Ere I had reached the age of sixty.
I spun, I wove, I kept the house, I nursed the sick,
I made the garden, and for holiday
Rambled over the fields where sang the larks,
And by Spoon River gathering many a shell,
And many a flower and medicinal weed —
Shouting to the wooded hills, singing to the green valleys.
At ninety-six I had lived enough, that is all,
And passed to a sweet repose.
What is this I hear of sorrow and weariness,
Anger, discontent and drooping hopes?
Degenerate sons and daughters,
Life is too strong for you —
It takes life to love Life.

— *Edgar Lee Masters*

ANNE RUTLEDGE

Out of me unworthy and unknown
The vibrations of deathless music;
"With malice toward none, with charity for all."
Out of me the forgiveness of millions toward millions,
And the beneficent face of a nation
Shining with justice and truth.
I am Anne Rutledge who sleep beneath these weeds,
Beloved in life of Abraham Lincoln,
Wedded to him, not through union,
But through separation.
Bloom forever, O Republic,
From the dust of my bosom!

— *Edgar Lee Masters*

JOHNNY APPLESEED

When the air of October is sweet and cold as the wine of apples
Hanging ungathered in frosted orchards along the Grand
          River,
I take the road that winds by the resting fields and wander
From Eastmanville to Nunica down to the Villa Crossing.

I look for old men to talk with, men as old as the orchards,
Men to tell me of ancient days, of those who built and planted,
Lichen gray, branch broken, bent and sighing,
Hobbling for warmth in the sun and for places to sit and
          smoke.

For there is a legend here, a tale of the croaking old ones
That Johnny Appleseed came here, planted some orchards
          around here,

When nothing was here but the pine trees, oaks and the
      beeches,
And nothing was here but the marshes, lake and the river.

Peter Van Zylen is ninety and this he tells me:
My father talked with Johnny Appleseed there on the hill-
      side,
There by the road on the way to Fruitport, saw him
Clearing pines and oaks for a place for an apple orchard.

Peter Van Zylen says: He got that name from the people
For carrying apple-seed with him and planting orchards
All the way from Ohio, through Indiana across here,
Planting orchards, they say, as far as Illinois.

Johnny Appleseed said, so my father told me:
I go to the place forgotten, the orchards will thrive and be
      here
For children to come, who will gather and eat hereafter.
And few will know who planted, and none will understand.

I laugh, said Johnny Appleseed: Some fellow buys this
      timber
Five years, perhaps from to-day, begins to clear for barley.
And here in the midst of the timber is hidden an apple
      orchard.
How did it come here?   Lord!   Who was it here before me?

Yes, I was here before him, to make these places of worship,
Labor and laughter and gain in the late October.
Why did I do it, eh?   Some folks say I am crazy.
Where do my labors end?   Far west, God only knows!

Said Johnny Appleseed there on the hillside: Listen!
Beware the deceit of nurseries, sellers of seeds of the apple.
Think!   You labor for years in trees not worth the raising
You planted what you knew not, bitter or sour for sweet.

No luck more bitter than poor seed, but one as bitter:
The planting of perfect seed in soil that feeds and fails,
Nourishes for a little, and then goes spent forever.
Look to your seed, he said, and remember the soil.

And after that is the fight: the foe curled up at the root,
The scale that crumples and deadens, the moth in the
        blossoms
Becoming a life that coils at the core of a thing of beauty:
You bite your apple, a worm is crushed on your tongue!

And it's every bit the truth, said Peter Van Zylen.
So many things love an apple as well as ourselves.
A man must fight for the thing he loves, to possess it:
Apples, freedom, heaven, said Peter Van Zylen.

                                    — *Edgar Lee Masters*

WILLIAM VAUGHN MOODY

William Vaughn Moody was born at Spencer, Indiana, in 1869. He was educated at Harvard University. He travelled and studied and taught for a number of years at the University of Chicago. He died in 1910.

The Masque of Judgment, his first book, was published in 1900. His *Poems* appeared in 1901. He then began to write for the stage, and his prose dramas, *The Great Divide* and *The Faith Healer,* appeared in 1907 and 1909. A complete edition of his poems and poetic dramas was published in 1912.

The place that Moody holds in American poetry is secure and high. It is safe to say, however, that he is underestimated at the present time and that the future will add new leaves to his crown of laurel. He is one of the few who can merit the word "great." He spoke out of a rich mind, out of a passionate heart, out of certain spiritual insight, and his speech will be heard when thinner, cleverer, shallower words now echoing in our minds have long been dead and forgotten. Moreover, his intellectual riches, his social passion, his spiritual insight were not dissipated and lost by reason of any artistic laxity. He knew all the restraints of a good craftsman. In particular let me recommend for study "Gloucester Moors" and "An Ode In Time of Hesitation." In my opinion "Pandora's Song" from *The Firebringer* is the finest short lyric ever written by an American. It is unfortunate that his publishers will not permit the reprinting of his work in this book.

Arthur Guiterman was born of American parentage at Vienna, Austria, in 1871 and was educated at the College of the City of New York. He has worked in New York City as a teacher, a lecturer, an editor, and a writer. His verse, both humorous and serious, has been printed and reprinted in many periodicals and is always carefully and accurately written.

Orestes (with Andre Tridon) was published in 1909. *The Laughing Muse* (1915), *The Mirthful Lyre* (1918), and *Ballads of Old New York* (1919) followed. Of these books by far the most interesting and important as poetry is the last, *The Ballads of Old New York*. In it Mr. Guiterman takes up the old tales of early days in the Empire State and makes them into ballads that have a decided historical interest. "The Flying Dutchman of the Tappan Zee" is an engaging ghost story. The places named can be found on a map that shows the towns along the Hudson River. The Tappan Zee (zee is Dutch for sea) is a wide part of the river near Tarrytown.

THE FLYING DUTCHMAN OF THE TAPPAN ZEE

On Tappan Zee a shroud of gray
　　Is heavy, dank, and low.
And dimly gleams the beacon-ray
　　Of white Pocantico.

No skipper braves old Hudson now
　　Where Nyack's Headlands frown,
And safely moored is every prow
　　Of drowsy Tarrytown;

Yet, clear as word of human lip,
  The river sends its shores
The rhythmic rullock-clank and **drip**
  Of even-rolling oars.

What rower plies a reckless oar
  With mist on flood and strand?
That Oarsman toils forevermore
  And ne'er shall reach the land.

  .   .   .   .   .

Roystering, rollicking Ram van Dam,
Fond of a frolic and fond of a dram,
Fonder — yea, fonder, proclaims renown, —
Of Tryntje Bogardus of Tarrytown,
Leaves Spuyten Duyvil to roar his song!
Pull!   For the current is sly and strong;
Nestles the robin and flies the bat.
Ho! for the frolic at Kakiat!

Merry, the sport at the quilting bee
Held at the farm on the Tappan Zee!
Jovial labor with quips and flings,
Dances with wonderful pigeon wings,
Twitter of maidens and clack of dames,
Honest flirtations and rousing games;
Platters of savory beef and brawn,
Buckets of treacle and good suppawn,
Oceans of cider, and beer in lakes,
Mountains of crullers and honey-cakes —
Such entertainment could never pall!
Rambout van Dam took his fill of all;
Laughed with the wittiest, worked with a zest,
Danced with the prettiest, drank with the best.

Oh! that enjoyment should breed annoy!
Tryntje grew fickle or cold or coy;
Rambout, possessed of a jealous sprite,
Scowled like the sky on a stormy night,
Snarled a good-bye from his sullen throat,
Blustered away to his tugging boat.
After him hastened Jacobus Horn:
"Stay with us, Rambout, till Monday morn.
Soon in the east will the dawn be gray,
Rest from thy oars on the Sabbath Day."

Angrily Rambout van Dam ripped back:
"Dunder en Blitzen! du Schobbejak!
Preach to thy children! and let them know
Spite of the duyvil and thee, I'll row
Thousands of Sundays, if need there be,
Home o'er this ewig-vervlekte zee!"
Muttering curses, he headed south.
Jacob, astounded, with open mouth
Watched him receding, when — crash on crash
Volleyed the thunder! A hissing flash
Smote on the river! He looked again.
Rambout was gone from the sight of men!

. . . . .

Old Dunderberg with grumbling roar
    Hath warned the fog to flee,
But still that never-wearied oar
    Is heard on Tappan Zee.

A moon is closed on Hudson's breast
    And lanterns gem the town;
The phantom craft that may not rest
    Plies ever, up and down,

'Neath skies of blue and skies of gray,
   In spite of wind or tide,
Until the trump of Judgment Day —
   A sound — and naught beside.

— Arthur Guiterman

THOMAS AUGUSTINE DALY

Thomas Augustine Daly was born at Philadelphia, Pennsylvania, in 1871. He was educated in the public schools and at Villanova College and at Fordham University. He has several honorary degrees. He has been prominent for some years as an author and journalist.

His books are *Canzoni* (1906), *Carmina* (1909), *Madrigali* (1912), *Songs of Wedlock* (1916), and *McAroni Ballads* (1919). Mr. Daly's fame as a poet is due to his beautiful way of using the dialect of Italian and Irish immigrants in half-humorous, half-pathetic verse that tells odd little tales of their adventures. In this field his work has unique distinction. His work in the usual English of literature is pleasant, but not distinguished. "Da Leetla Boy" is an exquisitely tender and loving account of the death of a poor man's child. "Perennial May" is a sweet domestic lyric.

DA LEETLA BOY

Da spreeng ees com'! but oh, da joy
    Eet ees too late!
He was so cold, my leetla boy,
    He no could wait.

I no can count how manny week,
How manny day, dat he ees seeck;
How manny night I seet an' hold
Da leetla hand dat was so cold.
He was so patience, oh, so sweet!
Eet hurts my throat for theenk of eet;
An' all he evra ask ees w'en
Ees gona com' da spreeng agen.

Wan day, wan brighta sunny day,
He see, across da alleyway,
Da leetla girl dat's livin' dere
Ees raise her window for da air,
An' put outside a leetla pot
Of — w'at-you-call? — forgat-me-not.
So smalla flower, so leetla theeng!
But steel eet mak' hees hearta seeng:
"Oh, now, at las', ees com' da spreeng!
Da leetla plant ees glad for know
Da sun ees com' for mak' eet grow.
So, too, I am grow warm and strong."
So lika dat he seeng hees song.
But, Ah! da night com' down an' den
Da weenter ees sneak back agen,
An' een da alley all da night
Ees fall da snow, so cold, so white,
An 'cover up da leetla pot
Of — w'at-you-call? — forgat-me-not.
All night da leetla hand I hold
Ees grow so cold, so cold, so cold!

Da spreeng ees com'; but oh, da joy
    Eet ees too late!
He was so cold, my leetla boy.
    He no could wait.

— *Thomas Augustine Daly*

PERENNIAL MAY

May walks the earth again,
This old earth, and the same
Green spurts of tender flame

Burn now on sod and tree
That burned when first she came,
Dear love, to you and me.
If any change there be —
A greater or a less
Degree of loveliness —
It is not ours to see,
Dear love,
Not ours to feel or see.

May thrills our hearts again,
These old hearts, and the bough
Burns not with blossoms now
That blow more splendidly.
For, since our wedded vow
Made one of you and me,
If any change there be —
A greater or a less
Degree of tenderness —
It is not ours to see,
Dear love,
Not ours to feel or see.

— *Thomas Augustine Daly*

ANNA HEMPSTEAD BRANCH

Anna Hempstead Branch was born at New London, Connecticut, and was educated at the Adelphi Academy, Brooklyn, at Smith College, and at the American Academy of Dramatic Art in New York. Since 1898 she has been a contributor of verse and prose to leading magazines.

She is the author of *The Heart of the Road* (1901), *The Shoes that Danced* (1905), *Rose of the Wind* and *Nimrod and Other Poems* (1910), and a play called *Rose of the Wind*, produced at the Carnegie Lyceum and at the Empire Theater. Her work is invariably excellent and few women writing to-day can share laurels equally with her. Aside from its lyrical excellence, it has always this to distinguish it — a certain quaint "other-worldliness" that could never be imitated. "The Monk in the Kitchen" is more than a plea for orderliness in life; it is a benediction on common things and a recognition of the sacredness of humble occupations.

THE MONK IN THE KITCHEN

I

Order is a lovely thing;
On disarray it lays its wing,
Teaching simplicity to sing.
It has a meek and lowly grace,
Quiet as a nun's face.
Lo — I will have thee in this place!
Tranquil well of deep delight,
All things that shine through thee appear
As stones through water, sweetly clear.
Thou clarity,
That with angelic charity

Revealest beauty where thou art,
Spread thyself like a clean pool.
Then all the things that in thee are,
Shall seem more spiritual and fair,
Reflection from serener air —
Sunken shapes of many a star
In the high heavens set afar.

II

Ye stolid, homely, visible things,
Above you all brood glorious wings
Of your deep entities, set high,
Like slow moons in a hidden sky.
But you, their likenesses, are spent
Upon another element.
Truly ye are but seemings —
The shadowy cast-off gleamings
Of bright solidities.   Ye seem
Soft as water, vague as dream;
Image, cast in a shifting stream.

III

What are ye?
I know not.
Brazen pan and iron pot,
Yellow brick and gray flag-stone
That my feet have trod upon —
Ye seem to me
Vessels of bright mystery.
For ye do bear a shape, and so
Though ye were made by man, I know
An inner Spirit also made,
And ye his breathings have obeyed.

IV

Shape, the strong and awful Spirit,
Laid his ancient hand on you.
He waste chaos doth inherit;
He can alter and subdue.
Verily, he doth lift up
Matter, like a sacred cup.
Into deep substance he reached, and lo
Where ye were not, ye were; and so
Out of useless nothing, ye
Groaned and laughed and came to be.
And I use you, as I can,
Wonderful uses, made for man,
Iron pot and brazen pan.

V

What are ye?
I know not;
Nor what I really do
When I move and govern you.
There is no small work unto God.
He required of us greatness;
Of his least creature
A high angelic nature,
Stature superb and bright completeness.
He sets to us no humble duty.
Each act that he would have us do
Is haloed round with strangest beauty;
Terrific deeds and cosmic tasks
Of his plainest child he asks.
When I polish the brazen pan
I hear a creature laugh afar

In the gardens of a star,
And from his burning presence run
Flaming wheels of many a sun.
Whoever makes a thing more bright,
He is an angel of all light.
When I cleanse this earthen floor
My spirit leaps to see
Bright garments trailing over it,
A cleanness made by me.
Purger of all men's thoughts and ways,
With labor do I sound Thy praise,
My work is done for Thee.
Whoever makes a thing more bright,
He is an angel of all light.
Therefore let me spread abroad
The beautiful cleanness of my God.

VI

One time in the cool of dawn
Angels came and worked with me.
The air was soft with many a wing.
They laughed amid my solitude
And cast bright looks on everything.
Sweetly of me did they ask
That they might do my common task.
And all were beautiful — but one
With garments whiter than the sun
Had such a face
Of deep, remembered grace;
That when I saw I cried — "Thou art
The great Blood-Brother of my heart.
Where have I seen thee?" — And he said,

"When we are dancing round God's throne,
How often thou art there.
Beauties from thy hands have flown
Like white doves wheeling in mid air.
Nay — thy soul remembers not?
Work on, and cleanse thy iron pot."

VII

What are we?   I know not.

— *Anna Hempstead Branch*

AMY LOWELL

Amy Lowell was born at Brookline, Massachusetts, in 1874 and educated by private tutors and by travel abroad. As a young girl she decided to be a poet, but instead of offering her immature work to the public in magazines, she wrote and studied for about ten years before attempting to publish anything.

Her first book, *A Dome of Many-Colored Glass*, appeared in 1912. Her later books are *Sword Blades and Poppy Seed* (1914), *Six French Poets* (criticism) (1915), *Men, Women and Ghosts* (1916), *Tendencies in Modern American Poetry* (criticism) (1917), *Can Grande's Castle* (1918), *Pictures of the Floating World* (1919), *Legends* (1921), and *Fir-Flower Tablets — Poems Translated from the Chinese* (with Florence Ayscough) (1921).

Miss Lowell has a brilliant imagination and extraordinary powers of inventiveness which are displayed in the forms that she uses and in the imagery in which she clothes her feelings and ideas. Although she is best known for her work in unrhymed cadence (see introduction) and although she introduced polyphonic prose (see introduction) into American literature, a very large part of her work has been done in the conservative way by the use of metrical stanzas, and she has even written sonnets. The colors, scents, textures, and outlines of life are the materials Miss Lowell uses in her poetry. Out of them she makes her vivid descriptions of moods and her swiftly moving stories. In the opinion of this writer she does her best work as a teller of tales and her finest book is *Can Grande's Castle*.

"The Paper Windmill" is a story of a little boy's deep disappointment told in polyphonic prose. "Purple Grackles" describes the mood that comes to her with the visitation of the grackles.

THE PAPER WINDMILL

The little boy pressed his face against the windowpane and looked out at the bright sunshiny morning. The cobble-stones of the square glistened like mica. In the trees, a breeze danced and pranced, and shook drops of sunlight like falling golden coins into the brown water of the canal. Down stream slowly drifted a long string of galliots piled with crimson cheeses. The little boy thought they looked as if they were roc's eggs, blocks of big ruby eggs. He said, "Oh!" with delight, and pressed against the window with all his might.

The golden cock on the top of the *Stadhuis* gleamed. His beak was open like a pair of scissors and a narrow piece of blue sky was wedged in it. "Cock-a-doodle-do," cried the little boy. "Can't you hear me through the window, Gold Cocky? Cock-a-doodle-do! You should crow when you see the eggs of your cousin, the great roc." But the golden cock stood stock still, with his fine tail blowing in the wind. He could not understand the little boy, for he said *"Cocorico"* when he said anything. But he was hung in the air to swing, not to sing. His eyes glittered to the bright West wind, and the crimson cheeses drifted away down the canal.

It was very dull there in the big room. Outside in the square, the wind was playing tag with some fallen leaves. A man passed, with a dogcart beside him full of smart, new milkcans. They rattled out a gay tune: "Tiddity-tum-ti-ti. Have some milk for your tea. Cream for your coffee to drink to-night, thick, and smooth, and sweet, and white," and the man's sabots beat an accompaniment: "Plop! trop! milk for your tea. Plop! trop! drink it to-night." It was very pleasant out there, but it was lonely here in the big room.   The little boy gulped at a tear.

It was queer how dull all his toys were.   They were so still.   Nothing was still in the square.   If he took his eyes away a moment it had changed.   The milkman had disappeared round the corner, there was only an old woman with a basket of green stuff on her head, picking her way over the shiny stones.   But the wind pulled the leaves in the basket this way and that, and displayed them to beautiful advantage.   The sun patted them condescendingly on their flat surfaces, and they seemed sprinkled with silver.   The little boy sighed as he looked at his disordered toys on the floor.   They were motionless, and their colours were dull. The dark wainscoting absorbed the sun.   There was none left for toys.

The square was quite empty now.   Only the wind ran round and round it, spinning.   Away over in the corner where a street opened into the square, the wind had stopped. Stopped running, that is, for it never stopped spinning. It whirred, and whirled, and gyrated, and turned.   It burned like a great coloured sun.   It hummed, and buzzed, and sparked, and darted.   There were flashes of blue, and long smearing lines of saffron, and quick jabs of green.   And over it all was a sheen like a myriad cut diamonds.   Round and round it went, the huge windwheel, and the little boy's head reeled with watching it.   The whole square was filled with its rays, blazing and leaping round after one another, faster and faster.   The little boy could not speak, he could only gaze, staring in amaze.

The wind-wheel was coming down the square.   Nearer and nearer it came, a great disk of spinning flame.   It was opposite the window now, and the little boy could see it plainly, but it was something more than the wind which he saw. A man was carrying a huge fan-shaped frame on his shoulder, and stuck in it were many little painted paper windmills, each one scurrying round in the breeze. They were bright and beautiful, and the sight was one to please anybody; and how much more a little boy who had only stupid, motionless toys to enjoy.

The little boy clapped his hands, and his eyes danced and whizzed, for the circling windmills made him dizzy. Closer and closer came the windmill man, and held up his big fan to the little boy in the window of the Ambassador's house. Only a pane of glass between the boy and the windmills. They slid round before his eyes in rapidly revolving splendour. There were wheels and wheels of colours — big, little, thick, thin — all one clear, perfect spin. The windmill vendor dipped and raised them again, and the little boy's face was glued to the windowpane. Oh! What a glorious, wonderful plaything! Rings and rings of windy colour always moving! How had any one ever preferred those other toys which never stirred. "Nursie, come quickly. Look! I want a windmill. See! It is never still. You will buy me one, won't you? I want that silver one, with the big ring of blue."

So a servant was sent to buy that one: silver, ringed with blue, and smartly it twirled about in the servant's hands as he stood a moment to pay the vendor. Then he entered the house, and in another minute he was standing in the nursery door, with some crumpled paper on the end of a stick which he held out to the little boy. "But I wanted a windmill which went round," cried the little boy. "That is the one you asked for, Master Charles," Nursie was a bit impatient, she had mending to do. "See, it is silver, and here is the blue." "But it is only a blue streak," sobbed the little boy. "I wanted a blue ring, and this silver doesn't sparkle." "Well, Master Charles, that is what you wanted, now run away and play with it, for I am very busy."

The little boy hid his tears against the friendly window-pane. On the floor lay the motionless, crumpled bit of paper on the end of its stick. But far away across the square was the windmill vendor, with his big wheel of whirring splendour. It spun round in a blaze like a whirling rainbow, and the sun gleamed upon it, and the wind whipped it, until it seemed a maze of spattering diamonds. *"Cocorico!"* crowed the golden cock on the top of the *Stadhuis.* "That is something worth crowing for." But the little boy did not hear him, he was sobbing over the crumpled bit of paper on the floor.

— Amy Lowell

PURPLE GRACKLES

The grackles have come.
The smoothness of the morning is puckered with their
       incessant chatter.
A sociable lot, these purple grackles,
Thousands of them strung across a long run of wind,
Thousands of them beating the air-ways with quick
       wing-jerks,
Spinning down the currents of the South.
Every year they come,
My garden is a place of solace and recreation evidently,
For they always pass a day with me.

With high good nature they tell me what I do not
          want to hear.
The grackles have come.

I am persuaded that grackles are birds;
But when they are settled in the trees,
I am inclined to declare them fruits
And the trees turned hybrid blackberry vines.
Blackness shining and bulging under leaves,
Does not that mean blackberries, I ask you?
Nonsense!   The grackles have come.

Nonchalant highwaymen, pickpockets, second-story
          burglars,
Stealing away my little hope of Summer.
There is no stealthy robbing in this.
Whoever heard such a gabble of thieves' talk!
It seems they delight in unmasking my poor pretense.
Yes, now I see that the hydrangea blooms are rusty;
That the hearts of the golden glow are ripening to
          lustreless seeds;
That the garden is dahlia-coloured,
Flaming with its last over-hot hues;
That the sun is pale as a lemon too small to fill the
          picking-ring.
I did not see this yesterday,
But to-day the grackles have come.

They drop out of the trees
And strut in companies over the lawn,
Tired of flying, no doubt;
A grand parade to limber legs and give wings a rest.

I should build a great fish-pond for them,
Since it is evident that a bird-bath, meant to accommodate
        two gold-finches at most,
Is slight hospitality for these hordes.
Scarcely one can get in,
They all peck and scrabble so,
Crowding, pushing, chasing one another up the bank with
        spread wings.
"Are we ducks, you owner of such inadequate comforts,
That you offer us lily-tanks where one must swim or drown,
Not stand and splash like a gentleman?"
I feel the reproach keenly, seeing them perch on the edges
        of the tanks, trying the depth with a chary foot,
And hardly able to get their wings under water in the
        bird-bath.
But there are resources I have not considered,
If I am bravely ruled out of count.
What is that thudding against the eaves just beyond my
        window?
What is that spray of water blowing past my face?
Two — three — grackles bathing in the gutter,
The gutter providentially choked with leaves.
I pray they think I put the leaves there on purpose;
I would be supposed thoughtful and welcoming
To all guests, even thieves.
But considering that they are going South and I am not,
I wish they would bathe more quietly,
It is unmannerly to flaunt one's good fortune.

They rate me of no consequence,
But they might reflect that it is my gutter.
I know their opinion of me,

Because one is drying himself on the window-sill
Not two feet from my hand.
His purple neck is sleek with water,
And the fellow preens his feathers for all the world as if I
      were a fountain statue.
If it were not for the window,
I am convinced he would light on my head.
Tyrian-feathered freebooter,
Appropriating my delightful gutter with so extravagant
      an ease,
You are as cool a pirate as ever scuttled a ship,
And are you not scuttling my Summer with every peck of
      your sharp bill?

But there is a cloud over the beech-tree.
A quenching cloud for lemon-livered suns.
The grackles are all swinging in the tree-tops.
And the wind is coming up, mind you.
That boom and reach is no Summer gale,
I know that wind,
It blows the Equinox over seeds and scatters them,
It rips petals from petals, and tears off half-turned leaves.
There is rain on the back of that wind.
Now I would keep the grackles,
I would plead with them not to leave me.
I grant their coming, but I would not have them go.
It is a milestone, this passing of grackles.
A day of them, and it is a year gone by.
There is magic in this and terror,
But I only stare stupidly out of the window.
The grackles have come.

Come! Yes, they surely came.
But they have gone.
A moment ago the oak was full of them,
They are not there now.
Not a speck of a black wing,
Not an eye-peep of a purple head.
The grackles have gone,
And I watch an Autumn storm
Stripping the garden,
Shouting black rain challenges
To an old, limp Summer
Laid down to die in the flower-beds.

— *Amy Lowell*

(Frederic) Ridgely Torrence was born at Xenia, Ohio, in 1875 and was educated at Miami and at Princeton University. For a time after leaving college he was librarian of the Astor Library and of the Lenox Library. He has been on the editorial staffs of several magazines. He is a member of the National Institute of Arts and Letters.

He is the author of *The House of a Hundred Lights* (1900), *El Dorado, a Tragedy* (1903), *Abelard and Heloise* (poetic drama) (1907), also three plays for a negro theater, *Granny Maumee, The Rider of Dreams,* and *Simon the Cyrenian,* published together in 1917.

The best of his work in verse, however, is not to be found in any book. His uncollected lyrics are exceedingly fine in thought and feeling and are written with great distinction. "Eye-witness" is a narrative of a religious vision written with a most unusual delicacy and insight. It is poised and sane and inspiring from beginning to end, never degenerating into sentimentality, in spite of its mysticism, and always placing the emphasis on loving service of our kind. It is most difficult to offer interpretation of a lyric as gravely beautiful as "The Singers in a Cloud." It seems to be a poem of the eternal world of unseen realities that touches this world nearly and yet can never be explained or defined in prose.

EYE-WITNESS

Down by the railroad in a green valley
By dancing water, there he stayed awhile
Singing, and three men with him, listeners,
All tramps, all homeless reapers of the wind,
Motionless now and while the song went on
Transfigured into mages thronged with visions;

There with the late light of the sunset on them
And on clear water spinning from a spring
Through little cones of sand dancing and fading,
Close beside pine woods where a hermit thrush
Cast, when love dazzled him, shadows of music
That lengthened, fluting, through the singer's pauses
While the sure earth rolled eastward bringing stars
Over the singer and the men that listened
There by the roadside, understanding all.

A train went by but nothing seemed to be changed.
Some eye at a car window must have flashed
From the plush world inside the glassy Pullman,
Carelessly bearing off the scene forever,
With idle wonder what the men were doing,
Seeing they were so strangely fixed and seeing
Torn papers from their smeary dreary meal
Spread on the ground with old tomato cans
Muddy with dregs of lukewarm chicory,
Neglected while they listened to the song.
And while he sang the singer's face was lifted,
And the sky shook down a soft light upon him
Out of its branches where like fruits there were
Many beautiful stars and planets moving,
With lands upon them, rising from their seas,
Glorious lands with glittering sands upon them,
With soils of gold and magic mould for seeding,
The shining loam of lands afoam with gardens
On mightier stars with giant rains and suns
There in the heavens; but on none of all
Was there ground better than he stood upon:
There was no world there in the sky above him

Deeper in promise than the earth beneath him
Whose dust had flowered up in him the singer
And three men understanding every word.

The Tramp Sings:

I will sing, I will go, and never ask me "Why?"
I was born a rover and a passer-by.

I seem to myself like water and sky,
A river and a rover and a passer-by.

But in the winter three years back
We lit us a night fire by the track,

And the snow came up and the fire it flew
And we couldn't find the warming room for two.

One had to suffer, so I left him the fire
And I went to the weather from my heart's desire.

It was night on the line, it was no more fire,
But the zero whistle through the icy wire.

As I went suffering through the snow
Something like a shadow came moving slow.

I went up to it and I said a word;
Something flew above it like a kind of bird.

I leaned in closer and I saw a face;
A light went round me but I kept my place.

My heart went open like an apple sliced;
I saw my Saviour and I saw my Christ.

Well, you may not read it in a book,
But it takes a gentle Saviour to give a gentle look.

I looked in his eyes and I read the news;
His heart was having the railroad blues.

Oh, the railroad blues will cost you dear,
Keeps you moving on for something that you don't see here.

We stood and whispered in a kind of moon;
The line was looking like May and June.

I found he was a roamer and a journeyman
Looking for a lodging since the night began.

He went to the doors but he didn't have the pay.
He went to the windows, then he went away.

Says, "We'll walk together and we'll both be fed."
Says, "I will give you the 'other' bread."

Oh, the bread he gave and without money!
O drink, O fire, O burning honey!

It went all through me like a shining storm:
I saw inside me, it was light and warm.

I saw deep under and I saw above,
I saw the stars weighed down with love.

They sang that love to burning birth,
They poured that music to the earth.

I heard the stars sing low like mothers.
He said: "Now look, and help feed others."

I looked around, and as close as touch
Was everybody that suffered much.

They reached out, there was darkness only;
They could not see us, they were lonely.

I saw the hearts that deaths took hold of,
With the wounds bare that were not told of;

Hearts with things in them making gashes;
Hearts that were choked with their dreams' ashes;

Women in front of the rolled-back air,
Looking at their breasts and nothing there;

Good men wasting and trapped in hells;
Hurt lads shivering with the fare-thee-wells.

I saw them as if something bound them;
I stood there but my heart went round them.

I begged him not to let me see them wasted.
Says, "Tell them then what you have tasted."

Told him I was weak as a rained-on bee:
Told him I was lost. — Says: "Lean on me."

Something happened then I could not tell,
But I knew I had the water for every hell.

Any other thing it was no use bringing;
They needed what the stars were singing,

What the whole sky sang like waves of light,
The tune that it danced to, day and night.

Oh, I listened to the sky for the tune to come;
The song seemed easy, but I stood there dumb.

The stars could feel me reaching through them
They let down light and drew me to them.

I stood in the sky in a light like day,
Drinking in the word that all things say

Where the worlds hang growing in clustered shapes
Dripping the music like wine from grapes.

With, "Love, Love, Love," above the pain,
— The vine-like song with its wine-like rain.

Through heaven under heaven the song takes root
Of the turning, burning, deathless fruit.

I came to the earth and the pain so near me,
I tried that song but they couldn't hear me.

I went down into the ground to grow,
A seed for a song that would make men know.

Into the ground from my roamer's light
I went; he watched me sink to night

Deep in the ground from my human grieving,
His pain ploughed in me to believing.

Oh, he took earth's pain to be his bride,
While the heart of life sang in his side.

For I felt that pain, I took its kiss,
My heart broke into dust with his.

Then sudden through the earth I found life springing;
The dust men trampled on was singing.

Deep in my dust I felt its tones;
The roots of beauty went round my bones.

I stirred, I rose like a flame, like a river,
I stood on the line, I could sing forever.

Love had pierced into my human sheathing,
Song came out of me simple as breathing.

A freight came by, the line grew colder,
He laid his hand upon my shoulder.

Says, "Don't stay on the line such nights,"
And led me by the hand to the station lights.

I asked him in front of the station-house wall
If he had lodging.   Says, "None at all."

I pointed to my heart and looked in his face. —
"Here, — if you haven't got a better place."

He looked and he said: "Oh, we still must roam
But if you'll keep it open, well, I'll call it 'home.'"

The thrush now slept whose pillow was his wing.
So the song ended and the four remained
Still in the faint starshine that silvered them,
While the low sound went on of broken water
Out of the spring and through the darkness flowing
Over a stone that held it from the sea.
Whether the men spoke after could not be told,
A mist from the ground so veiled them, but they waited
A little longer till the moon came up;
Then on the gilded track leading to the mountains,
Against the moon they faded in common gold
And earth bore East with all toward the new morning.

— *Ridgely Torrence*

THE SINGERS IN A CLOUD

OVERHEAD at sunset all heard the choir.
Nothing could be seen except jewelled grey
Raining beauty earthward, flooding with desire
All things that listened there in the broken day;
Songs from freer breathers, their unprisoned fire
Out of cloudy fountains, flying and hurled,
Fell and warmed the world.

Sudden came a wind and birds were laid bare,
Only music warmed them round their brown breasts.
They had sent the splendours pouring through the air,
Love was their heat and home far above their nests.
Light went softly out and left their voices there.
Starward passed forever all that great cry,
Burning, round the sky.

On the earth the battles war against light,
Heavy lies the harrow, bitter the field.
Beauty, like a river running through the night,
Streams past the stricken one whom it would have healed,
But the darkened faces turn away from sight.
Blind, bewildered nations sow, reap, and fall,
Shadows gather all.

Far above the birdsong bright shines the gold.
Through the starry orchards earth's paths are hung;
As she moves among them glowing fruits unfold,
Such that the heavens there reawaken young.
Overhead is beauty, healing for the old.
Overhead is morning, nothing but youth,
Only lovely youth.

—Ridgely Torrence

HARRIET MONROE

Harriet Monroe was born at Chicago and is a graduate of The Visitation Academy at Georgetown, D. C. She is founder and editor of *Poetry, A Magazine of Verse*.

Her books are *Valeria and Other Poems* (1892), *The Columbian Ode* (1893), *The Passing Show* (1903), *You and I* (1914). She is co-editor with Alice Corbin Henderson of *The New Poetry*. "The Water Ouzel" needs no explanation.

THE WATER OUZEL

Little brown surf-bather of the mountains!
Spirit of foam, lover of cataracts, shaking your wings in
      falling waters!
Have you no fear of the roar and rush when Nevada
      plunges —
Nevada, the shapely dancer, feeling her way with slim,
      white fingers?
How dare you dash at Yosemite the mighty —
Tall, white limbed Yosemite, leaping down, down over the
      cliff?
Is it not enough to lean on the blue air of mountains?
Is it not enough to rest with your mate at timberline, in
      bushes that hug the rocks?
Must you fly through mad waters where the heaped-up
      granite breaks them?
Must you batter your wings in the torrent?
Must you plunge for life or death through the foam?

—Harriet Monroe

ROBERT FROST

Robert (Lee) Frost was born at San Francisco, California, in 1875. When he was ten years old he was brought home to the New England hills where his family had lived for eight generations. After his graduation from the high school in Lawrence, Massachusetts, he went to Dartmouth for a few months, but did not like the routine of college life and gave it up to enter one of the mills in Lawrence as a bobbin boy. *The Independent* was the first magazine to publish any of his verse and for many years the only one. Mr. Frost's work was so decidedly original that it had to make its way slowly with editors accustomed to mild, innocuous, vacuous, and jingling lyrics. For twenty years Robert Frost went on writing, but remained unknown. Surely that was keeping faith with his art! While he was making his poems whose value the world did not recognize, he was farming and teaching in New England to earn a living for himself and for his family.

But in 1912 he decided to make a change. He sold his farm and sailed to England. There, for the first time in his life, he met literary people and lived among them. He took his collection of poems — so often rejected! — to an English publisher and it was accepted and published in 1913 under the title *A Boy's Will*. Moreover, it was received with enthusiasm. A year later *North of Boston* was published and made Mr. Frost famous both in England and at home. Almost at once he became a leading figure in American literature and he has remained a leader ever since. *Mountain Interval*, which contains some of Mr. Frost's most exquisite lyrics, appeared in 1916. Three slender volumes, these, proclaiming a mastery of life and art!

It is difficult to give a brief characterization of his work because the temptation is to write at length about it. In the first place, it has grown and blossomed out of the soil of New England, and no other part of the world could have produced it. It is poetry of a locality. Somebody has wisely said that many people have written about New England, but that Robert Frost *is* New England. It is poetry that uses the turns of human speech, all the tricks and twists of conversation, and makes them lyrical. I do not mean that Mr. Frost writes in dialect, for he does not. He does not hear a dialect spoken in the New England that he knows. But he uses language just as it is used by the hearth or under the trees or on the haymow, full of fresh, keen emotion, shrewd thought, pungent humor. And he gives to this language overtones of melody and meaning that do not belong to it except by his gift. Nobody can fully enjoy the music of his verse who does not understand this, who does not realize that he has departed just far enough from the norm of literary language to make his work true to life — and no farther. He has been called a realist because of his love for facts. But he is certainly not the typical realist. This is what he thinks about realism.

A man who makes really good literature is like a fellow who goes into the fields to pull carrots. He keeps on pulling them patiently enough until he finds a carrot that suggests something else to him. It is not shaped like other carrots. He takes out his knife and notches it here and there, until the two pronged roots become legs and the carrot takes on something of the semblance of a man. The real genius takes hold of that bit of life which is suggestive to him and gives it form. But the man who is merely a realist, and not a genius, will leave the carrot just as he finds it. The man who is merely an idealist and not a genius, will try to carve a donkey where no donkey is suggested by the carrot he pulls.

BIRCHES

When I see birches bend to left and right
Across the line of straighter darker trees,
I like to think some boy's been swinging them.
But swinging doesn't bend them down to stay.
Ice-storms do that. Often you must have seen them
Loaded with ice a sunny winter morning

After a rain.   They click upon themselves
As the breeze rises, and turn many-colored
As the stir cracks and crazes their enamel.
Soon the sun's warmth makes them shed crystal shells
Shattering and avalanching on the snow-crust —
Such heaps of broken glass to sweep away
You'd think the inner dome of heaven had fallen.
They are dragged to the withered bracken by the load,
And they seem not to break; though, once they are bowed
So low for long, they never right themselves:
You may see their trunks arching in the woods
Years afterwards, trailing their leaves on the ground
Like girls on hands and knees that throw their hair
Before them over their heads to dry in the sun.
But I was going to say when Truth broke in
With all her matter-of-fact about the ice-storm
I should prefer to have some boy bend them
As he went out and in to fetch the cows —
Some boy too far from town to learn baseball,
Whose only play was what he found himself,
Summer or winter, and could play alone.
One by one he subdued his father's trees
By riding them down over and over again
Until he took the stiffness out of them,
And not one but hung limp, not one was left
For him to conquer.   He learned all there was
To learn about not launching out too soon
And so not carrying the tree away
Clear to the ground.   He always kept his poise
To the top branches, climbing carefully
With the same pains you use to fill a cup
Up to the brim, and even above the brim.

Then he flung outward, feet first, with a swish,
Kicking his way down through the air to the ground.

So was I once myself a swinger of birches;
And so I dream of going back to be.
It's when I'm weary of considerations, ·
And life is too much like a pathless wood
Where your face burns and tickles with the cobwebs
Broken across it, and one eye is weeping
From a twig's having lashed across it open.
I'd like to get away from earth awhile
And then come back to it and begin over.
May no fate wilfully misunderstand me
And half grant what I wish and snatch me away
Not to return.   Earth's the right place for love:
I don't know where it's likely to go better.
I'd like to go by climbing a birch tree,
And climb black branches up a snow-white trunk
Toward heaven, till the tree could bear no more,
But dipped its top and set me down again.
That would be good both going and coming back.
One could do worse than be a swinger of birches.

—*Robert Frost*

MENDING WALL

Something there is that doesn't love a wall,
That sends the frozen-ground-swell under it,
And spills the upper boulders in the sun;
And makes gaps even two can pass abreast.
The work of hunters is another thing:
I have come after them and made repair
Where they have left not one stone on a stone,

But they would have the rabbit out of hiding,
To please the yelping dogs.   The gaps I mean,
No one has seen them made or heard them made,
But at spring mending-time we find them there.
I let my neighbor know beyond the hill;
And on a day we meet to walk the line
And set the wall between us once again.
We keep the wall between us as we go.
To each the boulders that have fallen to each.
And some are loaves and some so nearly balls
We have to use a spell to make them balance:
"Stay where you are until our backs are turned!"
We wear our fingers rough with handling them.
Oh, just another kind of outdoor game,
One on a side.   It comes to little more:
He is all pine and I am apple-orchard.
My apple trees will never get across
And eat the cones under his pines, I tell him.
He only says, "Good fences make good neighbors."
Spring is the mischief in me, and I wonder
If I could put a notion in his head:
"*Why* do they make good neighbors?   Isn't it
Where there are cows?   But here there are no cows.
Before I built a wall I'd ask to know
What I was walling in or walling out,
And to whom I was like to give offence.
Something there is that doesn't love a wall,
That wants it down!"   I could say "Elves" to him,
But it's not elves exactly, and I'd rather
He said it for himself.   I see him there,
Bringing a stone grasped firmly by the top
In each hand, like an old-stone savage armed.

He moves in darkness as it seems to me,
Not of woods only and the shade of trees.
He will not go behind his father's saying,
And he likes having thought of it so well
He says again, "Good fences make good neighbors."

—*Robert Frost*

THE ONSET

Always the same when on a fated night
At last the gathered snow lets down as white
As may be in dark woods and with a song
It shall not make again all winter long —
Of hissing on the yet uncovered ground, —
I almost stumble looking up and round,
As one who, overtaken by the end,
Gives up his errand and lets death descend
Upon him where he is, with nothing done
To evil, no important triumph won
More than if life had never been begun.

Yet all the precedent is on my side:
I know that winter death has never tried
The earth but it has failed; the snow may heap
In long storms an undrifted four feet deep
As measured against maple, birch and oak;
It cannot check the Peeper's silver croak;
And I shall see the snow all go down hill
In water of a slender April rill
That flashes tail through last year's withered brake
And dead weeds like a disappearing snake.
Nothing will be left white but here a birch
And there a clump of houses with a church.

—*Robert Frost*

SARAH N. CLEGHORN

Sarah N. Cleghorn was born at Norfolk, Virginia, in 1876. She was graduated from Burr and Burton Seminary in Manchester, Vermont, and was a student at Radcliffe College for a year. She is a pacifist, a socialist, and an anti-vivisectionist, and she is also a poet. Perhaps it would be wiser to call her an exponent of radical Christianity.

Her books are *A Turnpike Lady* (1907), *The Spinster* (1916), *Fellow Captains* (with Dorothy Canfield Fisher, 1916), *and Portraits and Protests* (1917). The last named volume is her collection of verse. It is well named. Some of the poems are keen and kindly portraits of people she has known and studied. Others are fiery protests against social injustice.

PORTRAIT OF A LADY

Her eyes are sunlit hazel;
　　Soft shadows round them play.
Her dark hair, smoothly ordered,
　　Is faintly touched with grey.
Full of a gentle kindness
　　Her looks and language are;
Kind tongue that never wounded,
　　Sweet mirth that leaves no scar.

Her dresses are of lilac
　　And silver pearly grey.
She wears, on meet occasion,
　　Modes of a bygone day,
But moves with soft composure
　　In fashion's pageant set,

116

Until her world she teaches
  Its costume to forget.

With score of friends foregathered
  About a cheerful blaze,
She loves good ranging converse
  Of past and future days;
Her best delight (too seldom)
  From olden friends to hear
How fares the small old city
  She left this many a year.

There is a still more pleasant,
  A cosier converse still,
When, all our guests departed,
  Close comrades talk their fill.
Beside our smouldering fire
  We muse and wonder late,
Commingling household gossip
  With talk of gods and fate.

All seemly ways of living,
  Proportion, comeliness,
Authority and order,
  Her loyal heart possess;
Then with what happy fingers
  She spreads the linen fair
In that great Church of Bishops
  That is her darling care!

And yet I dare to forecast
  What her new name shall be,

Writ in the mystic volume
    Beside the silver sea;
Instead of "True Believer,"
    The golden quill hath penned
"Of the poor beasts that perish,
    The brave and gentle friend."

—*Sarah N. Cleghorn*

WILLIAM GRIFFITH

William Griffith was born at Memphis, Mo., in 1876. He is well known in New York as an editor and as the author of a number of books of verse. Perhaps the best known of his books, and certainly one of the most charming of them, is *Loves and Losses of Pierrot* (1916). His later books are *City Pastorals* (1918) and *Candles in the Sun* (1921). His lyrics are written with unusual delicacy and refinement.

CANTICLE

Devoutly worshipping the oak
Wherein the barred owl stares,
The little feathered forest folk
Are praying sleepy prayers:

Praying the summer to be long
And drowsy to the end,
And daily full of sun and song,
That broken hopes may mend.

Praying the golden age to stay
Until the whippoorwill
Appoints a windy moving-day,
And hurries from the hill.

— *William Griffith*

CARL SANDBURG

Carl Sandburg was born at Galesburg, Illinois, in 1878. He was educated by life rather than by schools, for at thirteen years of age he took a milk route and from that time on worked at many trades until the time of the war with Spain. Then, in 1898, he enlisted in Company C, Sixth Illinois Volunteers. When the campaign in Porto Rico was over he entered Lombard College in Galesburg and began to get another sort of education out of books. After he left college he did many things to earn a living; was a salesman, an advertiser, a journalist, and a political organizer.

In 1904 Mr. Sandburg published a small collection of his early poems. His first important book, however, was *Chicago Poems*, published in 1916. It was followed by *Cornhuskers* (1918), and *Smoke and Steel* (1920). Perhaps the most valuable of the three collections is *Cornhuskers*, but all are individual to a degree and particularly interesting to other poets and critics and to those who wish to understand the industrial problems of this period. It is not that Mr. Sandburg writes primarily to inform us or to argue with us, for he does not do that, although information and argument are plentiful in his books. It is simply that he gives, or tries to give, the people's feeling, the force that is behind the argument, beneath the information. Frequently he is merely eloquent and oratorical — a popular preacher — not a restrained and creative artist. It is interesting to remember that his unrhymed eloquence made its first appeal to poets and critics who had learned to inveigh against the "rhymed eloquence" of an earlier period. The question of the advisability of using slang as freely as Mr. Sandburg uses it is one that must be faced alike by those who admire his work and by those who do not. The use of slang in literature as a part of the characterization of people is permissible. Is it permissible for a poet to speak lyrically and subjectively in slang? That is the question. Perhaps the use of slang and of the coarser folk words gives a directness and reality and pungency to what Mr. Sandburg has to say about this period to the people of this period. But no fashions change faster than fashions in slang. Will Mr. Sandburg's language be obsolete fifty years hence, or will he be strong enough to make it immortal? It seems to the writer of this book to be fairly probable that Mr. Sandburg's noisy, eloquent, oratorical, and slangy poems are chiefly important now and in the near future, and that immortality will be reserved for his quieter poems, which express his spirit.

Of these, surely, one of the loveliest is "Monotone" with its gentle music and perfect picturing. "Cool Tombs" is characteristic alike of his deep friendliness and of his way of writing. "Fog" is simply a small, masterly metaphor.

COOL TOMBS

When Abraham Lincoln was shoveled into the tombs, he
    forgot the copperheads and the assassin . . . in
    the dust, in the cool tombs.

And Ulysses Grant lost all thought of con men and Wall
    Street, cash and collateral turned ashes . . . in
    the dust, in the cool tombs.

Pocahontas' body, lovely as a poplar, sweet as a red haw
    in November or a pawpaw in May, did she wonder?
    does she remember? . . . in the dust, in the cool
    tombs?

Take any streetful of people buying clothes and groceries,
    cheering a hero or throwing confetti and blowing
    tin horns . . . tell me if the lovers are losers
    . . . tell me if any get more than the lovers . . .
    in the dust . . . in the cool tombs.

                                —*Carl Sandburg*

MONOTONE

The monotone of the rain is beautiful,
And the sudden rise and slow relapse
Of the long multitudinous rain.

The sun on the hills is beautiful,
Or a captured sunset, sea-flung,
Bannered with fire and gold.

A face I know is beautiful —
With fire and gold of sky and sea,
And the peace of long warm rain.

—Carl Sandburg

FOG

The fog comes
on little cat feet.

It sits looking
over harbor and city
on silent haunches
and then moves on.

—Carl Sandburg

FLORENCE WILKINSON EVANS

Florence Wilkinson Evans (née Wilkinson) was born at Tarrytown, New York. She was educated at home and at several colleges and then traveled abroad and studied at the Sorbonne and at the Bibliotheque Nationale in Paris.

She is the author of *The Lady of the Flag Flowers* (1899), *The Strength of the Hills* (1902), *Kings and Queens* (1903), *Two Plays of Israel* (1904), *The Far Country* (1905), *The Marriage of Guineth* and *Two is Company* (1902), and *The Ride Home* (1913). "The Flower Factory," printed here, is a protest against child labor, one of the most beautiful poems of protest against iniquitous industrialism that has been given to us in this period.

THE FLOWER FACTORY

Lisabetta, Marianina, Fiametta, Teresina,
They are winding stems of roses, one by one, one by one,
Little children, who have never learned to play;
Teresina softly crying that her fingers ache to-day;
Tiny Fiametta nodding when the twilight slips in, gray.
High above the clattering street, ambulance and fire-gong
    beat,
They sit, curling crimson petals, one by one, one by one.

Lisabetta, Marianina, Fiametta, Teresina,
They have never seen a rosebush nor a dewdrop in the sun.
They will dream of the vendetta, Teresina, Fiametta,
Of a Black Hand and a face behind a grating;
They will dream of cotton petals, endless, crimson, suffocat-
    ing,
Never of a wild-rose thicket nor the singing of a cricket,

But the ambulance will bellow through the wanness of their
    dreams,
And their tired lids will flutter with the street's hysteric
    screams.
Lisabetta, Marianina, Fiametta, Teresina,
They are winding stems of roses, one by one, one by one.
Let them have a long, long playtime, Lord of Toil, when toil
    is done,
Fill their baby hands with roses, joyous roses of the sun!

                               —*Florence Wilkinson*

JOSEPHINE PRESTON PEABODY

Josephine Preston Peabody Marks (née Peabody) was born at New York City and educated in the Girls' Latin School of Boston and at Radcliffe. She taught at Wellesley College for two years and then gave up teaching for literature. She died in 1922.

Her most important books are *The Wayfarers — A Book of Verse* (1898), *Fortune and Men's Eyes — New Poems with a Play* (1900), *Marlowe* (1901), *The Singing Leaves* (1903), *Pan, A Choric Idyl* (for music) (1904), *The Wings* (1905), *The Piper* (which obtained the Stratford-on-Avon prize in 1910 and was then produced in England and in America), *The Singing Man* (1911), *The Wolf of Gubbio* (1913), and *Harvest Moon* (1916). "The House and the Road" is one of the best beloved of her short lyrics. Perhaps it tells of the time when young people have to leave home to go out into the world and earn their living. There are other interpretations, however. The house may symbolize all that stays and is permanent, the road all that leads up and out and away, all that never rests.

THE HOUSE AND THE ROAD

The little Road says, Go,
The little House says, Stay:
And O, it's bonny here at home,
But I must go away.

The little Road, like me,
Would seek and turn and know;
And forth I must, to learn the things
The little Road would show!

And go I must, my dears,
And journey while I may,
Though heart be sore for the little House
That had no word but Stay.

Maybe, no other way
Your child could ever know
Why a little House would have you stay,
When a little Road says, Go.

—Josephine Preston Peabody

OLIVE TILFORD DARGAN

Olive Tilford Dargan was born at Grayson, Kentucky, and educated at the University of Nashville and at Radcliffe College. Before her marriage to Mr. Dargan she taught and traveled abroad.

Her books are *Semiramis and Other Plays* (1904-08), *Lords and Lovers and Other Dramas* (1906), *The Mortal Gods and Other Dramas* (1912), *Path Flower and Other Poems* (1914), *The Cycle's Rim* (1916) and *Lute and Furrow* (1922). *The Cycle's Rim* received the prize of five hundred dollars offered by The Southern Society of New York for the best book of the year by a Southern writer.

"Path Flower" is a gracious and charming ballad. It uses one of the typical stanzas of balladry and is at once very simple and very conventional. It deals with the simplest of incidents, something that might happen at any time in the life of any kindly person, the giving of a small coin to a young girl who looked ragged and hungry. But the poem is so magically made that we are as much interested in this little incident as we could be in an event far more important. The interest is sustained from line to line and from stanza to stanza. "Path Flower" is remarkable for its tact, fineness, delicacy of perception, and quaintness of manner.

PATH FLOWER

A red-cap sang in Bishop's wood,
  A lark o'er Golder's lane,
As I the April pathway trod
  Bound west for Willesden.

At foot each tiny blade grew big
  And taller stood to hear,
And every leaf on every twig
  Was like a little ear.

127

As I too paused, and both ways tried
    To catch the rippling rain, —
So still, a hare kept at my side
    His tussock of disdain, —

Behind me close I heard a step,
    A soft pit-pat surprise,
And looking round my eyes fell deep
    ' Into sweet other eyes;

The eyes like wells, where sun lies too,
    So clear and trustful brown,
Without a bubble warning you
    That here's a place to drown.

"How many miles?"   Her broken shoes
    Had told of more than one.
She answered like a dreaming Muse,
    "I came from Islington."

"So long a tramp?"   Two gentle nods
    Then seemed to lift a wing,
And words fell soft as willow-buds,
    "I came to find the Spring."

A timid voice, yet not afraid
    In ways so sweet to roam,
As it with honey bees had played
    And could no more go home.

Her home!   I saw the human lair,
    I heard the hucksters bawl,

I stifled with the thickened air
  Of bickering mart and stall.

Without a tuppence for a ride,
  Her feet had set her free.
Her rags, that decency defied,
  Seemed new with liberty.

But she was frail.   Who would might note
  The trail of hungering
That for an hour she had forgot
  In wonder of the Spring.

So shriven by her joy she glowed
  It seemed a sin to chat.
(A tea-shop snuggled off the road;
  Why did I think of that?)

Of, frail, so frail!   I could have wept, —
  But she was passing on,
And I but muddled "You'll accept
  A penny for a bun?"

Then up her little throat a spray
  Of rose climbed for it must;
A wilding lost till safe it lay
  Hid by her curls of rust;

And I saw modesties at fence
  With pride that bore no name;
So old it was she knew not whence
  It sudden woke and came;

But that which shone of all most clear
   Was startled, sadder thought
That I should give her back the fear
   Of life she had forgot.

And I blushed for the world we'd made,
   Putting God's hand aside,
Till for the want of sun and shade
   His little children died;

And blushed that I who every year
   With Spring went up and down,
Must greet a soul that ached for her
   With "penny for a bun!"

Struck as a thief in holy place
   Whose sin upon him cries,
I watched the flowers leave her face,
   The song go from her eyes.

Then she, sweet heart, she saw my rout,
   And of her charity
A hand of grace put softly out
   And took the coin from me.

A red-cap sang in Bishop's wood,
   A lark o'er Golder's lane;
But I, alone, still glooming stood,
   And April plucked in vain;

Till living words rang in my ears
   And sudden music played:

Out of such sacred thirst as hers
  The world shall be remade.

Afar she turned her head and smiled
  As might have smiled the Spring,
And humble as a wondering child
  I watched her vanishing.

— *Olive Tilford Dargan*

ANGELA MORGAN

Angela Morgan was born at Washington, D. C., and educated in the public schools and under tutors. She was a special student at Columbia University and at Chautauqua, New York.

She is the author of *The Hour Has Struck* (1914), *Utterance and Other Poems* (1916), *Forward, March!* (1918), *Hail Man!* (1919), *The Luminous Heart* (1922). The poem quoted here, "Song of the New World," is typical of Miss Morgan's fervor and optimism.

SONG OF THE NEW WORLD

I sing the song of a new Dawn waking,
A new wind shaking
  The children of men.
I say the hearts that are nigh to breaking
  Shall leap with gladness and live again.
Over the woe of the world appalling,
  Wild and sweet as a bugle cry,
Sudden I hear a new voice calling —
  "Beauty is nigh!"
Beauty is nigh! Let the world believe it.
  Love has covered the fields of dead.
Healing is here! Let the earth receive it,
  Greeting the Dawn with lifted head.
I sing the song of the sin forgiven,
  The deed forgotten, the wrong undone.
Lo, in the East, where the dark is riven,
  Shines the rim of the rising sun.
Healing is here! O brother, sing it!
  Laugh, O heart, that has grieved so long.
Love will gather your woe and fling it

Over the world in waves of song.
Hearken, mothers, and hear them coming —
Heralds crying the day at hand.
Faint and far as the sound of drumming,
Hear their summons across the land.
Look, O fathers! Your eyes were holden —
Armies throng where the dead have lain.
Fiery steeds and chariots golden —
Gone is the dream of soldiers slain.
Sing, O sing of a new world waking,
Sing of creation just begun.
Glad is the earth when morn is breaking —
Man is facing the rising sun!

—Angela Morgan

GRACE HAZARD CONKLING

Grace Hazard Conkling (née Hazard) was born at New York City and educated at Smith College and at Harvard Summer School. She also studied music and languages at the University of Heidelberg and in Paris. She has been for some time a teacher, first in the Graham School in New York and later at Smith College as an associate professor of English.

She is the author of *Afternoons of April* (1915) and of *Wilderness Songs* (1920). Her work is remarkable for finished and exquisite technique, charming fancy, and winning moods. "Maine Woods in Winter" has all the grace of some of her lighter lyrics and is more seriously thoughtful than most of them. It is not simply excellent description, but suggests more than is said of life and death and immortality and the outward reaching of our spirits.

MAINE WOODS IN WINTER

Now I have climbed the hillside to discover
The forest sitting in its silver clothes
With ermine pulled about its knees.   I know
There is no better place than trees have found
To live their lives in, past the million years
That life has toiled to make them perfect trees;
And I shall listen to their thoughts a while,
For I would share the minds of men no longer.
Here the rich snow might be a floor of cloud;
Or sifted hawthorn-bloom cloud-like and soft
Poured thick from Maytime hedges; or the drift
Down a pear-orchard when a gust has passed;
Or all the captive foam of a coral island;
Or feathers of a comet lost in air

And fallen forgotten from the flying star.
And not a sound of the world can leap the wall
Of thrilling quiet where great trees stand still
As though one gesture might unhinge the moon
And bring it down too close to show its deeps
Of alabaster valley any more,
Or send the sun astray with the moon to follow
Out of their reach, and blot the sky with dark.
They would not break the spell of any dream.
And God is dreaming too.
                                    So they stand still.
I wonder when I go among such trees
Far from the fields and deeper in alone,
If I shall find a silence before sound
That was in the beginning?   Will there be rest
And room for music in my mind again
After the interval?   I shall creep close
To watch the wind writing upon dry leaves
With pencil of sunlight words I cannot read,
And I shall write too, with an icicle
That withers like a rainbow from my grasp.
I shall forget the passionate hastes of men
Among the swarthy hemlocks; and Orion
Will pierce the forest-thatch with casual eye
Before I miss the sun.   Oh, I shall be
The imagining spirit of that solitude,
Bold to create a stillness of my own
Above the cataract of the universe
Where it pours down obscure and infinite
Under a whirling surface-foam of worlds:
The trees will keep me listening all day long!
And I shall know them, learn their evening look,

Gray that is purple, purple that is dusk,
Or running with the lean and supple wind
Follow the dawn along their mighty columns
That loom and glitter in an air like bronze.

— *Grace Hazard Conkling*

WILLIAM STANLEY BRAITHWAITE

William Stanley Braithwaite was born at Boston in 1878, was self-educated, but has taken several honorary degrees from universities. For a number of years he has been one of our foremost reviewers of poetry and his numerous anthologies are well known.

He is the author of *Lyrics of Life and Love* (1904) and of *The House of Falling Leaves* (1908). "Sic Vita," offered here, is one of his most likeable lyrics.

SIC VITA

Heart free, hand free,
    Blue above, brown under,
All the world to me
    Is a place of wonder.
Sun shine, moon shine,
    Stars, and winds a-blowing,
All into this heart of mine
    Flowing, flowing, flowing!

Mind free, step free,
    Days to follow after,
Joys of life sold to me
    For the price of laughter,
Girl's love, man's love,
    Love of work and duty,
Just a will of God's to prove
    Beauty, beauty, beauty.

—*William Stanley Braithwaite*

137

ROBERT HAVEN SCHAUFFLER

Robert Haven Schauffler was born at Brunn, Austria, of American parents in 1879. He came to this country in 1881 and was educated at Northwestern University and at Princeton University. Later he studied at the University of Berlin. He is a 'cellist and a sculptor as well as a poet, and has written and edited many books of prose.

His poetry is to be found in *Scum o' the Earth and Other Poems* (1912) and in *The White Comrade and Other Poems* (1920). The title poem of his first book was exceedingly popular when it first appeared because of the spirit of racial tolerance and national hospitality in which it was written. It is still a favorite with people who believe that America is the "Melting Pot" wherein will be mingled the great traditions of many races and kinds of men. All to whom this idea is less congenial can still find in the poem a wise way of admiring and liking other nations and races for their unique qualities and for their greatest heroes.

"SCUM O' THE EARTH"

I

At the gate of the West I stand,
On the isle where the nations throng.
We call them "scum o' the earth";

Stay, are we doing you wrong,
Young fellow from Socrates' land? —
You, like a Hermes so lissome and strong
Fresh from the master Praxiteles' hand?
So you're of Spartan birth?
Descended, perhaps, from one of the band —
Deathless in story and song —
Who combed their long hair at Thermopylae's pass? . . .
Ah, I forget what straits, (alas!)

More tragic than theirs, more compassion-worth,
Have doomed you to march in our "immigrant class"
Where you're nothing but "scum o' the earth."

II

You Pole with the child on your knee,
What dower brings you to the land of the free?
Hark! does she croon
The sad little tune
That Chopin once found on his Polish lea
And mounted in gold for you and for me?
Now a ragged young fiddler answers
In wild Czech melody
That Dvořak took whole from the dancers.
And the heavy faces bloom
In the wonderful Slavic way;
The little, dull eyes, the brows a-gloom,
Suddenly dawn like the day.
While, watching these folk and their mystery,
I forget that they're nothing worth;
That Bohemians, Slovaks, Croatians,
And men of all Slavic nations
Are "polacks" — and "scum o' the earth."

III

Genoese boy of the level brow,
Lad of the lustrous, dreamy eyes
Agaze at Manhattan's pinnacles now
In the first, sweet shock of a hushed surprise;
Within your far-rapt seer's eyes
I catch the glow of the wild surmise
That played on the Santa Maria's prow
In that still gray dawn,
Four centuries gone,

When a world from the wave began to rise.
Oh, who shall foretell what high emprise
Is the goal that gleams
When Italy's dreams
Spread wing and sweep into the skies.
Caesar dreamed him a world ruled well;
Dante dreamed Heaven out of Hell;
Angelo brought us there to dwell;
And you, are you of a different birth? —
You're only a "dago," — and "scum o' the earth"!

IV

Stay, are we doing you wrong
Calling you "scum o' the earth,"
Man of the sorrow-bowed head,
Of the features tender yet strong, —
Man of the eyes full of wisdom and mystery
Mingled with patience and dread?
Have not I known you in history,
Sorrow-bowed head?
Were you the poet-king, worth
Treasures of Ophir unpriced?
Were you the prophet, perchance, whose art
Foretold how the rabble would mock
That shepherd of spirits, ere long,
Who should gather the lambs to his heart
And tenderly feed his flock?
Man — lift that sorrow-bowed head.
Behold the face of the Christ!
The vision dies at its birth.
You're merely a butt for our mirth.
You're a "sheeny" — and therefore despised
And rejected as "scum o' the earth."

V

Countrymen, bend and invoke
Mercy for us blasphemers,
For that we spat on these marvelous folk,
Nations of darers and dreamers,
Scions of singers and seers,
Our peers, and more than our peers.
"Rabble and refuse," we name them
And "scum o' the earth" to shame them.
Mercy for us of the few, young years,
Of the culture so callow and crude,
Of the hands so grasping and rude,
The lips so ready for sneers
At the sons of our ancient more-than-peers.
Mercy for us who dare despise
Men in whose loins our Homer lies;
Mothers of men who shall bring to us
The glory of Titian, the grandeur of Huss;
Children in whose frail arms shall rest
Prophets and singers and saints of the West.

Newcomers all from the eastern seas,
Help us incarnate dreams like these.
Forget, and forgive, that we did you wrong.
Help us to father a nation, strong
In the comradeship of an equal birth,
In the wealth of the richest bloods of earth.

—Robert Haven Schauffler

VACHEL LINDSAY

(Nicholas) Vachel Lindsay was born at Springfield, Illinois, in 1879. His mother was an ardent prohibitionist. His home was next door to the executive mansion of the State of Illinois. Perhaps such influences account, in part, for his interest in politics and reform. He was educated at Hiram College and at the Chicago Art Institute. Later he studied at the New York School of Art under Chase and Henri. He lectured for the Y. M. C. A. for several years, and later for the Anti-Saloon League of Central Illinois.

In 1912 he took up the rambling task of an American minstrel. He walked from Illinois to New Mexico, distributing his "rhymes to be traded for bread," visiting with the people of the countryside and preaching his "gospel of beauty." This gospel was intended to give people a deeper insight into the beauty of holiness and into the holiness of beauty. It was not a narrow aesthetic program of a formal nature that Mr. Lindsay desired and preached, but a broad-spirited, democratic development of American life in harmony with all kinds of beauty and goodness. He has tried to bring into poetry the best elements in the popular life — the politics, religion, labors, and amusements of the American people. He has glorified these things in his poetry by his humor, his understanding, his depth and warmth of feeling, and his inimitable sense of rhythm. (See Introduction.) To hear him read or intone any of his vivid American masterpieces is an experience that no American should miss if opportunity to enjoy it comes to him.

Mr. Lindsay's books of poetry are *General William Booth Enters Heaven and Other Poems* (1913), *The Congo and Other Poems* (1914), *The Chinese Nightingale and Other Poems* (1917), and *The Golden Whales of California and Other Poems* (1920). His books of prose are *Adventures while Preaching the Gosepl of Beauty* (1914), *A Handy Guide for Beggars* (1916), and *The Golden Book of Springfield* (1920).

In "The Santa Fé Trail" we have a scene taken out of American

142

ife on the western plains.   Beside the double-tracked railroad is a
oad on which the automobiles run, where, as Mr. Lindsay says,
'The United States goes by."   Over this road the poet takes us and
shares his vision of the goal with us, "the mystery the beggars win."
It is a marvelously accurate picture, this poem, and full of quaint
and delightful suggestions.   "The Eagle Forgotten" is a quiet,
profound poem commemorating the life and work of John P. Altgeld,
the fearless Governor of Illinois.   The eagle — our national sym-
bol — is used as a symbol of the man Mr. Lindsay would honor.
"Abraham Lincoln Walks at Midnight" is a plea for peace and
brotherhood.   "The Broncho that Would Not be Broken" is a
tragic short story and a plea for gentleness in our dealings with
dumb brutes.   It is all the better because it does not preach at us.
It simply tells a tale that touches our hearts.

THE SANTA FÉ TRAIL — A HUMORESQUE

I asked the old negro, "What is that bird that sings so well?"
He answered, "That is the Rachel-Jane." "Hasn't it
another name — lark, or thrush, or the like?" "No, jus'
Rachel-Jane."

I

In which a Racing Auto comes from the East.

This is the order of the music of the morning: —
First, from the far East comes but a crooning;
The crooning turns to a sunrise singing.
Hark to the calm-horn, balm-horn, psalm-horn;
Hark to the faint-horn, quaint-horn, saint-horn . . . .

Hark to the pace-horn, chase-horn, race-horn!
And the holy veil of the dawn has gone,
Swiftly the brazen car comes on.

To be sung
delicately to an
improvised
tune

To be sung or
read with
great speed

It burns in the East as the sunrise burns,
I see great flashes where the far trail turns.
Its eyes are lamps like the eyes of dragons.
It drinks gasoline from big red flagons.
Butting through the delicate mists of the morning,
It comes like lightning, goes past roaring.
It will hail all the wind-mills, taunting, ringing,
Dodge the cyclones,
Count the milestones,
On through the ranges the prairie-dog tills,
Scooting past the cattle on the thousand hills . . . .
Ho for the tear-horn, scare-horn, dare-horn,
Ho for the gay-horn, bark-horn, bay-horn.

To be read or sung in a rolling bass with some deliberation

Ho for Kansas, land that restores us
When houses choke us, and great books bore us!
Sunrise Kansas, harvester's Kansas,
A million men have found you before us.

II

In which Many Autos pass Westward.

In an even, deliberate, narrative manner

I want live things in their pride to remain.
I will not kill one grasshopper vain
Though he eats a hole in my shirt like a door.
I let him out, give him one chance more.
Perhaps, while he gnaws my hat in his whim,
Grasshopper lyrics occur to him.

I am a tramp by the long trail's border,
Given to squalor, rags and disorder.
I nap and amble and yawn and look,
Write fool-thoughts in my grubby book,

Recite to the children, explore at my ease,
Work when I work, beg when I please,
Give crank drawings, that make folks stare,
To the half-grown boys in the sunset-glare;
And get me a place to sleep in the hay
At the end of a live-and-let-live day.

I find in the stubble of the new-cut weeds
A whisper and a feasting, all one needs:
The whisper of the strawberries, white and red,
Here where the new-cut weeds lie dead.
But I would not walk all alone till I die
Without some life-drunk horns going by.
Up round this apple-earth they come,
Blasting the whispers of the morning dumb: —
Cars in a plain realistic row.
And fair dreams fade
When the raw horns blow.

On each snapping pennant
A big black name —
The careering city
Whence each car came.

Like a train-caller in Union Depot

They tour from Memphis, Atlanta, Savannah,
Tallahassee and Texarkana.
They tour from St. Louis, Columbus, Manistee,
They tour from Peoria, Davenport, Kankakee.
Cars from Concord, Niagara, Boston,
Cars from Topeka, Emporia and Austin.
Cars from Chicago, Hannibal, Cairo,
Cars from Alton, Oswego, Toledo.
Cars from Buffalo, Kokomo, Delphi,
Cars from Lodi, Carmi, Loami.

Ho for Kansas, land that restores us
When houses choke us, and great books bore us!
While I watch the highroad
And look at the sky,
While I watch the clouds in amazing grandeur
Roll their legions without rain
Over the blistering Kansas plain —
While I sit by the milestone
And watch the sky,
The United States
Goes by!

To be given
very harshly
with a
snapping ex-
plosiveness

Listen to the iron horns, ripping, racking.
Listen to the quack horns, slack and clacking!
Way down the road, trilling like a toad,
Here come the dice-horn, here comes the vice-horn,
Here comes the snarl-horn, brawl-horn, lewd-horn,
Followed by the prude-horn, bleak and squeaking: —
(Some of them from Kansas, some of them from Kansas).
Here comes the hod-horn, plod-horn, sod-horn,
Nevermore-to-roam-horn, loam-horn, home-horn,
(Some of them from Kansas, some of them from Kansas).

To be read or
sung well-nigh
in a whisper

Far away the Rachel-Jane,
Not defeated by the horns,
Sings amid a hedge of thorns;
"Love and life,
Eternal youth —
Sweet, sweet, sweet, sweet!
Dew and glory,
Love and truth,
Sweet, sweet, sweet, sweet!"

While smoke-black freights on the double-tracked railroad, *Louder and louder, faster and faster*
Driven as though by the foul-fiend's ox-goad,
Screaming to the west coast, screaming to the east,
Carry off a harvest, bring back a feast,
Harvesting machinery and harness for the beast.
The hand-cars whiz, and rattle on the rails;
The sunlight flashes on the tin dinner-pails.
And then, in an instant, *In a rolling bass with increasing deliberation*
Ye modern men,
Behold the procession once again!
Listen to the iron-horns, ripping, racking! *With a snapping explosiveness*
Listen to the wise-horn, desperate-to-advise horn,
Listen to the fast-horn, kill-horn, blast-horn . . . .

> *Far away the Rachel-Jane,* *To be sung or read well-nigh in a whisper*
> *Not defeated by the horns,*
> *Sings amid a hedge of thorns: —*
> *"Love and life,*
> *Eternal youth —*
> *Sweet, sweet, sweet, sweet!*
> *Dew and glory,*
> *Love and Truth —*
> *Sweet, sweet, sweet, sweet!"*

The mufflers open on a score of cars
With wonderful thunder,
CRACK, CRACK, CRACK,
CRACK-CRACK, CRACK-CRACK, *To be brawled in the beginning with a snapping explosiveness ending in languorous chant*
CRACK-CRACK-CRACK, ...
Listen to the gold-horn . . . .
Old-horn . . . .
Cold-horn . . . .

And all of the tunes, till the night comes down
On hay-stack, and ant-hill, and wind-bitten town.

To be sung to exactly the same whispered tune as the first five lines

Then far in the west, as in the beginning,
Dim in the distance, sweet in retreating,
Hark to the faint-horn, quaint-horn, saint-horn,
Hark to the calm-horn, balm-horn, psalm-horn . . . .

This section beginning sonorously, ending in a languorous whisper

They are hunting the goals that they understand: —
San Francisco and the brown sea-sand.
My goal is the mystery the beggars win.
I am caught in the web the night-winds spin.
The edge of the wheat-ridge speaks to me;
I talk with the leaves of the mulberry tree.
And now I hear, as I sit all alone
In the dusk, by another big Santa Fé stone,
The souls of the tall corn gathering round,
And the gay little souls of the grass in the ground.
Listen to the tale the cotton-wood tells.
Listen to the wind-mills singing o'er the wells.
Listen to the whistling flutes without price
Of myriad prophets out of paradise . . . .

To the same whispered tune as the Rachel-Jane song—but very slowly

Harken to the wonder that the night-air carries.
Listen . . . to . . . the . . . whisper . . .
Of . . . the . . . prairie . . . fairies
Singing over the fairy plain:
"Sweet, sweet, sweet, sweet!
Love and glory, stars and rain,
Sweet, sweet, sweet, sweet!"

— *Vachel Lindsay*

THE EAGLE THAT IS FORGOTTEN

John P. Altgeld: Dec. 30, 1847–March 12, 1902.

Sleep softly . . . eagle forgotten . . . under the stone.
Time has its way with you there, and the clay has its own.

"We have buried him now," thought your foes, and in secret
    rejoiced.
They made a brave show of their mourning, their hatred
    unvoiced.
They had snarled at you, barked at you, foamed at you day
    after day;
Now you are ended.   They praised you . . . and laid you
    away.

The others that mourned you in silence and terror and truth,
The widow bereft of her crust, and the boy without youth,
The mocked and the scorned and the wounded, the lame and
    the poor,
That should have remembered forever . . . remember no
    more.

Where are those lovers of yours, on what name do they call —
The lost, that in armies wept over your funeral pall?
They call on the names of a hundred high-valiant ones;
A hundred white eagles have risen, the sons of your sons.
The zeal in their wings is a zeal that your dreaming began,
The valor that wore out your soul in the service of man.

Sleep softly . . . eagle forgotten . . . under the stone.
Time has its way with you there and the clay has its own.

Sleep on, O brave-hearted, O wise man, that kindled the
    flame —
To live in mankind is far more than to live in a name;
To live in mankind, far, far more . . . than to live in a name.

                                      — *Vachel Lindsay*

THE BRONCHO THAT WOULD NOT BE BROKEN

A little colt — broncho, loaned to the farm
To be broken in time without fury or harm,
Yet black crows flew past you, shouting alarm,
Calling "Beware," with lugubrious singing . . .
The butterflies there in the bush were romancing,
The smell of the grass caught your soul in a trance,
So why be a-fearing the spurs and the traces,
O broncho that would not be broken of dancing?

You were born with the pride of the lords great and olden
Who danced, through the ages, in corridors golden.
In all the wide farm-place the person most human.
You spoke out so plainly with squealing and capering,
With whinnying, snorting, contorting and prancing,
As you dodged your pursuers, looking askance,
With Greek-footed figures, and Parthenon paces,
O broncho that would not be broken of dancing.

The grasshoppers cheered. "Keep whirling," they said.
The insolent sparrows called from the shed
"If men will not laugh, make them wish they were dead."
But arch were your thoughts, all malice displacing,
Though the horse-killers came, with snake-whips advancing.
You bantered and cantered away your last chance.

And they scourged you; with Hell in their speech and their
    faces,
O broncho that would not be broken of dancing.

"Nobody cares for you," rattled the crows,
As you dragged the whole reaper next day down the rows.
The three mules held back, yet you danced on your toes.
You pulled like a racer, and kept the mules chasing.
You tangled the harness with bright eyes side-glancing,
While the drunk driver bled you — a pole for a lance —
And the giant mules bit at you — keeping their places.
O broncho that would not be broken of dancing.

In that last afternoon your boyish heart broke.
The hot wind came down like a sledge-hammer stroke.
The blood-sucking flies to a rare feast awoke.
And they searched out your wounds, your death-warrant
    tracing.
And the merciful men, their religion enhancing,
Stopped the red reaper to give you a chance.
Then you died on the prairie, and scorned all disgraces,
O broncho that would not be broken of dancing.

                    — *Vachel Lindsay*

ABRAHAM LINCOLN WALKS AT MIDNIGHT

It is portentous, and a thing of state
That here at midnight, in our little town
A mourning figure walks, and will not rest,
Near the old court-house pacing up and down,

Or by his homestead, or in shadowed yards
He lingers where his children used to play,

Or through the market, on the well-worn stones
He stalks until the dawn-stars burn away.

A bronzed, lank man! His suit of ancient black,
A famous high-top hat and plain worn shawl
Make him the quaint great figure that men love,
The prairie lawyer, master of us all.

He cannot sleep upon his hillside now.
He is among us: — as in times before!
And we who toss and lie awake for long
Breathe deep, and start, to see him pass the door.

His head is bowed. He thinks on men and kings.
Yea, when the sick world cries, how can he sleep?
Too many peasants fight, they know not why,
Too many homesteads in black terror weep.

The sins of all the war-lords burn his heart.
He sees the dreadnaughts scouring every main.
He carries on his shawl-wrapped shoulders now
The bitterness, the folly and the pain.

He cannot rest until a spirit-dawn
Shall come; — the shining hope of Europe free:
The league of sober folk, the Workers' Earth,
Bringing long peace to Cornland, Alp and Sea.

It breaks his heart that kings must murder still,
That all his hours of travail here for men
Seem yet in vain. And who will bring white peace
That he may sleep upon his hill again?

— *Vachel Lindsay*

JOHN G. NEIHARDT

John Gneisenau Neihardt was born near Sharpsburg, Illinois, in 1881. He was educated at the Nebraska Normal College. For a number of years he lived among the Omaha Indians to study their history, traditions, and characteristics. In 1921 he was appointed poet laureate of Nebraska by act of the legislature.

He is the author of *The Divine Enchantment* (1900), *The Lonesome Trail* (1907), *A Bundle of Myrrh* (1908), *Man-Song* (1909), *The River and I* (1910), *The Dawn-Builder* (1911), *The Stranger at the Gate* (1912), *The Death of Agrippina* (1913), *Life's Lure* (1914), *The Song of Hugh Glass* (1915), *The Quest* (1916), *The Song of Three Friends* (1919), *The Splendid Wayfaring* (1920), and *Two Mothers* (1921). Of these books probably the most important are the five latest. *The Song of Hugh Glass* and *The Song of Three Friends* are excellent American epics dealing with manly adventures that would interest boys and men immensely. They are too long to be reprinted in full and quotations do not do them justice since they are stories. They are founded on fact — these epics — made out of the heroic deeds and personalities that were a part of the early history of the country. The poem quoted here is simply one more protest against industrial wrong, one more paean of democracy.

CRY OF THE PEOPLE

Tremble before your chattels,
Lords of the scheme of things!
Fighters of all earth's battles,
Ours is the might of kings!
Guided by seers and sages,
The world's heart-beat for a drum,
Snapping the chains of ages,
Out of the night we come!

153

Lend us no ear that pities!
Offer no almoner's hand!
Alms for the builders of cities!
When will you understand?
Down with your pride of birth
And your golden gods of trade!
A man is worth to his mother, Earth,
All that a man has made!

We are the workers and makers.
We are no longer dumb!
Tremble, O Shirkers and Takers!
Sweeping the earth — we come!
Ranked in the world-wide dawn,
Marching into the day!
The night is gone and the sword is drawn
And the scabbard is thrown away!

— *John G. Neihardt*

WITTER BYNNER

Witter Bynner was born at Brooklyn, New York, in 1881. He was educated at Harvard University. He has done various kinds of editorial work, has acted as instructor in English at the University of California, and has lectured on poetry to many audiences.

He is the author of a number of plays and of a book of epigrams, *Pins for Wings*, which characterizes his contemporaries. His best books of verse are *The New World* (1915), a long poem which gives a vision of democracy and of immortality by presenting the personality of a gracious woman, Celia; *Grenstone Poems* (1917), *A Canticle of Praise* (1919), and *A Canticle of Pan* (1920), Mr. Bynner has written many melodious lyrics, of which "To a Phœbe-Bird," given below, is an excellent example. He has made a translation of Emile Cammaert's *La Patrie*. The translation is called *The Homeland* and is so musical and natural that it might be taken for an original poem.

TO A PHŒBE-BIRD

Under the eaves, out of the wet,
    Your nest within my reach;
You never sing for me and yet
    You have a golden speech.

You sit and quirk a rapid tail,
    Wrinkle a ragged crest,
Then pirouette from tree to rail
    And vault from rail to nest.

And when in frequent, witty fright
    You grayly slip and fade,

And when at hand you re-alight
   Demure and unafraid,

And when you bring your brood its fill
   Of iridescent wings
And green legs dewy in your bill,
   Your silence is what sings.

Not of a feather that enjoys
   To prate or praise or preach,
O phœbe, with your lack of noise,
   What eloquence you teach!

— Witter Bynner

JAMES OPPENHEIM

James Oppenheim was born at St. Paul, Minnesota in 1882. He studied at Columbia University as a special student, and was, for a time, teacher and acting superintendent at the Hebrew Technical School for Girls.

His first book of verse appeared in 1909 under the title *Monday Morning*. In it was the well known and much beloved "Saturday Night." A number of novels followed. Then came *Songs for the New Age* (1914), *War and Laughter* (1916), *The Book of Self* (1917) and *The Solitary* (1919). Mr. Oppenheim has written a beautiful, poetic, one-act play called *Night*, published in a small booklet unaccompanied by other work. Some of his best poems are brief, concise lyrics in unrhymed cadence (see Introduction) like the following selections.

THE SLAVE

They set the slave free, striking off his chains . . .
Then he was as much of a slave as ever.

He was still chained to servility,
He was still manacled to indolence and sloth,
He was still bound by fear and superstition,
By ignorance, suspicion, and savagery . . .
His slavery was not in the chains,
But in himself. . . .

They can only set free men free . . .
And there is no need of that:
Free men set themselves free.

— James Oppenheim

From *Songs of the New Age*

THE RUNNER IN THE SKIES

Who is the runner in the skies,
With her blowing scarf of stars,
And our earth and sun hovering like bees about her blossom-
  ing heart?
Her feet are on the winds, where space is deep,
Her eyes are nebulous and veiled;
She hurries through the night to a far lover . . .

— James Oppenheim

From *Songs of the New Age*

ALFRED KREYMBORG

Alfred Kreymborg was born at New York City in 1883 and was educated there by life and experience. He became an expert chess player, and earned a living by teaching the game and playing exhibition games. He worked for a time as a bookkeeper. After working hours his hobby — or passion — was music. He became the organizer and leader of a group of whimsical, radical poets who called themselves "Others."

His books are *Mushrooms* (1916), *Plays for Poet-Mimes* (1918), *Plays for Merry Andrews* (1920) and *Blood of Things* (1920). These books are full of quaint, merry, audacious, and more or less thoughtful sayings. Mr. Kreymborg's love of humor sometimes carries him much too far toward absurdity and his love of the odd sometimes carries him much too far toward eccentricity. But an elfin imagination and the force of brevity sometimes make it possible for him to work exquisite little miracles with language. Such are the two poems offered here. "Idealists" says more by its indirection than could ever have been said in direct statement. "Old Manuscript" gives fresh and original expression to man's ancient wonder in beholding the sky.

OLD MANUSCRIPT

The sky
is that beautiful old parchment
in which the sun
and the moon
keep their diary.
To read it all,
one must be a linguist
more learned than Father Wisdom;
and a visionary
more clairvoyant than Mother Dream.

But to feel it,
one must be an apostle:
one who is more than intimate
in having been, always,
the only confidant —
like the earth
or the sea.

— *Alfred Kreymborg*

IDEALISTS

Brother Tree:
Why do you reach and reach?
do you dream some day to touch the sky?
Brother Stream:
Why do you run and run?
do you dream some day to fill the sea?
Brother Bird:
Why do you sing and sing?
do you dream —

Young Man:
Why do you talk and talk and talk?

— *Alfred Kreymborg*

BADGER CLARK

Badger Clark was born at Albia, Iowa, in 1883, but when he was still a baby he was taken to Dakota Territory and still lives in South Dakota. He was educated by the plains and the hills, by the ranchers and cow-punchers.

His two books are *Sun and Saddle Leather* (1915) and *Grass-Grown Trails* (1917). "The Glory Trail," sometimes called "High-Chin Bob," is probably his best known poem. It is a true ballad, stirring and vigorous as a narrative and also as verse. It has all the merits of the ballads of old — humor, pathos, fancy and adventure. It has been so widely circulated, sung, and revised by the cowboys that it has become a true folk-ballad and another version of it can be found in a collection of cowboy ballads made by Professor Lomax.

"Mogollons" is pronounced as if it were spelled "Mókiónes."

THE GLORY TRAIL

'Way high up the Mogollons,
   Among the mountain tops,
A lion cleaned a yearlin's bones
   And licked his thankful chops,
When on the picture who should ride,
   A-trippin' down a slope,
But High-Chin Bob, with sinful pride
   And mav'rick-hungry rope.

     "Oh, glory be to me," says he,
      "And fame's unfadin' flowers!
     All meddlin' hands are far away;
     I ride my good top-hawse today

161

And I'm top-rope of the Lazy J —
　Hi! kitty cat, you're ours!"

That lion licked his paw so brown
　And dreamed soft dreams of veal —
And then the circlin' loop sung down
　And roped him 'round his meal.
He yowled quick fury to the world
　Till all the hills yelled back;
The top-hawse gave a snort and whirled
　And Bob caught up the slack.

　　"Oh, glory be to me," laughs he.
　　　"We've hit the glory trail.
　　No human man as I have read
　　Darst loop a ragin' lion's head,
　　Nor ever hawse could drag one dead
　　　Until we told the tale."

'Way high up the Mogollons
　That top-hawse done his best,
Through whippin' brush and rattlin' stones,
　From canyon-floor to crest.
But ever when Bob turned and hoped
　A limp remains to find,
A red-eyed lion, belly roped
　But healthy, loped behind.

　　"Oh, glory be to me," grunts he.
　　　"This glory trail is rough,
　　Yet even till the Judgment Morn
　　I'll keep this dally 'round the horn,
　　For never any hero born
　　　Could stoop to holler: 'Nuff!'"

Three suns had rode their circle home
   Beyond the desert's rim,
And turned their star-herds loose to roam
   The ranges high and dim;
Yet up and down and 'round and 'cross
   Bob pounded, weak and wan,
For pride still glued him to his hawse
   And glory drove him on.

> *"Oh, glory be to me," sighs he.*
> * "He kaint be drug to death,*
> *But now I know beyond a doubt*
> *Them heroes I have read about*
> *Was only fools that stuck it out*
> * To end of mortal breath."*

'Way high up the Mogollons
   A prospect man did swear
That moon dreams melted down his bones
   And hoisted up his hair:
A ribby cow-hawse thundered by,
   A lion trailed along,
A rider, ga'nt but chin on high,
   Yelled out a crazy song.

> *"Oh, glory be to me!" cries he,*
> * "And to my noble noose!*
> *Oh, stranger, tell my pards below*
> *I took a rampin' dream in tow,*
> *And if I never lay him low,*
> * I'll never turn him loose!"*

— Badger Clark

MARGUERITE WILKINSON

Marguerite Wilkinson was born at Halifax, Nova Scotia, Canada, in 1883. She was educated at the Evanston Township High School of Evanston, Ill., at The Misses Ely's School, then in New York City, and at Northwestern University. She writes both prose and verse and lectures on contemporary poetry.

Her most important books are *In Vivid Gardens* (1911), *Bluestone* (1920), and *The Great Dream* (1923). In 1919 her *New Voices* appeared, a critical and friendly introduction to contemporary poetry, and in 1922, *The Dingbat of Arcady*, a narrative of adventures in the open air, written in poetic prose.

"The Somerset Farmer" is a description of country life in England. "Ghosts" is an out-of-door picture set down in free verse. (For a discussion of free verse see Introduction.) Both of these poems are slightly whimsical and should be read gayly, and with lightheartedness. "A Chant Out of Doors" is more serious, a song of worship and wonder. It might be used antiphonally.

THE SOMERSET FARMER

I said,

      It is good to live in the country,
   To have a small cottage in a big green field,
   A neat little garden inside of a gateway,
   To see how much you can make it yield;
   To have dusty chickens and a spotted calf
   And a good stout cow with a silky skin,
   This, I suppose, is better by half
   Than the winning of much men die to win?
The Somerset Farmer rubbed his head
And smiled at me. "Oh-ay," he said.

I said again,
> It is good to be friendly,
> To have a small door where neighbors knock,
> To get up early and work while you listen
> To a cuckoo singing as well as a clock;
> And to lie down when the West is ruddy
> With hardly a thought that is not kind;
> With the earth to con and the sky to study
> A man need never be dull of mind?

The Somerset Farmer nodded at me
And smiled again, "Oh-ay," said he.

I said,
> It is good to have young things near you,
> Children to play with, children to hold;
> To hear them laughing; to have them hear you
> Calling to them as you grow old;
> To know that you have a part in the ages
> Through all to-morrows, though silently,
> Immortal as singers and saints and sages
> While youth buds out on the ancient tree —

The Somerset Man looked out at the sky.
Solemn and soft he said, "Oh-ay."

— Marguerite Wilkinson

GHOSTS

You say you saw a ghost, in the house, at night,
Standing stiff and chilly in evanescent silver,
In your room, near the bed where your grandfather died.
But I saw ghosts, hundreds of them, dancing,
Out of doors, by day, in a dazzle of sunlight,

Climbing through the air of a clearing near the river,
Flying dizzily there in a brief puff of the breeze,
Yes, hundreds of ghosts, where a little while ago
Died hundreds of the purple blooms of the thistle.

— *Marguerite Wilkinson*

A CHANT OUT OF DOORS

God of grave nights,
God of brave mornings,
God of silent noon,
Hear my salutation!

    For where the rapids rage white and scornful,
    I have passed safely, filled with wonder;
    Where the sweet pools dream under willows,
    I have been swimming, filled with life.

God of round hills,
God of green valleys,
God of clear springs,
Hear my salutation!

    For where the moose feeds, I have eaten berries,
    Where the moose drinks, I have drunk deep.
    When the storms crashed through broken heavens—
    And under clear skies — I have known joy.

God of great trees,
God of wild grasses,
God of little flowers,
Hear my salutation!

For where the deer crops and the beaver plunges,
Near the river I have pitched my tent;
Where the pines cast aromatic needles
On a still floor, I have known peace.

God of grave nights,
God of brave mornings,
God of silent noon,
Hear my salutation!

— Marguerite Wilkinson

MAX EASTMAN

Max Eastman was born at Canandaigua, New York, in 1883, the son of parents who were both in the ministry of the Congregational Church. He received his A.B. from Williams College and was, for a time, on the faculty of Columbia University.

He is the author of *Child of the Amazons* (1913) and of *Colors of Life* (1918). These books are both small, but a number of excellent poems are to be found in them. In particular I should like to name "Coming into Port" and "A Rainy Song." Mr. Eastman has also written the most interesting book about poetry which this period has produced. It is called *The Enjoyment of Poetry*.

INVOCATION

Truth, be more precious to me than the eyes,
Of happy love; burn hotter in my throat
Than passion, and possess me like my pride;
More sweet than freedom, more desired than joy,
More sacred than the pleasing of a friend.

— *Max Eastman*

FANNIE STEARNS GIFFORD

Fannie Stearns Gifford (née Davis) was born at Cleveland, Ohio, in 1884. She was educated at Smith College.

Her books are *Myself and I* (1913) and *Crack o' Dawn* (1915). Her verse is always graceful and musical. The first of the "Songs of Conn the Fool," "Moon Folly," is included here because of its delightfully wild and whimsical imagining. Poems of this sort are not to be taken too seriously, although it is possible for any reader to give his own meaning to the symbols. It is wisest to read them joyfully, taking part in the imagining as in a delightful intellectual play. And intellectual play is just as good for our minds, sometimes, as intellectual work. It makes us gay and whimsical and imaginative ourselves.

THE SONGS OF CONN THE FOOL

MOON FOLLY

I will go up the mountain after the Moon:
She is caught in a dead fir-tree.
Like a great pale apple of silver and pearl,
Like a great pale apple is she.

I will leap and will catch her with quick cold hands
And carry her home in my sack.
I will set her down safe on the oaken bench
That stands at the chimney-back.

And then I will sit by the fire all night,
And sit by the fire all day.
I will gnaw at the Moon to my heart's delight
Till I gnaw her slowly away.

And while I grow mad with the Moon's cold taste
The World will beat at my door,
Crying "Come out!" and crying "Make haste,
And give us the Moon once more!"

But I shall not answer them ever at all.
I shall laugh, as I count and hide
The great black beautiful Seeds of the Moon
In a flower-pot deep and wide.

Then I shall lie down and go fast asleep,
Drunken with flame and aswoon.
But the seeds will sprout and the seeds will leap,
The subtle swift seeds of the Moon.

And some day, all of the World that cries
And beats at my door shall see
A thousand moon-leaves spring from my thatch
On a wonderful white Moon-tree!

Then each shall have Moons to his heart's desire:
Apples of silver and pearl;
Apples of orange and copper fire
Setting his five wits aswirl!

And then they will thank me, who mock me now,
"Wanting the Moon is he," —
Oh, I'm off to the mountain after the Moon,
Ere she falls from the dead fir-tree!

                     — *Fannie Stearns Davis*

EUNICE TIETJENS

Eunice Tietjens (née Hammond) was born at Chicago, Illinois, in 1884. She has written a novel, *Jake*, and has worked as an editor. In 1917-18 she was a war correspondent in France.

Profiles from China, her first book of poetry, appeared in 1917. It is a collection of sketches and studies of Chinese places, people, and events, written in free verse. Her *Body and Raiment* appeared in 1919. In it are to be found her well-known poems, "The Drug Clerk," and "The Steam Shovel," and her very popular poem, "The Bacchante to her Babe." Her two books are remarkable for an astonishing versatility of thought and technique and her best work has an assured brilliance. "The Most Sacred Mountain," quoted below, is more than brilliant because it is beautiful. It has in it the "swift white peace, the stinging exultation" of a mountain top. It is written about Tai Shan, the holy mountain of China.

THE MOST-SACRED MOUNTAIN

Space, and the twelve clean winds of heaven,
And this sharp exultation, like a cry, after the slow six
. thousand feet of climbing!
This is Tai Shan, the beautiful, the most holy.

Below my feet the foot-hills nestle, brown with flecks of
green; and lower down the flat brown plain, the floor of
earth, stretches away to blue infinity.
Beside me in this airy space the temple roofs cut their slow
curves against the sky.
And one black bird circles above the void.

Space, and the twelve clean winds are here;
And with them broods eternity — a swift, white peace, a
presence manifest.

171

The rhythm ceases here.   Time has no place.
This is the end that has no end.

Here when Confucius came, a half a thousand years before
     the Nazarene, he stepped with me, thus into timelessness.
The stone beside us waxes old, the carven stone that says:
     On this spot once Confucius stood and felt the smallness
     of the world below.

The stone grows old.
Eternity
Is not for stones.

But I shall go down from this airy space, this swift white
     peace, this stinging exultation;
And time will close about me, and my soul stir to the rhythm
     of the daily round.
Yet, having known, life will not press so close, and always I
     shall feel time ravel thin about me;
For once I stood
In the white windy presence of eternity.

                                  — *Eunice Tietjens*

SARA TEASDALE

Sara Teasdale was born at St. Louis, Missouri, in 1884. She was educated in the private schools of that city and later by travel in Europe and in the near East.

She is the author of *Helen of Troy and Other Poems* (1911), *Rivers to the Sea* (1915), *Love Songs* (1917), and *Flame and Shadow* (1920). She is also the editor of two anthologies, *The Answering Voice*, a collection of a hundred love lyrics by women, and *Rainbow Gold*, a collection of poems for young children.

Many of her lyrics are quite perfect as poetry. They have a subtle and exquisite verbal music, an austere simplicity in the use of imagery, symbolism, and diction, and a marvelous precision and brevity. Aside from these technical qualities they are remarkable for the depth and clarity of feeling in them, and for the steel-strong, defiant intellect that formulates a philosophy not to be found in any one of them studied alone, but apparent in her work as a whole, a philosophy that implies and even states the triumph of beauty over death. Sara Teasdale's work has grown steadily in power and loveliness.

"The Coin" is simply a wise little maxim admirably made into verse. "Stars" is a really noble lyric of exultation in the beauty of the marching constellations. It could never be explained to a person who could not feel it, and the person who can feel it needs no explanation. "Let It Be Forgotten" is sheer song unburdened by any message, a lyrical miracle that should liberate the reader from little things that it is wiser to forget. "Lovely Chance" and "May Day" are blithe thanksgivings. Every one of these little songs is unique, the result of Sara Teasdale's own personal reaction to life, but every one of them is also universal because thousands of people know what is felt and said in them. They are poems to be enjoyed and memorized.

MAY DAY

A delicate fabric of bird song
    Floats in the air,
The smell of wet wild earth
    Is everywhere.

Red small leaves of the maple
    Are clenched like a hand,
Like girls at their first communion
    The pear trees stand.

Oh I must pass nothing by
    Without loving it much,
The raindrop try with my lips,
    The grass with my touch;

For how can I be sure
    I shall see again
The world on the first of May
    Shining after the rain?

— Sara Teasdale

STARS

Alone in the night
    On a dark hill
With pines around me
    Spicy and still,

And a heaven full of stars
    Over my head,
White and topaz
    And misty red;

Myriads with beating
Hearts of fire
That aeons
Cannot vex or tire;

Up the dome of heaven
Like a great hill,
I watch them marching
Stately and still,

And I know that I
Am honored to be
Witness
Of so much majesty.

—Sara Teasdale

THE COIN

Into my heart's treasury
I slipped a coin
That time cannot take
Nor a thief purloin, —
Oh better than the minting
Of a gold-crowned king
Is the safe-kept memory
Of a lovely thing.

—Sara Teasdale

"LET IT BE FORGOTTEN"

Let it be forgotten, as a flower is forgotten,
Forgotten as a fire that once was singing gold,
Let it be forgotten for ever and ever,
Time is a kind friend, he will make us old.

If anyone asks, say it was forgotten
   Long and long ago,
As a flower, as a fire, as a hushed footfall
   In a long forgotten snow.

                — Sara Teasdale

LOVELY CHANCE

O lovely chance, what can I do
To give my gratefulness to you?
You rise between myself and me
With a wise persistency;
I would have broken body and soul,
But by your grace, still I am whole.
Many a thing you did to save me,
Many a holy gift you gave me,
Music and friends and happy love
More than my dearest dreaming of;
And now in this wide twilight hour
With earth and heaven a dark blue flower,
In a humble mood I bless
Your wisdom — and your waywardness,
You brought me even here, where I
Live on a hill against the sky
And look on mountains and the sea
And a thin white moon in the pepper tree.

                —Sara Teasdale

"LIKE BARLEY BENDING"

Like barley bending
   In low fields by the sea,
Singing in hard wind
   Ceaselessly;

Like barley bending
   And rising again,
So would I, unbroken,
   Rise from pain;

So would I softly,
   Day long, night long,
Change my sorrow
   Into song.

               — *Sara Teasdale*

LOUIS UNTERMEYER

Louis Untermeyer was born at New York City in **1885 and** educated at the DeWitt Clinton High School. He has been in the jewelry business since he was seventeen years of age, but has found time for much lecturing and writing and editing. He has written clever criticism and brilliant parodies.

His books of poetry are *First Love* (1911), *Challenge* (1914), *These Times* (1917), and *The New Adam* (1920). Of these by far the best are *Challenge* and *These Times*. His best collections of parodies are ————*and Other Poets* (1916), and *Including Horace* (1919). His best book of criticism is *The New Era in Contemporary Poetry* (1919), which is heartily recommended to readers of this book who wish to know more about contemporary poetry.

Much of his best work is concerned, in one way or another, with protest against wrong and injustice and we sometimes believe that if Mr. Untermeyer had followed this trail of the mind still higher into the mountains, he might have reached the heights as a prophet. However that may be, "Daybreak" is a stern and searching poem against war, and "Caliban in the Coal Mines" is an eloquent plea for industrial justice.

CALIBAN IN THE COAL MINES

God, we don't like to complain —
    We know that the mine is no lark —
But — there's the pools from the rain;
    But — there's the cold and the dark.

God, You don't know what it is —
    You, in your well-lighted sky,
Watching the meteors whizz;
    Warm, with the sun always by.

God, if You had but the moon
　　Stuck in Your cap for a lamp,
Even You'd tire of it soon,
　　Down in the dark and the damp.

Nothing but blackness above,
　　And nothing that moves but the cars —
God, if You wish for our love,
　　Fling us a handful of stars!
　　　　　　　　　　— Louis Untermeyer

ON THE BIRTH OF A CHILD

(Jerome Epstein —August 8, 1912)

Lo — to the battle-ground of Life,
　　Child, you have come, like a conquering shout,
Out of a struggle — into strife;
　　Out of a darkness — into doubt.

Girt with the fragile armor of Youth,
　　Child, you must ride into endless wars,
With the sword of protest, the buckler of truth,
　　And a banner of love to sweep the stars.

About you the world's despair will surge;
　　Into defeat you must plunge and grope —
Be to the faltering an urge;
　　Be to the hopeless years a hope!

Be to the darkened world a flame;
　　Be to its unconcern a blow —
For out of its pain and tumult you came,
　　And into its tumult and pain you go.
　　　　　　　　　　— Louis Untermeyer

JEAN STARR UNTERMEYER

Jean Starr Untermeyer (née Starr) was born at Zanesville, Ohio, in 1886. She was educated at Putnam's Seminary, Zanesville, and at the Kohut School for Girls in New York, and took an Extension Course with Columbia University. She married Louis Untermeyer in 1907. She was a contributor to magazines for several years before her books were published.

Growing Pains appeared in 1918 and *Dreams Out of Darkness* in 1921. Most of Mrs. Untermeyer's early work was written in free verse, but her later poems achieve greater rhythmical symmetry. Moreover, they show growing spiritual insight. "Clay Hills" is an admirable expression of idealism.

CLAY HILLS

It is easy to mould the yielding clay.
And many shapes grow into beauty
Under the facile hand.
But forms of clay are lightly broken;
They will lie shattered and forgotten in a dingy corner.

But underneath the slipping clay
Is rock. . . .
I would rather work in stubborn rock
All the years of my life,
And make one strong thing
And set it in a high, clean place,
To recall the granite strength of my desire.

— *Jean Starr Untermeyer*

JOHN GOULD FLETCHER

John Gould Fletcher was born at Little Rock, Arkansas, in 1886. He was educated at Phillips Academy, Andover, and at Harvard University. He lives in England.

He is the author of *Irradiations — Sand and Spray* (1915), *Goblins and Pagodas* (1916), *The Tree of Life* (1918), and *Breakers and Granite* (1921). Of these by far the strongest is the latest, *Breakers and Granite*. Its salient quality is its Americanism. It is a moving picture of American vistas and a panorama of the moods and meanings that they suggest to Mr. Fletcher. Mr. Fletcher knows this land of his and of ours where wild beauty is a tremendous challenge, where nature is aptly symbolized by large things, — the Grand Canyon, the Rockies, the Bad Lands, the Mississippi, giant sequoias, breakers and granite; where all the elemental forces of life declare that only godlike men will ever be able to dominate them spiritually. Mr. Fletcher feels this as few American poets have felt it, and has succeeded in getting it into his book.

Most of the poems are written in unrhymed cadence (see Introduction), but the best, "Clipper Ships" is in polyphonic prose (see Introduction) that has a startling vitality.

CLIPPER-SHIPS

Beautiful as a tiered cloud, skysails set and shrouds twanging, she emerges from the surges that keep running away before day on the low Pacific shore. With the roar of the wind blowing half a gale after, she heels and lunges, and buries her bows in the smother, lifting them swiftly, and scattering the glistening spray-drops from her jib-sails with laughter. Her spars are cracking, her royals are half splitting, her lower stunsail booms are bent aside, like bow-strings ready to loose, and the water is roaring into her scuppers, but she still staggers out under a full press of sail, her upper trucks enkindled by the sun into shafts of rosy flame.

Oh, the anchor is up and the sails they are set, and it's 'way Rio; 'round Cape Stiff and up to Boston, ninety days hauling at the ropes: the decks slope and the stays creak as she lurches into it, sending her jib awash at every thrust, and a handful of dust and a thirst to make you weep, are all we get for being two years away to sea.

Topgallant stunsail has carried away! Ease the spanker! The anchor is rusted on the deck. Men in short duck trousers, wide-brimmed straw hats, with brown mahogany faces, pace up and down, spinning the wornout yarns they told a year ago. Some are coiling rope; some smoke; "Chips" is picking oakum near the boats. Ten thousand miles away lies their last port. In the rigging climbs a hairy monkey, and a green parakeet screams at the masthead. In the dead calm of a boiling noonday near the line, she lifts her spread of shining canvas from heel to truck, from jib o' jib to ringtail, from moonsails to watersails. Men have hung their washing in the stays so she can get more way on her. She ghosts along before an imperceptible breeze, the sails hanging limp in the cross-trees, and clashing against the masts. She is a proud white albatross skimming across the ocean, beautiful as a tiered cloud. Oh, a Yankee ship comes down the river; blow, boys, blow: her masts and yards they shine like silver: blow, my bully boys, blow; she's a crack ship, a dandy clipper, nine hundred miles from land; she's a down-Easter from Massachusetts, and she's bound to the Rio Grande!

Where are the men who put to sea in her on her first voyage? Some have piled their bones in California among the hides; some died frozen off the Horn in snowstorms; some slipped down between two greybacks, when the yards were joggled suddenly. Still she glistens beautifully, her decks snow-white with constant scrubbing as she sweeps into some empty sailless bay which sleeps all day, where the wild deer skip away when she fires her eighteen pounder, the sound reverberating about the empty hills. San Francisco? No: San Francisco will not be built for a dozen years to come. Meanwhile she hums with the tumult of loading. The mutineers, even, are let out of their irons and flogged and fed. Every day from when the dawn flares up red amid the hills to the hour it drops dead to westward, men walk gawkily, balancing on their heads the burden of heavy, stiff hides. Now the anchor is up and the sails they are set and its 'way, Rio. Boston girls are pulling at the ropes: only three months of trouble yet: time for us to go!

Beautiful as a tiered cloud she flies out seaward, and on her decks loaf and stumble a luckless crowd; the filthy sweepings of the stews. In a week, in a day, they have spent a year's wages, swilling it away and letting the waste of it run down among the gutters. How were these deadbeats bribed to go? Only the Ann Street runners know. Dagos, Dutchmen, Souwegians, niggers, crimp-captured greenhorns, they loaf up on the after deck, some of them already wrecks, so sick they wish they had never been born. Before them all the "old man" calls for a bucket of salt water to wash off his shore face. While he is at it, telling them how he will haze them till they are dead if they try soldiering, but it will be good grub and easy work if they hand, reef and steer and heave the lead, his officers are below, rummaging, through the men's dunnage, pulling out heavers, prickers, rum bottles, sheath knives, and pistols. On each grizzled half-cowed face appears something between a sheepish grin, a smirk of fear, a threat of treachery, and the dogged resignation of a brute. But the mate — Bucko Douglas is his name — is the very same that booted three men off the masthead when they were shortening sail in the teeth of a Cape Horn snorter. Two of them fell into the sea, and the third was tossed still groaning into the water. Only last night the captain stuck his cigar butt into one poor swabber's face for not minding the compass, and gave Jim Baines a taste of ratline hash for coming up on deck with dirty hands. Meanwhile under a grand spread of canvas, one hundred feet from side to side, the ship rides up the parallels. From aloft through the blue stillness of a tropic night, crammed with stars, with thunder brewing in the horizon, a mournful echo rises and swells:

> Oh, my name is hanging Johnny,
> Hooray, hooray!
> Oh, my name is hanging Johnny,
> So hang, boys, hang.

The *Great Republic*, launched before thirty thousand people, her main truck overlooking the highest steeple of the town, the eagle at her bows and colours flying, now in her first and last port, is slowly dying. She is a charred hulk, with toppling masts, seared gilding, and blistered sides. The *Alert* no more slides pertly through the bergs of the Horn. The desolate barrens of Staten Island, where no man was ever born, hold her bones. The Black Baller *Lightning*, that took eighty thousand dollars' worth of cargo around the world in one quick trip, was hurled and ripped to pieces on some unchartered reef or other. The *Dreadnought* disappeared in a hurricane's smother of foam. The *Sovereign of the Seas*, that never furled her topsails for ten years, was sheared clean amidships by the bows of an iron steamer as she left her last port. The slaver, *Bald Eagle*, cut an unlucky career short when she parted with her anchor and piled up on the Paracels where the pirate junks are waiting for every ship that swells out over the horizon.   The *Antelope* was caught off the Grande Ladrone in the northeast monsoon; she's gone.   The *Flying Cloud*, proud as she was of beating every ship that carried the Stars and Stripes or the St. George's flag, could not race faster than a thunder-bolt that fell one day on her deck and turned her to a cloud of flame — everything burned away but her fame!   No more will California hear the little *Pilgrim's* parting cheer.   The crew took to an open boat when their ship was scuttled by a privateer.   So they die out, year after year.

Sometimes the lookout on a great steamer wallowing and threshing through the heavy seas by night, sees far off on his lee quarter something like a lofty swinging light.   Beautiful as a tiered cloud, a ghostly clipper-ship emerges from the surges that keep running away before day on the low Pacific shore.   Her upper works are enkindled by the sun into shafts of rosy flame.   Swimming like a duck, steering like a fish, easy yet dry, lively yet stiff, she lifts cloud on cloud of crowded stainless sail.   She creeps abeam, within hail, she dips, she chases, she outpaces like a mettlesome racer the lumbering tea-kettle that keeps her company.   Before she fades into the weather quarter, the lookout cries: "Holy Jiggers, are you the *Flying Dutchman*, that you go two knots to our one?" Hoarsely comes back this answer from the sail: "*Challenge* is our name: America our nation: Bully Waterman our master: we can beat Creation."

> And it's 'way, Rio;
> Way — hay — hay, Rio;
> O, fare you well, my pretty young girl,
> For we're bound to the Rio Grande.

—John Gould Fletcher

"H. D."

Hilda Doolittle was born at Bethlehem, Pennsylvania, in 1886. She was educated at private schools and in Bryn Mawr College.

Her books are *Sea Garden* (1916) and *Hymen* (1921). They are examples of the Imagist spirit and technique at its very best (for a discussion of the Imagists see the Introduction), but they are more than that, for they are books of authentic poetry. H. D. is an artist. The apostrophe to the sea gods given here can be passionately felt only by those who feel beauty as H. D. feels it, but the beautiful language and the beautiful picturing are for us all to a certain extent, and the longer we know the poem the better we are going to like it.

SEA GODS

I

They say there is no hope —
Sand — drift — rocks — rubble of the sea —
The broken hulk of a ship,
Hung with shreds of rope,
Pallid under the cracked pitch.

They say there is no hope
To conjure you —
No whip of the tongue to anger you —
No hate of words
You must rise to refute.

They say you are twisted by the sea,
You are cut apart
By wave-break upon wave-break,

That you are misshapen by the sharp rocks,
Broken by the rasp and after-rasp.

That you are cut, torn, mangled,
Torn by the stress and beat,
No stronger than the strips of sand
Along your ragged beach.]

II

But we bring violets,
Great masses — single, sweet,
Wood-violets, stream-violets,
Violets from a wet marsh.

Violets in clumps from hills,
Tufts with earth at the roots,
Violets tugged from rocks,
Blue violets, moss, cliff, river-violets.

Yellow violets' gold,
Burnt with a rare tint —
Violets like red ash
Among tufts of grass.

We bring deep-purple
Bird-foot violets.
We bring the hyacinth-violet,
Sweet, bare, chill to the touch —
And violets whiter than the in-rush
Of your own white surf.

III

For you will come,
You will yet haunt men in ships,
You will trail across the fringe of strait
And circle the jagged rocks.

You will trail across the rocks
And wash them with your salt,
You will curl between sand-hills —
You will thunder along the cliff —
Break — retreat — get fresh strength —
Gather and pour weight upon the beach.

You will draw back,
And the ripple on the sand-shelf
Will be witness of your track.
O privet-white, you will paint
The lintel of wet sand with froth.
You will bring myrrh-bark
And drift laurel-wood from hot coasts.
When you hurl high — high —
We will answer with a shout.

For you will come,
You will come,
You will answer our taut hearts,
You will break the lie of men's thoughts,
And cherish and shelter us.

—H. D.

WILLIAM ROSE BENÉT

William Rose Benét was born at Fort Hamilton, New York Harbor, in 1886. He was educated at Albany Academy and at Yale University. He has worked as an editor and free-lance writer and, in war times, was in the United States Air Service.

His books are *Merchants of Cathay* (1913), *The Falconer of God* (1914), *The Great White Wall* (1916), *The Burglar of the Zodiac* (1918), *Perpetual Light* (1919), and *Moons of Grandeur* (1920). Mr. Benét's work is chiefly remarkable for the invigorating power of his rhythms and the wild delightfulness of his sky-treading imagination. Sometimes his imagination does not merely play — it romps! But in more serious moods it is a shaft of strong, steady light, a searchlight on human nature. Such a light is thrown upon life by his "The Falconer of God." It tells a story of personal religious experience in brave and satisfying symbols. The falcon is the human spirit, always rising and trying to capture a flying loveliness. The flying loveliness is symbolized by the heron. When we interpret symbols we must be guarded. We must speak finely and delicately. It is better to say very little than to say too much. But perhaps this is more than a poem of personal experience. Perhaps it tells a spiritual story of Everyman and of the race.

"The Horse Thief" is a poem of quite another kind, a rollicking ballad telling the adventures of a horse thief caught, presumably, by the sheriff and his posse, in the days and in the country when the penalty was death. In marvelously vivid, imaginative language the horse thief tells the story of his temptation — the splendor of the horse whose lines were "beyond all wonder," and the story of his thrilling ride — how he fancied that he was riding across the sky on Pegasus, pursued by the constellations. This poem should be read for the sheer joy of it, without making any attempt to find analogies.

189

THE FALCONER OF GOD

I flung my soul to the air like a falcon flying.
I said, "Wait on, wait on, while I ride below!
    I shall start a heron soon
    In the marsh beneath the moon —
A strange white heron rising with silver on its wings,
        Rising and crying
    Wordless, wondrous things;
    The secret of the stars, of the world's heart-strings
        The answer to their woe.
Then stoop thou upon him, and grip and hold him so!"

My wild soul waited on as falcons hover.
I beat the reedy fens as I trampled past.
    I heard the mournful loon
    In the marsh beneath the moon.
And then, with feathery thunder, the bird of my desire
        Broke from the cover
    Flashing silver fire.
    High up among the stars I saw his pinions spire.
        The pale clouds gazed aghast
As my falcon stooped upon him, and gript and held him fast.

My soul dropped through the air — with heavenly plunder?—
Gripping the dazzling bird my dreaming knew?
    Nay! but a piteous freight,
    A dark and heavy weight
Despoiled of silver plumage, its voice forever stilled, —
        All of the wonder
    Gone that ever filled
    Its guise with glory. O bird that I have killed,
        How brilliantly you flew
Across my rapturous vision when first I dreamed of you!

Yet I fling my soul on high with new endeavor,
And I ride the world below with a joyful mind.
    I shall start a heron soon
    In the marsh beneath the moon —
A wondrous silver heron its inner darkness fledges!
      I beat forever
        The fens and the sedges.
      The pledge is still the same—for all disastrous pledges,
        All hopes resigned!
My soul still flies above me for the quarry it shall find!

                      —William Rose Benét

THE HORSE THIEF

There he moved, cropping the grass at the purple canyon's
    lip.
  His mane was mixed with the moonlight that silvered his
    snow-white side,
For the moon sailed out of a cloud with the wake of a spectral
    ship.
  I crouched and I crawled on my belly, my lariat coil looped
    wide.

Dimly and dark the mesas broke on the starry sky.
  A pall covered every color of their gorgeous glory at noon.
I smelt the yucca and mesquite, and stifled my heart's quick
    cry,
  And wormed and crawled on my belly to where he moved
    against the moon!

Some Moorish barb was that mustang's sire. His lines were
    beyond all wonder.
  From the prick of his ears to the flow of his tail he ached in
    my throat and eyes.

Steel and velvet grace! As the prophet says, God had
"clothed his neck with thunder."
  Oh, marvelous with the drifting cloud he drifted across the
  skies!

And then I was near at hand — crouched, and balanced, and
cast the coil;
  And the moon was smothered in cloud, and the rope
  through my hands with a rip!
But somehow I gripped and clung, with the blood in my
brain aboil, —
  With a turn round the rugged tree-stump there on the
  purple canyon's lip.

Right into the stars he reared aloft, his red eye rolling and
raging.
  He whirled and sunfished and lashed, and rocked the
  earth to thunder and flame.
He squealed like a regular devil horse. I was haggard and
spent and aging —
  Roped clean, but almost storming clear, his fury too fierce
  to tame.

And I cursed myself for a tenderfoot moon-dazzled to play
the part,
  But I was doubly desperate then, with the posse pulled
  out from town,
Or I'd never have tried it. I only knew I must get a mount
and a start.
  The filly had snapped her foreleg short. I had had to shoot
  her down.

So there he struggled and strangled, and I snubbed him
   around the tree.
   Nearer, a little nearer — hoofs planted, and lolling
      tongue —
Till a sudden slack pitched me backward. He reared right on
   top of me.
   Mother of God — that moment! He missed me . . .
      and up I swung.

Somehow, gone daft completely and clawing a bunch of his
   mane,
   As he stumbled and tripped in the lariat, there I was — up
      and astride
And cursing for seven counties! And the mustang? *Just
   insane!*
   Crack-bang! went the rope; we cannoned off the tree —
      then — gods, that ride!

A rocket — that's all, a rocket! I dug with my teeth and
   nails.
   Why, we never hit even the high spots (though I hardly
      remember things),
But I heard a monstrous booming like a thunder of flapping
   sails
   When he spread — well, *call* me a liar! — when he spread
      those wings, those wings!

So white that my eyes were blinded, thick-feathered and wide
   unfurled
   They beat the air into billows. We sailed, and the earth
      was gone.
Canyon and desert and mesa withered below, with the world.
   And then I knew that mustang; for I — was Bellerophon!

Yes, glad as the Greek, and mounted on a horse of the elder
        gods,
    With never a magic bridle or a fountain-mirror nigh!
My chaps and spurs and holster must have looked it?   What's
        the odds?
    I'd a leg over lightning and thunder, careering across the
        sky!

And forever streaming before me, fanning my forehead cool,
    Flowed a mane of molten silver; and just before my thighs
(As I gripped his velvet-muscled ribs, while I cursed myself
        for a fool),
    The steady pulse of those pinions — their wonderful fall
        and rise!

The bandanna I bought in Bowie blew loose and whipped
        from my neck.
    My shirt was stuck to my shoulders and ribboning out
        behind.
The stars were dancing, wheeling and glancing, dipping with
        smirk and beck.
    The clouds were flowing, dusking and glowing. We
        rode a roaring wind.

We soared through the silver starlight to knock at the planets'
        gates.
    New shimmering constellations came whirling into our ken.
Red stars and green and golden swung out of the void that
        waits
    For man's great last adventure; the Signs took shape —
        and then

I knew the lines of that Centaur the moment I saw him come!
  The musical-box of the heavens all around us rolled to a
    tune
That tinkled and chimed and thrilled with silver sounds that
    struck you dumb,
  As if some archangel were grinding out the music of the
    moon.

Melody-drunk on the Milky Way, as we swept and soared
    hilarious,
  Full in our pathway, sudden he stood—the Centaur of the
    Stars,
Flashing from head and hoofs and breast! I knew him for
    Sagittarius.
  He reared, and bent and drew his bow. He crouched as a
    boxer spars.

Flung back on his haunches, weird he loomed — then
    leapt — and the dim void lightened.
  Old White Wings shied and swerved aside, and fled from
    the splendor-shod.
Through a flashing welter of worlds we charged. I knew why
    my horse was frightened.
  He *had* two faces — a dog's and a man's — that Baby-
    lonian god!

Also, he followed us real as fear. Ping! went an arrow past.
  My broncho buck-jumped, humping high. We plunged
    . . . I guess that's all!
I lay on the purple canyon's lip, when I opened my eyes at
    last —
  Stiff and sore and my head like a drum, but I broke no
    bones in the fall.

So you know — and now you may string me up. Such was
    the way you caught me.
  Thank you for letting me tell it straight, though you
    never could greatly care.
For I took a horse that wasn't mine! . . . But there's
    one the heavens brought me,
  And I'll hang right happy, because I know he is waiting for
    me up there.

From creamy muzzle to cannon-bone, by God, he's a peerless
    wonder!
  He is steel and velvet and furnace-fire, and death's
    supremest prize;
And never again shall be roped on earth that neck that is
    "clothed with thunder" . . .
  String me up, Dave! Go dig my grave! *I rode him across
  the skies.*

                        — *William Rose Benét*

JOHN HALL WHEELOCK

John Hall Wheelock was born at Far Rockaway, New York, in 1886. He was educated at Harvard University, at the University of Göttingen and at the University of Berlin. He has been with Charles Scribner's Sons, the publishers, since 1911.

He is the author of *The Human Fantasy* (1911), *The Beloved Adventure* (1912), *Love and Liberation* (1913), and *Dust and Light* (1919). Mr. Wheelock's lyrics have to do chiefly with love and with nature. But his thought of both is mystical rather more than it is naturalistic. Perhaps ''Earth'' is the noblest of his lyrics of nature. All perfection is seen in it as growing up out of the soil —

> Even as the growing grass
> Up from the soil religions pass,
> And the field that bears the rye
> Bears parables and prophecy.
> * * * *
> Yea, the quiet and cool sod
> Bears in her breast the dream of God.

Mr. Wheelock would have to take but a short step in advance to declare the oneness of life through all creation and the immanence of God in all life. But the poem is not so important for us doctrinally as it is emotionally. It should give us what life's difficulties and defilements sometimes take away, a sense of reverence for even the physical beginnings of all life.

EARTH

> Grasshopper, your fairy song
> And my poem alike belong
> To the dark and silent earth
> From which all poetry has birth;
> All we say and all we sing

Is but as the murmuring
Of that drowsy heart of hers
When from her deep dream she stirs:
If we sorrow, or rejoice,
You and I are but her voice.

Deftly does the dust express
In mind her hidden loveliness,
And from her cool silence stream
The cricket's cry and Dante's dream:
For the earth that breeds the trees
Breeds cities too, and symphonies,
Equally her beauty flows
Into a savior, or a rose —
Looks down in dream, and from above
Smiles at herself in Jesus' love.
Christ's love and Homer's art
Are but the workings of her heart;
Through Leonardo's hand she seeks
Herself, and through Beethoven speaks
In holy thunderings around
The awful message of the ground.

The serene and humble mould
Does in herself all selves enfold —
Kingdoms, destinies, and creeds,
Great dreams and dauntless deeds,
Science that metes the firmament,
The high, inflexible intent
Of one for many sacrificed —
Plato's brain, the heart of Christ:
All love, all legend, and all lore
Are in the dust forevermore.

Even as the growing grass
Up from the soil religions pass,
And the field that bears the rye
Bears parables and prophecy.
Out of the earth the poem grows
Like the lily, or the rose;
And all man is, or yet may be,
Is but herself in agony
Toiling up the steep ascent
Toward the complete accomplishment
When all dust shall be, the whole
Universe, one conscious soul.

Yea, the quiet and cool sod
Bears in her breast the dream of God.

If you would know what earth is, scan
The intricate, proud heart of man,
Which is the earth articulate,
And learn how holy and how great,
How limitless and how profound
Is the nature of the ground —
How without terror or demur
We may entrust ourselves to her
When we are wearied out, and lay
Our faces in the common clay.

For she is pity, she is love,
All wisdom she, all thoughts that move
About her everlasting breast
Till she gathers them to rest:
All tenderness of all the ages,
Seraphic secrets of the sages,

Vision and hope of all the seers
All prayer, all anguish, and all tears
Are but the dust, that from her dream
Awakes, and knows herself supreme —
Are but earth when she reveals
All that her secret heart conceals
Down in the dark and silent loam,
Which is ourselves asleep, at home.

Yea, and this my poem, too,
Is part of her as dust and dew,
Wherein herself she doth declare
Through my lips, and say her prayer.

— *John Hall Wheelock*

JOYCE KILMER

Joyce Kilmer was born at New Brunswick, New Jersey, in 1886. He was educated at Rutgers College and at Columbia University. He worked for several years as a teacher and then as a journalist, but when this country went into the world war he enlisted as a private in the Seventh Regiment, National Guard, New York. Later, at his own request, he was transferred to the 165th Infantry. On July 30, 1918, he was killed in action in a battle for the heights beyond the River Ourcq.

His books are *Summer of Love* (1911), *Trees and Other Poems* (1914), and *Main Street and Other Poems* (1917). After his death his publishers brought out a collection of his letters. His later poetry, which was his best, was imbued with the religious spirit of Roman Catholicism, the faith which he accepted in his young manhood. It reveals a buoyant, lovable, chivalrous personality and is aflame with zeal for the Church Militant. "Trees" needs no explanation. It has become one of the most popular poems ever written by an American. "Martin" is not quite so well known, but is a finer achievement, a delightful and memorable character study.

MARTIN

When I am tired of earnest men,
    Intense and keen and sharp and clever,
Pursuing fame with brush or pen
    Or counting metal disks forever,
Then from the halls of shadowland
    Beyond the trackless purple sea

Old Martin's ghost comes back to stand
   Beside my desk and talk to me.

Still on his delicate pale face
   A quizzical thin smile is showing,
His cheeks are wrinkled like fine lace,
   His kind blue eyes are gay and glowing.
He wears a brilliant-hued cravat,
   A suit to match his soft gray hair,
A rakish stick, a knowing hat,
   A manner blithe and debonair.

How good, that he who always knew
   That being lovely was a duty,
Should have gold halls to wander through
   And should himself inhabit beauty.
How like his old unselfish way
   To leave those halls of splendid mirth
And comfort those condemned to stay
   Upon the bleak and sombre earth.

Some people ask: What cruel chance
   Made Martin's life so sad a story?
Martin?   Why, he exhaled romance
   And wore an overcoat of glory.
A fleck of sunlight in the street,
   A horse, a book, a girl who smiled, —
Such visions made each moment sweet
   For this receptive, ancient child.

Because it was old Martin's lot
   To be, not make, a decoration
Shall we then scorn him, having not

His genius of appreciation?
Rich joy and love he got and gave;
 His heart was merry as his dress.
Pile laurel wreaths upon his grave
 Who did not gain, but was, success.

       — *Joyce Kilmer*

TREES

I think that I shall never see
A poem lovely as a tree.

A tree whose hungry mouth is prest
Against the earth's sweet flowing breast;

A tree that looks at God all day,
And lifts her leafy arms to pray;

A tree that may in summer wear
A nest of robins in her hair;

Upon whose bosom snow has lain;
Who intimately lives with rain.

Poems are made by fools like me,
But only God can make a tree.

       — *Joyce Kilmer*

ALINE KILMER

Aline (Murray) Kilmer was born at Norfolk, Virginia, in 1888. She was educated at the Rutgers Preparatory School in New Brunswick, New Jersey, and at the Vail-Deane School in Elizabeth, New Jersey. She married Joyce Kilmer, the poet. Her mother, Ada Foster Murray, is also a poet of fortunate achievement.

Mrs. Kilmer's books are *Candles That Burn* (1919) and *Vigils* (1921). Her gift is distinctly lyrical and her brief poems are all fine and clean-cut. They have in them that concise strength of personality that makes them both unique and universal.

SONG AGAINST CHILDREN

O the barberry bright, the barberry bright!
It stood on the mantelpiece because of the height.
Its stems were slender and thorny and tall
And it looked most beautiful against the grey wall.
But Michael climbed up there in spite of the height
And he ate all the berries off the barberry bright.

O the round holly wreath, the round holly wreath!
It hung in the window with ivy beneath.
It was plump and prosperous, spangled with red
And I thought it would cheer me although I were dead.
But Deborah climbed on a table beneath
And she ate all the berries off the round holly wreath.

O the mistletoe bough, the mistletoe bough!
Could anyone touch it?   I did not see how.
I hung it up high that it might last long,

I wreathed it with ribbons and hailed it with song.
But Christopher reached it, I do not know how,
And he ate all the berries off the mistletoe bough.

— Aline Kilmer

THE GIFT

He has taken away the things that I love best
  Love and youth and the harp that knew my hand.
Laughter alone is left of all the rest.
  Does He mean that I may fill my days with laughter,
  Or will it, too, slip through my fingers like spilt sand?

Why should I beat my wings like a bird in a net,
  When I can be still and laugh at my own desire?
The wise may shake their heads at me, but yet
  I should be sad without my little laughter.
  The crackling of thorns is not so bad a fire.

Will he take away even the thorns from under the pot,
  And send me cold and supperless to bed?
He has been good to me.   I know He will not.
  He gave me to keep a little foolish laughter.
  I shall not lose it even when I am dead.

— Aline Kilmer

MARGARET WIDDEMER

Margaret Widdemer was born at Doylestown, Pennsylvania, and began writing when she was still a little girl. She was educated by tutors and at the Drexel Institute Library School.

Her books are *The Factories with Other Lyrics* (1915), *The Old Road to Paradise* (1918), and *Cross-Currents* (1921). She has also written many light novels and stories for young girls, but her name is likely to live in the annals of American literature by virtue of her lyrics. Her lyrics are of two kinds — the grim and the graceful. The grim lyrics express her determined protestantism, her lively wrath against social and industrial evil. They are usually far more human and beautiful than those which she writes about her own soul and its experiences. "The Factories," "Teresina's Face," and "God and the Strong Ones" (given below) are unforgettable if one reads them with sensitive heart and conscience. Many of the graceful lyrics are simply graceful — pleasant, sentimental songs made out of popular folklore and feeling. But occasionally, when there is a real and passionate self-revelation the graceful lyric becomes a true poem. Such genuine achievements are "Barter," "Remembrance: Greek Folk Song," and "Winter Branches."

"God and the Strong Ones" is a poem against industrial exploitation. "Winter Branches" is a fine lyric of evanescence and change with a quiet depth of faith in it admirably suggested through the symbolism of the trees in winter.

GOD AND THE STRONG ONES

"We have made them fools and weak!" said the Strong Ones,
  "We have bound them, they are dumb and deaf and blind,
We have crushed them in our hands like a heap of crumbling
      sands,
  We have left them naught to seek or find:
They are quiet at our feet!" said the Strong Ones,

"We have made them one with wood and stone and clod;
Serf and laborer and woman, they are less than wise or
    human! —"
    "I shall raise the weak!" saith God.

"They are stirring in the dark!" said the Strong Ones,
    "They are struggling, who were moveless like the dead,
We can hear them cry and strain hand and foot against the
        chain,
    We can hear their heavy upward tread.   .   .   .
What if they are restless?" said the Strong Ones,
    "What if they have stirred beneath the rod?
Fools and weak and blinded men, we can tread them down
        again —"
    "Shall ye conquer Me?" saith God.

"They are evil and are brutes!" said the Strong Ones,
    "They are ingrates of the ease and peace we give,
We have stooped to them in grace and they mock us to our
        face —
    How shall we give light to them and live?
They are all unworthy grace!" said the Strong Ones,
    "They that cowered at our lightest look or nod —"
*"This that now ye pause and weigh of your grace may prove
        one day
    Mercy that ye need!" saith God.*

"They will trample us and bind!" said the Strong Ones;
    "We are crushed beneath the blackened feet and hands,
All the strong and fair and great they will crush from out the
        state,
    They will whelm it with the weight of pressing sands —
They are maddened and are blind!" saith the Strong Ones,

"Black decay has come where they have trod,
They will break the world in twain if their hands are on the
    rein —"
"What is that to Me?" saith God.

"Ye have made them in their strength, who were Strong Ones,
    Ye have only taught the blackness ye have known;
These are evil men and blind? — Ay, but molded to your mind
    How shall ye cry out against your own?
Ye have held the light and beauty I have given
    Far above the muddied ways where they must plod,
Ye have builded this your lord with the lash and with the sword—
    Reap what ye have sown! " saith God

                            — Margaret Widdemer

WINTER BRANCHES

When winter-time grows weary, I lift my eyes on high
And see the black trees standing, stripped clear against the
    sky;
They stand there very silent, with the cold flushed sky
    behind,
The little twigs flare beautiful and restful and kind;
Clear-cut and certain they rise, with summer past,
For all that trees can ever learn they know now, at last;
Slim and black and wonderful, with all unrest gone by,
The stripped tree-boughs comfort me, drawn clear against the
    sky.

                            — Margaret Widdemer

ALAN SEEGER

Alan Seeger was born at New York City in 1888 and spent most of his childhood on Staten Island. He was educated at Harvard University and then went to Paris in 1913. Less than three weeks after the beginning of the war he enlisted in the Foreign Legion of France and served on various fronts until he was mortally wounded in the attack on Belloy-en-Santerre, on July 4, 1916.

His collected *Poems* were published in 1916 with an Introduction by William Archer. In this collection will be found the poem by which he is known everywhere, "I have a Rendezvous with Death." It is inspired by that prescience of coming death which must have been common to many soldiers and it is most delicately and sensitively written, with as firm a note of courage in it as ever was sounded in any of the noisier and less lovely lyrics of the war.

"I HAVE A RENDEZVOUS WITH DEATH"

I have a rendezvous with Death
At some disputed barricade,
When Spring comes back with rustling shade
And apple-blossoms fill the air —
I have a rendezvous with Death
When Spring brings back blue days and fair.

It may be he shall take my hand
And lead me into his dark land
And close my eyes and quench my breath —
It may be I shall pass him still.
I have a rendezvous with Death
On some scarred slope of battered hill,
When Spring comes round again this year
And the first meadow-flowers appear.

God knows 'twere better to be deep
Pillowed in silk and scented down,
Where love throbs out in blissful sleep,
Pulse nigh to pulse, and breath to breath,
Where hushed awakenings are dear . . .
But I've a rendezvous with Death
At midnight in some flaming town,
When Spring trips north again this year,
And I to my pledged word am true,
I shall not fail that rendezvous.

— *Alan Seeger*

EDNA ST. VINCENT MILLAY

Edna St. Vincent Millay was born at Rockland, Maine, in 1892 and educated at Vassar College. She has been associated with The Provincetown Players both as playwright and actress. She has done many kinds of writing. But she excels as a poet and is, without question, one of our most brilliant lyrists.

Renascence, her first book, appeared in 1917. The title poem, originally printed in *The Lyric Year* in 1912, had already won her a substantial reputation. This first book was followed by *Figs from Thistles* (1920), *Second April* (1921), *Aria da Capo*, a brief and brilliant poetic tragedy (1921), and *The Lamp and the Bell* (1921). In everything that Miss Millay has written there is evidence of clear, keen, penetrative intellect, of subtle and fiery imaginative powers, of passionate feeling, and sensitiveness to beauty. Perhaps that very sensitiveness is the cause of the disillusionment and whimsical cynicism that we find in *Figs from Thistles* and *Aria da Capo*, and even in some of the lyrics in *Second April*. But her best lyrics are untouched by cynicism.

"Renascence," by which she is best known, is a beautiful and powerful poem, finely imagined and full of clean, wise, unworldly ecstasy.

TWO SONNETS

I

Euclid alone has looked on Beauty bare.
Let all who prate of Beauty hold their peace,
And lay them prone upon the earth and cease
To ponder on themselves, the while they stare
At nothing, intricately drawn nowhere
In shapes of shifting lineage; let geese
Gabble and hiss, but heroes seek release
From dusty bondage into luminous air.

O blinding hour, O holy, terrible day,
When first the shaft into his vision shone
Of light anatomized! Euclid alone
Has looked on Beauty bare. Fortunate they
Who, though once only and then but far away,
Have heard her massive sandal set on stone.

— Edna St. Vincent Millay

II

How healthily their feet upon the floor
Strike down! These are no spirits, but a band
Of children, surely, leaping hand in hand
Into the air in groups of three and four,
Wearing their silken rags as if they wore
Leaves only and light grasses, or a strand
Of black, elusive seaweed oozing sand,
And running hard, as if along a shore.

I know how lost forever and at length
How still, these lovely, tossing limbs shall lie,
And the bright laughter and the panting breath,
And yet before such beauty and such strength,
Once more, as always when the dance is high,
I am rebuked that I believe in death.

— Edna St. Vincent Millay

AUTUMN CHANT

Now the autumn shudders
   In the rose's root,
Far and wide the ladders
   Lean among the fruit,

Now the autumn clambers
  Up the trellised frame
And the rose remembers
  The dust from which it came.

Brighter than the blossom
  On the rose's bough
Sits the wizened, orange,
  Bitter berry now;

Beauty never slumbers;
  All is in her name,
But the rose remembers
  The dust from which it came.

— *Edna St. Vincent Millay*

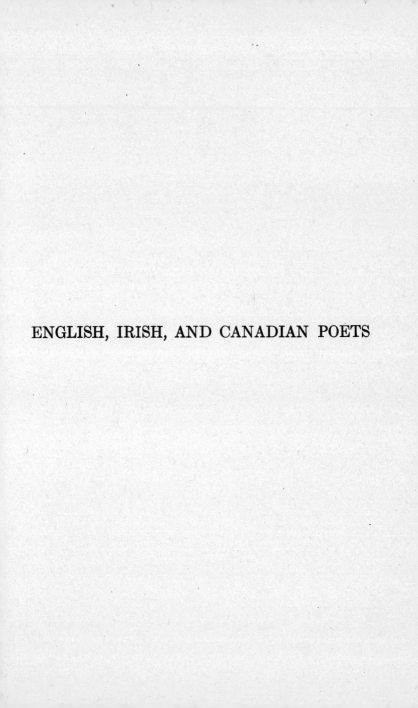

ENGLISH, IRISH, AND CANADIAN POETS

WILLIAM ERNEST HENLEY

William Ernest Henley was born in 1849, at Gloucester, England. He was the son of a bookseller and was educated at the Crypt School, Gloucester. Like many English poets, he suffered from tuberculosis. One foot had to be amputated before he was twenty years old and then he spent nearly two years in a hospital where Sir Joseph Lister, the physician, saved his other leg. In 1877 his literary life in London began. He was a critic and also an editor. He died in 1903 after having achieved an enviable reputation for a great deal of excellent work. He had become, in spite of lifelong illness, a leader in the literary and aesthetic life of his times. His verse was published under various titles between 1888 and 1892, when *London Voluntaries* appeared.

"Invictus," quoted here, is known and loved the world over for its indomitable courage. It is one of the most heartening poems ever written, for it seems to tell us that if man should lose everything else on earth, even his faith, he can still be brave. That, in itself, is a kind of faith, and a very robust kind. "Margaritae Sorori" is another fine poem of fortitude.

INVICTUS

Out of the night that covers me,
  Black as the pit from pole to pole,
I thank whatever gods may be
  ꞌ For my unconquerable soul.

In the fell clutch of circumstance
  I have not winced nor cried aloud.
Under the bludgeonings of chance
  My head is bloody, but unbowed.

217

Beyond this place of wrath and tears
   Looms but the Horror of the shade,
And yet the menace of the years
   Finds and shall find me unafraid.

It matters not how strait the gate,
   How charged with punishments the scroll,
I am the master of my fate:
   I am the captain of my soul.

                  —*William Ernest Henley*

MARGARITAE SORORI

A late lark twitters from the quiet skies:
And from the west,
Where the sun, his day's work ended,
Lingers as in content,
There falls on the old, gray city
An influence luminous and serene,
A shining peace.

The smoke ascends
In a rosy-and-golden haze.   The spires
Shine and are changed.   In the valley
Shadows rise.   The lark sings on.   The sun,
Closing his benediction,
Sinks, and the darkening air
Thrills with a sense of the triumphing night —
Night with her train of stars
And her great gift of sleep.

So be my passing!
My task accomplished and the long day done,
My wages taken, and in my heart
Some late lark singing,
Let me be gathered to the quiet west,
The sundown splendid and serene,
Death.

— *William Ernest Henley*

ROBERT LOUIS STEVENSON

Robert Louis Stevenson was born at Edinburgh, Scotland, in 1850. He was educated at private schools and by tutors, at Edinburgh Academy and at the University of Edinburgh. His father and uncles were harbor and lighthouse engineers and expected him to follow the same profession, but he was led away from it by inclination and rendered incapable of following it by ill health. The twenty years of his active life after 1873 were given up to writing — chiefly prose. He traveled far and wide in Europe, in America, in the South Seas. He was a patient invalid.

His prose books are well known and it is hardly necessary to name them all in a book devoted to poetry. *A Child's Garden of Verses*, his famous collection of lyrics for children, was put together and published in the period between 1884-7 when he was settled at Bournemouth — an invalid. *Underwoods* and then *Ballads* followed, and *Songs of Travel* was posthumously published. Sidney Colvin, writing of Stevenson in the fourth volume of *The English Poets* (Ward), says:

There was no time in his literary life when the chief part of his industry and effort was not given to prose: there was no time when he was not also accustomed occasionally to write verse. And though it was the preponderance and excellence of his work in prose that chiefly won and holds for him his place in literature, yet the charm and power of his spirit are to be felt scarcely less in the relatively small and unassuming body of his poetry.

The poems for children are deservedly beloved everywhere. And Stevenson's "Requiem" is one of the world's familiar poems. But surely Stevenson never made richer music than that of "I Will Make You Brooches" or paid a finer tribute of affection than that offered in "My Wife."

"I WILL MAKE YOU BROOCHES"

I will make you brooches and toys for your delight
Of bird-song at morning and star-shine at night.
I will make a palace fit for you and me
Of green days in forests and blue days at sea.

I will make my kitchen, and you shall keep your room,
Where white flows the river and bright blows the broom,
And you shall wash your linen and keep your body white
In rainfall at morning and dewfall at night.

And this shall be for music when no one else is near,
The fine song for singing, the rare song to hear!
That only I remember, that only you admire,
Of the broad road that stretches and the roadside fire.

— Robert Louis Stevenson

MY WIFE

Trusty, dusky, vivid, true,
With eyes of gold and bramble-dew,
Steel-true and blade-straight,
The great artificer
Made my mate.

Honour, anger, valour, fire;
A love that life could never tire,
Death quench or evil stir,
The mighty master
Gave to her.

Teacher, tender, comrade, wife,
A fellow-farer true through life,
Heart-whole and soul-free
The august father
Gave to me.

— *Robert Louis Stevenson*

ALICE MEYNELL

(Mrs.) Alice (Christina) Meynell was born in 1850. She is a sister of Lady Butler, the painter, and both she and her sister were carefully educated by their father. She is the wife of Wilfrid Meynell, the critic. Her daughter, Viola Meynell, is also a poet.

"The Shepherdess" is surely one of her most beautiful lyrics and one of the best known. The idea of guarding the thoughts of the mind as a shepherdess would guard little lambs is both religious and mannerly. In the good sense of the word it is aristocratic. The other poem, which has to do with Edith Cavell, will not need to be explained to people who remember the brave nurse who was executed, shot, in Belgium, in war times.

Mrs. Meynell died in 1922.

NURSE EDITH CAVELL

(*Two o'clock the morning of October 12, 1915*)

To her accustomed eyes
The midnight-morning brought not such a dread
As thrills the chance-awakened head that lies
In trivial sleep on the habitual bed.

'Twas yet some hours ere light;
And many, many, many a break of day
Had she outwatched the dying; but this night
Shortened her vigil was, briefer the way.

By dial of the clock
'Twas day in the dark above her lonely head.
"This day thou shalt be with me." Ere the cock
Announced that day she met the Immortal Dead.

— Alice Meynell

THE SHEPHERDESS

She walks — the lady of my delight —
　A shepherdess of sheep.
Her flocks are thoughts.　She keeps them white;
　She guards them from the steep.
She feeds them on the fragrant height,
　And folds them in for sleep.

She roams maternal hills and bright,
　Dark valleys safe and deep.
Her dreams are innocent at night;
　The chastest stars may peep.
She walks — the lady of my delight —
　A shepherdess of sheep.

She holds her little thoughts in sight,
　Though gay they run and leap.
She is so circumspect and right;
　She has her soul to keep.
She walks — the lady of my delight —
　A shepherdess of sheep.

— Alice Meynell

WILLIAM HENRY DRUMMOND

William Henry Drummond was born at Currawn, County Leitrim, Ireland, in 1854. He went to Canada as a boy, became a physician, and engaged in mining. He studied the French Canadian with sympathy, and has presented his life and thought with an interpretative skill that has won interest for the *habitant* and a reputation for the poet.

His books are *The Habitant* (1897), *Johnny Courteau* (1901), *The Voyageur* (1905), and *The Great Fight* (posthumous, 1908).

Dr. Drummond died in 1907.

THE WRECK OF THE "JULIE PLANTE"

A Legend of Lac St. Pierre

On wan dark night on Lac St. Pierre,
  De win' she blow, blow, blow,
An' de crew of the wood scow *Julie Plante*
  Got scar't an' run below —
For de win' she blow lak hurricane,
  Bimeby she blow some more,
An' de scow bus' up on Lac St. Pierre
  Wan arpent from de shore.

De captinne walk on de fronte deck,
  An' walk de hin' deck too —
He call de crew from up de hole,
  He call de cook also.
De cook she's name was Rosie,
  She come from Montreal,
Was chambre maid on lumber barge,
  On de Grande Lachine Canal.

De win' she blow from nor' — eas' — wes' —
   De sout' win' she blow too,
W'en Rosie cry "Mon cher captinne,
   Mon cher, w'at I shall do?"
Den de captinne t'row de big ankerre
   But still de scow she dreef,
De crew he can't pass on de shore,
   Becos' he los' hees skeef.

De night was dark lak' wan black cat,
   De wave run high an' fas',
W'en de captinne tak' de Rosie girl
   An' tie her to de mas'.
Den he also tak' de life preserve,
   An' jump off on de lak'.
An' say, "Good-bye, ma Rosie dear,
   I go drown for your sak'."

Nex' morning very early,
   'Bout ha'f-pas' two — t'ree — four —
De captinne — scow — an' de poor Rosie
   Was corpses on de shore,
For the win' she blow lak' hurricane
   Bimeby she blow some more,
An' de scow bus' up on Lac St. Pierre
   Wan arpent from de shore.

Moral

Now all good wood scow sailor man
   Tak' warning by dat storm
An' go an' marry some nice French girl
   An' leev on wan beeg farm.

De win' can blow lak' hurricane,
　　An' spose she blow some more,
You can't get drown on Lac St. Pierre
　　So long you stay on shore.

　　　　　　　　— William Henry Drummond

JOHNNIE'S FIRST MOOSE

De cloud is hide de moon, but dere's plaintee light above,
Steady, Johnnie, steady — kip your head down low,
Move de paddle leetle quicker, an' de ole canoe we'll shove
　　T'roo de water nice an' quiet
　　For de place we're goin' try it
　　Is beyon' de silver birch dere,
　　You can see it lak a church dere
W'en we're passin' on de corner w'ere de lily flower grow.

Wasn't dat correc' w'at I'm tolin' you jus' now?
Steady, Johnnie, steady — kip your head down low,
Never min', I'll watch behin' — me — an' you can watch de
　　　bow,
　　An' you'll see a leetle clearer
　　W'en canoe is comin' nearer —
　　Dere she is — now easy, easy,
　　For de win' is gettin' breezy,
An' we don't want not'ing smell us, till de horn begin to blow.

I remember long ago w'en ma fader tak' me out,
Steady, Johnnie, steady — kip your head down low,
Jus' de way I'm takin' you, sir, hello! was dat a shout?
　　Seems to me I t'ink I'm hearin'

Somet'ing stirrin' on de clearin'
W'ere it stan' de lumber shaintee;
If it's true, den you'll have plaintee
Work to do in half a minute, if de moose don't start to go.

An' now we're on de shore, let us hide de ole canoe,
Steady, Johnnie, steady — kip your head down low,
An' lie among de rushes, dat's bes' t'ing we can do,
    For de ole boy may be closer
    Dan anybody know, sir,
    An' look out you don't be shakin'
    Or de bad shot you'll be makin';
But I'm feelin' sam' way too, me, w'en I was young, also.

You ready for de call? here goes for number wan,
Steady, Johnnie, steady — kip your head down low,
Did you hear how nice I do it, an' how it travel on
    Till it reach across de reever
    Dat'll geev' some moose de fever!
    Wait now, Johnnie, don't you worry,
    No use bein' on de hurry,
But lissen for de answer, it'll come before you know.

For w'y you jomp lak dat? w'at's matter wit' your ear?
Steady, Johnnie, steady — kip your head down low —
Tak' your finger off de trigger, dat was only bird your hear.
    Can't you tell de pine tree crickin'
    Or de boule frog w'en he's spikin'?
    Don't you know de grey owl singin'
    From de beeg moose w'en he's ringin'
Out hees challenge on de message your ole gran'fader blow?

You're lucky boy to-night, wit' hunter man lak me!
Steady, Johnnie, steady — kip your head down low —
Can tole you all about it!   H-s-s-h! dat's somet'ing now I see,
    Dere he's comin' t'roo de bushes,
    So get down among de rushes,
    Hear heem walk! I t'ink, by tonder,
    He mus' go near fourteen honder.
Dat's de feller I been watchin' all de evening, I dunno.

I'll geev' anoder call, jus' a leetle wan or two,
Steady, Johnnie, steady — kip your head down low —
W'en he see dere's no wan waitin' I wonder w'at he'll do?
    But look out for here he's comin';
    Sa-pris-ti! ma heart is drummin'!
    You can never get heem nearer
    An' de moon is shinin' clearer,
W'at a fine shot you'll be havin'! now, Johnnie, let her go!

Bang! bang! you got heem sure! an' he'll never run away
Nor feed among de lily on de shore of Wessonneau.
So dat's your first moose, Johnnie! wall! remember all I say —
    Doesn't matter w'at you're chasin',
    Doesn't matter w'at you're facin',
    Only watch de t'ing you're doin';
    If you don't, ba gosh! you're ruin!
An' steady, Johnnie, steady — kip your head down low.

                      — *William Henry Drummond*

From *Poetical Works by W. H. Drummond*

JOHN DAVIDSON

John Davidson was born in 1857. He was educated at Edinburgh University and was, for several years, a schoolmaster. He was found drowned at Penzance in 1909.

His first book was *Bruce* (1886), a poetic drama. *Fleet Street Eclogues* (1893) made his reputation as a poet. He was the author of a number of novels and plays as well as of other books of verse. "Epping Forest" describes a storm in what is really a large grove near London. (Americans would not call it a forest.) It is a powerful bit of description, using strong rhythm, fresh imagery, and vigorous words to give us a sense of the beauty of wind and rain and moving trees. It is a terse, stout-hearted, masculine poem of nature and does a certain kind of justice to its theme. It is fortunately free from all the sentimental gush that is commonly used to prettify and misrepresent nature.

EPPING FOREST

Woods and coppice by tempest lashed;
   Pollard shockheads glaring in the rain;
Jet-black underwood with crimson splashed —
   Rich November, one wet crimson stain!

Turf that whispered moistly to the tread;
   Bursts of laughter from the shuffled leaves;
Pools of light in distant arbors spread;
   Depths of darkness under forest eaves.

High above the wind the clouds at rest
   Emptied every vast and steeply hurled
Reservoirs and floods; the wild nor'west
   Raked the downpour ere it reached the world;

Part in wanton sport and part in ire,
    Flights of rain on ruddy foliage rang:
Woven showers like sheets of silver fire
    Streamed; and all the forest rocked and sang.

— John Davidson

A. E. HOUSMAN

Alfred Edward Housman was educated at Oxford. He became a Higher Division Clerk in H. M. Patent Office (1882-92) and then Professor of Latin in University College, London (1892-1911). Since 1911 he has been Professor of Latin at Cambridge.

A Shropshire Lad, his first volume of verse, was published in 1896. But many poets have written at great length and for years without producing the deep impression made by this little book. The poems are wonderfully simple and direct expressions of the thought and feeling of a young man's life, of his love, his friendships, his tragedies. "Loveliest of Trees" is a lyric that defies explanation or comment because it is too simple and clear for analysis. It is unforgettable, and hundreds, perhaps thousands of people have memorized it.

His second book, *Last Poems*, appeared in 1922.

"LOVELIEST OF TREES"

Loveliest of trees, the cherry now
Is hung with bloom along the bough,
And stands about the woodland ride
Wearing white for Eastertide.

Now, of my threescore years and ten,
Twenty will not come again,
And take from seventy springs a score,
It only leaves me fifty more.

And since to look at things in bloom
Fifty springs are little room,
About the woodland I will go
To see the cherry hung with snow.

— *A. E. Housman*

REVEILLE

Wake: the silver dusk returning
　　Up the beach of darkness brims,
And the ship of sunrise burning
　　Strands upon the eastern rims.

Wake: the vaulted shadow shatters,
　　Tramples to the floor it spanned,
And the tent of night in tatters
　　Straws the sky-pavilioned land.

Up, lad, up, 'tis late for lying:
　　Hear the drums of morning play;
Hark, the empty highways crying
　　"Who'll beyond the hills away?"

Towns and countries woo together,
　　Forelands beacon, belfries call;
Never lad that trod on leather
　　Lived to feast his heart with all.

Up, lad: thews that lie and cumber
　　Sunlit pallets never thrive;
Morns abed and daylight slumber
　　Were not meant for man alive.

Clay lies still, but blood's a rover;
　　Breath's a ware that will not keep.
Up, lad: when the journey's over
　　There'll be time enough to sleep.

— A. E. Housman

FRANCIS THOMPSON

Francis Thompson was born at Preston, England, in 1859. His parents were Roman Catholics and it was intended at first that he should enter the priesthood. Later he studied medicine at Owens College, but it was not his destiny to become either a priest or a doctor. After a period of great poverty and distress in London, he was discovered by Mr. and Mrs. Meynell (Alice Meynell, the poet), who assisted him in every possible way and helped to make his genius known to the world.

His first volume, *Poems*, was published in 1893. *Sister Songs* appeared in 1895, and *New Poems* in 1897. In 1907 Thompson died in London of consumption.

His greatest poem is that stupendous mystical ode, "The Hound of Heaven." Majestic in movement and sublime in thought, it is a great gift to mankind. In it God is symbolized as the hound of Heaven, following the human soul through the universe in swift and loving pursuit. It is a daring symbol, and, in the hands of a merely talented poet, would become offensive. But Thompson was a genius, and, by putting his emphasis only on the noblest abstract qualities inherent in the nature of his symbol, — on strength, and speed, and certainty of approach, — he relieves it of all that might otherwise be distasteful and even lifts it, exalting the symbol by that which it symbolizes, into a higher range of meanings and suggestions. Briefly, this is what the poem tells:

A human soul has fled from God, hidden from Him, evaded Him. God has pursued the soul through all the nights and days, through tears and laughter. Yet the soul ignores God and turns to mankind for love and solace and understanding, being fearful lest, having God, it must give up everything else. Still the soul can not rest satisfied in any human heart and

"Fear wist not to evade as Love wist to pursue."

Then the soul turns to children, then to Nature, for satisfaction,

234

but is disappointed.   Nothing is left in which it may put confidence, and in utter desolation the soul pauses, awaiting love's uplifted stroke.   A superb dialogue between the soul and God follows, in which the soul asks the ancient, challenging, terrible questions, and is answered.   The footfall halts, and the soul learns that all which it blindly sought is kept for it in God.

> "I am He Whom thou seekest!
> Thou dravest love from thee, who dravest Me."

The pursuit is over and God has won, but the triumph is for the soul after all.

"The Hound of Heaven" merits careful study, not only for its emotional and intellectual values as feeling and thought, but for its rich and stately music, varying in accordance with them, and also for the fluent language and illuminating imagery.

"The Kingdom of God" is a much shorter and simpler poem with the same spiritual authenticity — the quality that makes us feel how real Thompson's belief was to him.   And "To a Snowflake" is a magical lyric in praise of one of the least things of creation.

THE HOUND OF HEAVEN

I fled Him, down the nights and down the days;
  I fled Him, down the arches of the years;
I fled Him, down the labyrinthine ways
  Of my own mind; and in the mist of tears
I hid from Him, and under running laughter.
          Up vistaed hopes, I sped;
          And shot, precipitated
Adown Titantic glooms of chasmèd fears,
    From those strong Feet that followed, followed after.
          But with unhurrying chase,
          And unperturbèd pace,
        Deliberate speed, majestic instancy,

They beat — and a Voice beat
More instant than the Feet —
"All things betray thee, who betrayest Me."

I pleaded, outlaw-wise,
By many a hearted casement, curtained red,
    Trellised with intertwining charities;
(For, though I knew His love Who followed,
            Yet was I sore adread
Lest, having Him, I must have naught beside)
But, if one little casement parted wide,
    The gust of His approach would clash it to.
    Fear wist not to evade as Love wist to pursue.
Across the margent of the world I fled,
    And troubled the gold gateways of the stars,
    Smiting for shelter on their clangèd bars;
            Fretted to dulcet jars
And silvern chatter the pale ports o' the moon.
I said to dawn: Be sudden — to eve: Be soon;
    With thy young skiey blossoms heap me over
            From this tremendous Lover!
Float thy vague veil about me, lest He see!
    I tempted all His servitors, but to find
My own betrayal in their constancy,
In faith to Him their fickleness to me,
    Their traitorous trueness, and their loyal deceit.
To all swift things for swiftness did I sue;
    Clung to the whistling mane of every wind.
        But whether they swept, smoothly fleet,
    The long savannahs of the blue;
            Or whether, Thunder-driven,
        They clanged His chariot 'thwart a heaven,

Plashy with flying lightnings round the spurn o' their feet: —
Fear wist not to evade as Love wist to pursue.
        Still with unhurrying chase,
        And unperturbèd pace,
    Deliberate speed, majestic instancy,
        Came on the following Feet,
        And a Voice above their beat —
"Naught shelters thee, who wilt not shelter Me."

I sought no more that, after which I strayed,
        In face of man or maid;
But still within the little children's eyes
        Seems something, something that replies,
They at least are for me, surely for me!
I turned me to them very wistfully;
But just as their young eyes grew sudden fair
        With dawning answers there,
Their angel plucked them from me by the hair.
"Come then, ye other children, Nature's — share
With me" (said I) "your delicate fellowship;
        Let me greet you lip to lip,
        Let me twine with you caresses,
            Wantoning
        With our Lady-Mother's vagrant tresses,
            Banqueting
        With her in her wind-walled palace,
        Underneath her azured dais,
        Quaffing, as your taintless way is,
            From a chalice
Lucent-weeping out of the dayspring."
        So it was done:

I in their delicate fellowship was one —
Drew the bolt of Nature's secrecies.
> *I* knew all the swift importings
> On the wilful face of skies;
> I knew how the clouds arise
> Spumèd of the wild sea-snortings;
>> All that's born or dies
Rose and drooped with — made them shapers
Of mine own moods, or wailful or divine —
> With them joyed and was bereaven
> I was heavy with the even,
When she lit her glimmering tapers
> Round the day's dead sanctities.
> I laughed in the morning's eyes.
I triumphed and I saddened with all weather,
> Heaven and I wept together,
And its sweet tears were salt with mortal mine;
Against the red throb of its sunset-heart
> I laid my own to beat,
> And share commingling heat;
But not by that, by that, was eased my human smart.
In vain my tears were wet on Heaven's grey cheek.
For, ah! we know not what each other says,
> These things and I; in sound *I* speak —
Their sound is but their stir, they speak by silences.
Nature, poor stepdame, cannot slake my drouth;
> ·Let her, if she would owe me,
Drop yon blue bosom-veil of sky, and show me
> The breasts o' her tenderness:
Never did any milk of hers once bless
>> My thirsting mouth.
>> Nigh and nigh draws the chase,

With unperturbèd pace,
Deliberate speed, majestic instancy,
And past those noisèd Feet
A Voice comes yet more fleet —
"Lo! naught contents thee, who content'st not Me."

Naked I wait Thy love's unlifted stroke!
My harness piece by piece Thou hast hewn from me,
And smitten me to my knee;
I am defenceless utterly.
I slept, methinks, and woke
And, slowly gazing, find me stripped in sleep.
In the rash lustihead of my young powers,
I shook the pillaring hours
And pulled my life upon me; grimed with smears,
I stand amid the dust 'o the mounded years —
My mangled youth lies dead beneath the heap,
My days have crackled and gone up in smoke,
Have puffed and burst as sun-starts on a stream.
Yea, faileth now even dream
The dreamer, and the lute the lutanist;
Even the linked fantasies, in whose blossomy twist
I swung the earth a trinket at my wrist,
Are yielding; cords of all too weak account
For earth with heavy griefs so overplussed.
Ah! is Thy love indeed
A weed, albeit an amaranthine weed,
Suffering no flowers except its own to mount?
Ah! must —
Designer Infinite! —
Ah! must Thou char the wood ere Thou canst limn with it?
My freshness spent its wavering shower i' the dust;

And now my heart is as a broken fount,
Wherein tear-drippings stagnate, spilt down ever
     From the dank thoughts that shiver
Upon the sighful branches of my mind.
     Such is; what is to be?
The pulp so bitter, how shall taste the rind?
I dimly guess what Time in mists confounds;
Yet ever and anon a trumpet sounds
From the hid battlements of Eternity;
Those shaken mists a space unsettle, then
Round the half-glimpsèd turrets slowly wash again;
     But not ere him who summoneth
     I first have seen, enwound
With glooming robes purpureal, cypress-crowned;
His name I know, and what his trumpet saith.
Whether man's heart or life it be which yields
     Thee harvest, must Thy harvest fields
     Be dunged with rotten death?
      Now of that long pursuit
     Comes on at hand the bruit;
That Voice is round me like a bursting sea;
     "And is thy earth so marred,
     Shattered in shard on shard?
Lo, all things fly thee, for thou fliest Me!
     Strange, piteous, futile thing!
Wherefore should any set thee love apart?
Seeing none but I make much of naught" (He said),
"And human love needs human meriting:
     How hast thou merited —
Of all man's clotted clay, the dingiest clot?
     Alack, thou knowest not
How little worthy of any love thou art!

Whom wilt thou find to love ignoble thee,
        Save Me, save only Me?
All which I took from thee I did but take,
        Not for thy harms,
But just that thou might'st seek it in My arms.
        All which thy child's mistake
Fancies as lost, I have stored for thee at home:
        Rise, clasp My hand, and come."

        Halts by me that footfall:
        Is my gloom, after all,
    Shade of His hand, outstretched caressingly?
        "Ah, fondest, blindest, weakest,
        I am He Whom thou seekest!
Thou dravest love from thee, who dravest Me."

— *Francis Thompson*

THE KINGDOM OF GOD

"In No Strange Land"

O world invisible, we view thee,
O world intangible, we touch thee,
O world unknowable, we know thee.
Inapprehensible, we clutch thee.

Does the fish soar to find the ocean,
The eagle plunge to find the air —
That we ask of the stars in motion
If they have rumour of thee there?

Not where the wheeling systems darken,
And our benumbed conceiving soars! —

The drift of pinions, would we harken,
Beats at our own clay-shuttered doors.

The angels keep their ancient places; —
Turn but a stone and start a wing!
'Tis ye, 'tis your estranged faces,
That miss the many-splendoured thing.

But when so sad thou canst not sadder,
Cry; and upon thy so sore loss
Shall shine the traffic of Jacob's ladder
Pitched betwixt Heaven and Charing Cross.

Yea, in the night, my Soul, my daughter,
Cry, — clinging Heaven by the hems:
And lo, Christ walking on the water
Not of Gennesareth, but Thames!

— *Francis Thompson*

TO A SNOWFLAKE

What heart could have thought you? —
Past our devisal
(O filigree petal)
Fashioned so purely,
Fragilely, surely,
From what Paradisal
Imagineless metal,
Too costly for cost?
Who hammered you, wrought you,
From argentine vapour? —
  God was my shaper,

Passing surmisal,
He hammered, He wrought me,
From curled silver vapour,
To lust of His mind: —
Thou couldst not have thought me!
So purely, so palely,
Tinily, surely,
Mightily, frailly,
Insculped and embossed,
With His hammer of wind,
And His graver of frost.

— *Francis Thompson*

HENRY CHARLES BEECHING

The Very Reverend Henry Charles Beeching was born in 1859 and educated at the City of London School and at Oxford. He was made Dean of Norwich Cathedral in 1911 and was Preacher to the Honorable Society of Lincoln's Inn from 1904 to 1912. He has written many books on religious and literary subjects.

In a Garden and Other Poems was published in 1895. The two poems quoted here, "Prayers" and "Going Down Hill on a Bicycle" are taken from that choicest of all small anthologies, *The Oxford Book of English Verse*. They need no explanation, for they are delightfully simple, full of fresh and spontaneous sympathy with boyhood. It is a good thing to remember that the England which produced the schools of which Dickens wrote, the schools which he did so much to banish from the land, also produced men who could write such poems of boyhood as these by Dean Beeching.

PRAYERS

God who created me
  Nimble and light of limb,
In three elements free,
  To run, to ride, to swim:
Not when the sense is dim,
  But now from the heart of joy,
I would remember Him:
  Take the thanks of a boy.

Jesus, King and Lord,
  Whose are my foes to fight,
Gird me with Thy sword
  Swift and sharp and bright.
Thee would I serve if I might:

244

And conquer if I can,
From day-dawn till night,
   Take the strength of a man.

Spirit of Love and Truth,
   Breathing in grosser clay,
The light and flame of youth,
   Delight of men in the fray,
Wisdom in strength's decay;
   From pain, strife, wrong to be free, —
This best gift I pray,
   Take my spirit to Thee.

— Henry Charles Beeching

GOING DOWN HILL ON A BICYCLE

A Boy's Song

With lifted feet, hands still,
I am poised, and down the hill
Dart, with heedful mind;
The air goes by in a wind.

Swifter and yet more swift,
Till the heart with a mighty lift
Makes the lungs laugh, the throat cry: —
'O bird, see; see, bird, I fly.

"Is this, is this your joy?
O bird, then I, though a boy,
For a golden moment share
Your feathery life in air!"

Say, heart, is there aught like this
In a world that is full of bliss?
'Tis more than skating, bound
Steel-shod to the level ground.

Speed slackens now, I float
Awhile in my airy boat;
Till, when the wheels scarce crawl,
My feet to the treadles fall.

Alas, that the longest hill
Must end in a vale; but still
Who climbs with toil, wheresoe'er,
Shall find wings waiting there.

— *Henry Charles Beeching*

CHARLES G. D. ROBERTS

Charles (George Douglas) Roberts was born in Canada in 1860. For many years he has been a writer of books about Canada. He has also written history, accounts of nature study and exploration, stories of animal life, and poetry.

His *Poems* were published in 1903. "The Recessional" is one of the loveliest of modern songs of autumn. It has a dignified marching music and moves solemnly from thought to thought.

HILL TOP SONGS

I

Here on the hill
At last the soul sees clear.
Desire being still
The High Unseen appear.
The thin grass bends
One way, and hushed attends
Unknown and gracious ends.
Where the sheep's pasturing feet
Have cleft the sods
The mystic light lies sweet;
The very clods,
In purpling hues elate,
Thrill to their fate;
The high rock-hollows wait,
Expecting gods.

II

When the lights come out in the cottages
Along the shores at eve,

And across the darkening water
   The last pale shadows leave;

And up from the rock-ridged pasture slopes
   The sheep-bell tinklings steal,
And the folds are shut, and the shepherds
   Turn to their quiet meal;

And even here, on the unfenced height,
   No journeying wind goes by,
But the earth-sweet smells, and the home-sweet sounds,
   Mount, like prayer, to the sky;

Then from the door of my opened heart
   Old blindness and pride are driven,
Till I know how high is the humble,
   The dear earth how close to heaven.

             — *Charles G. D. Roberts*

BLISS CARMAN

(William) Bliss Carman was born at Frederickton, New Brunswick, Canada in 1861. He was educated at the University of New Brunswick, the University of Edinburgh, and Harvard University. He read law for two years. Then, in 1890, he became office editor of *The Independent*. He went from that office to other editorial positions. He has lived in the United States most of the time since 1889.

His books are *Low Tide on Grand Pre* (1893), *Behind the Arras* (1895), *By the Aurelian Wall* (1897), *Songs from Vagabondia* (with Richard Hovey) (1894), *More Songs from Vagabondia* (with Richard Hovey) (1896), *Last Songs from Vagabondia* (with Richard Hovey) (1900), *Pipes of Pan* (five volumes in one) (1904-05), *Sappho* (100 lyrics not issued in America except in a limited edition out of print), *The Rough Rider* (1909), *Echoes from Vagabondia* (1912), *Daughters of Dawn* (with Mary Perry King) (1913), *Earth Deities* (with Mary Perry King) (1914), *April Airs* (1916).

His poetry is purely and clearly lyrical in type and is best when it is nearest to nature, whose true and loyal interpreter Mr. Carman is. "Lord of My Heart's Elation" is a song of faith that finds God immanent in nature.

THE GRAVEDIGGER

Oh, the shambling sea is a sexton old,
And well his work is done.
With an equal grave for lord and knave,
He buries them every one.

Then hoy and rip, with a rolling hip,
He makes for the nearest shore;

And God, who sent him a thousand ship,
Will send him a thousand more;

But some he'll save for a bleaching grave,
And shoulder them in to shore, —
Shoulder them in, shoulder them in,
Shoulder them in to shore.

Oh, the ships of Greece and the ships of Tyre
Went out, and where are they?
In the port they made, they are delayed
With the ships of yesterday.

He followed the ships of England far.
As the ships of long ago;
And the ships of France they led him a dance,
But he laid them all arow.

Oh, a loafing, idle lubber to him
Is the sexton of the town;
For sure and swift, with a guiding lift,
He shovels the dead men down.

But though he delves so fierce and grim,
His honest graves are wide,
As well they know who sleep below
The dredge of the deepest tide.

Oh, he works with a rollicking stave at lip,
And loud is the chorus skirled;
With the burly rote of his rumbling throat
He batters it down the world.

He learned it once in his father's house,
Where the ballads of eld were sung;
And merry enough is the burden rough,
But no man knows the tongue.

Oh, fair, they say, was his bride to see,
And wilful she must have been,
That she could bide at his gruesome side
When the first red dawn came in.

And sweet, they say, is her kiss to those
She greets to his border home;
And softer than sleep her hand's first sweep
That beckons, and they come.

Oh, crooked is he, but strong enough
To handle the tallest mast;
From the royal barque to the slaver dark,
He buries them all at last.

Then hoy and rip, with a rolling hip,
He makes for the nearest shore;
And God, who sent him a thousand ship,
Will send him a thousand more;
But some he'll save for a bleaching grave,
And shoulder them in to shore, —
Shoulder them in, shoulder them in,
Shoulder them in to shore.

— Bliss Carman

SIR HENRY NEWBOLT

Sir Henry (John) Newbolt was born in 1862. He was educated at Oxford and became a barrister at Lincoln's Inn. He practised law until 1899. He is best known for his ballads of the sea.

His *Admirals All* was published in 1897 and his *Collected Poems* in 1910.

"He Fell Among Thieves" is one of his most popular poems and has been reprinted many times. It seems to be simply a story of a young Englishman murdered by bandits in India. He can die bravely and quietly and with a thanksgiving on his lips because he has "lived" in the highest and best sense, has known the wonder and sweetness of life in home and school and college and in the service of England.

> O glorious Life, Who dwellest in earth and sun,
> I have lived, I praise and adore Thee.

For us, in this country, the poem has additional value for its picturing of home and school life in England and for its description of the meaning of these things in an Englishman's mind.

"HE FELL AMONG THIEVES"

"Ye have robbed," said he, "ye have slaughtered and made
    an end,
  Take your ill-got plunder and bury the dead:
What will ye more of your guest and sometime friend?"
    "Blood for our blood," they said.

He laughed: "If one may settle the score for five,
  I am ready; but let the reckoning stand till day:
I have loved the sunlight as dearly as any alive,"
    "You shall die at dawn," said they.

He flung his empty revolver down the slope,
   He climbed alone to the Eastward edge of the trees;
All night long in a dream untroubled of hope
   He brooded, clasping his knees.

He did not hear the monotonous roar that fills
   The ravine where the Yassin river sullenly flows;
He did not see the starlight on the Laspur hills
   Or the far Afghan snows.

He saw the April noon on his books aglow,
   The wistaria trailing in at the window wide,
He heard his father's voice from the terrace below
   Calling him down to ride.

He saw the gray little church across the park,
   The mounds that hide the loved and honored dead.
The Norman arch, the chancel softly dark,
   The brasses black and red.

He saw the School Close, sunny and green,
   The runner beside him, the stand by the parapet wall,
The distant tape, and the crowd roaring between
   His own name over all.

He saw the dark wainscot and timbered roof,
   The long tables, and the faces merry and keen;
The College Eight, and their trainer, dining aloof,
   The Dons on the dais serene.

He watched the liner's stem ploughing the foam,
   He felt her trembling speed and the thrash of her screw;

He heard her passengers' voices talking of home,
   He saw the flag she flew.

And now it was dawn. He rose strong on his feet,
   And strode to his ruined camp below the wood;
He drank the breath of the morning cool and sweet;
   His murderers round him stood.

Light on the Laspur hills was broadening fast,
   The blood-red snow-peaks chilled to a dazzling white:
He turned and saw the golden circle at last,
   Cut by the Eastern height.

"O glorious Life, Who dwellest in earth and sun,
   I have lived, I praise and adore Thee."
     A sword swept.
Over the pass the voices one by one
   Faded, and the hill slept.

            — *Sir Henry Newbolt*

SAILING AT DAWN

One by one the pale stars die before the day now,
   One by one the great ships are stirring from their sleep,
Cables all are rumbling, anchors all aweigh now,
   Now the fleet's a fleet again, gliding toward the deep.
     Now the fleet's a fleet again, bound upon the old ways,
     Splendor of the past comes shining in the spray,
     Admirals of old time, bring us on the bold ways!
     Souls of all the sea-dogs, lead the line to-day!

Far away behind us tower and town are dwindling,
   Home becomes a fair dream faded long ago;

Infinitely glorious the height of heaven is kindling,
　　Infinitely desolate the shoreless sea below.
　　　Now the fleet's a fleet again, bound upon the old ways!
　　　Splendor of the past comes shining in the spray!
　　　Admirals of old time, bring us on the bold ways
　　　Souls of all the sea-dogs, lead the line to-day

Once again with proud hearts we make the old surrender,
　　Once again with high hearts serve the age to be,
Not for us the warm life of Earth, secure and tender,
　　Ours the eternal wandering and warfare of the sea.
　　　Now the fleet's a fleet again, bound upon the old ways,
　　　Splendor of the past comes shining in the spray,
　　　Admirals of old time, bring us on the bold ways!
　　　Souls of all the sea-dogs, lead the line to-day!

　　　　　　　　　　　　　— Sir Henry Newbolt

STEPHEN PHILLIPS

Stephen Phillips was born at Summertown, near Oxford, England, in 1864. He was educated at the Grammar School, Stratford-on-Avon, and at Oundle School. He was intended for civil service, but went on the stage instead. He was not a success as an actor.

After the publication of a few relatively unimportant volumes of verse, his *Poems* appeared in 1897 and won him immediate popularity. He then began to write poetical drama and found that his experience on the stage was to his advantage. His best plays in verse are *Paolo and Francesca* (1899), *Herod* (1900), *Ulysses* (1902), *The Sin of David* (1904), and *Nero* (1906). His *New Poems* appeared in 1903 and *Lyrics and Dramas* in 1913. Stephen Phillips had the true poetic passion and, although he was a traditionalist rather than a creator of new forms and values, he had his own measure of originality, the result of his own personal conflict and contact with life.

The lyric quoted here is called "A Poet's Prayer." It is a subjective lyric and had, doubtless, certain meanings in the life of its maker that it could not have for anybody else. It has other meanings that belong especially to all poets, for it describes the ebb and flow of inspiration. But we must remember that poets are not the only inspired people in the world. If they were, nobody but poets would ever read poetry. Inspiration is for all who live in such a way as to make it a possible experience. To live without it all one's life is to know a living death. Do we not all know moments when we are brought near to high and lovely things? This poem is a prayer for inspiration, and a prayer for solace when it is withdrawn.

Stephen Phillips died in 1915.

A POET'S PRAYER

That I have felt the rushing wind of Thee:
That I have run before Thy blast to sea;

That my one moment of transcendent strife
Is more than many years of listless life;
Beautiful Power, I praise Thee: yet I send
A prayer that sudden strength be not the end.
Desert me not when from my flagging sails
Thy breathing dies away, and virtue fails:
When Thou hast spent the glory of that gust,
Remember still the body of this dust.
Not then when I am boundless, without bars,
When I am rapt in hurry to the stars;
When I anticipate an endless bliss,
And feel before my time the final kiss,
Not then I need Thee: for delight is wise,
I err not in the freedom of the skies;
I fear not joy, so joy might ever be,
And rapture finish in felicity.
But when Thy joy is past; comes in the test,
To front the life that lingers after zest:
To live in mere negation of Thy light,
A more than blindness after more than sight.
'Tis not in flesh so swiftly to descend,
And sudden from the spheres with earth to blend;
And I, from splendour thrown, and dashed from dream,
Into the flare pursue the former gleam.
Sustain me in that hour with Thy left hand,
And aid me, when I cease to soar, to stand;
Make me Thy athlete even in my bed,
Thy girded runner though the course be sped;
Still to refrain that I may more bestow,
From sternness to a larger sweetness grow.
I ask not that false calm which many feign,
And call that peace which is a dearth of pain.

True calm doth quiver like the calmest star;
It is that white where all the colours are;
And for its very vestibule doth own
The tree of Jesus and the pyre of Joan.
Thither I press: but O do Thou meanwhile
Support me in privations of Thy smile.
Spaces Thou hast ordained the stars between
And silences where melody hath been:
Teach me those absences of fire to face,
And Thee no less in silence to embrace,
Else shall Thy dreadful gift still people Hell,
And men not measure from what height I fell.

— *Stephen Phillips.*

RUDYARD KIPLING

Rudyard Kipling was born in 1865 and was associated with India from the time of his birth. He was educated at the United Service College. He began his career in India in 1882 as the associate editor of *The Civil and Military Gazette* and *The Pioneer*. Since 1910 he has published chiefly new editions of his famous novels, poems, and short stories.

He is the author of many books of prose and of the following volumes of verse: *Departmental Ditties and Other Verses* (1886), *Barrack Room Ballads and Other Verses* (1892), *The Jungle Book* (which contains some of his best verse) (1894), *The Second Jungle Book* (1895). His *Collected Poems* appeared in 1920. Mr. Kipling's poetry is remarkable for its vigorous rhythms, its occasional brilliant images, its use of the out-of-door life and activities of plain men as subject matter, and for its popularity with people who read very little poetry.

"The Recessional," which was rescued from the waste basket into which he had thrown it, has taken its place among great patriotic hymns as one of the best. "The Ballad of East and West" has a moving, masculine strenuousness that makes us think of men like Roosevelt and Lincoln, even though it has nothing to do with their lives or personalities. It is a song of man's strength.

RECESSIONAL

God of our fathers, known of old —
   Lord of our far-flung battle-line —
Beneath whose awful hand we hold
   Dominion over palm and pine —
Lord God of Hosts, be with us yet,
Lest we forget, lest we forget!

The tumult and the shouting dies —
　　The captains and the kings depart —
Stills stands Thine ancient sacrifice,
　　An humble and a contrite heart.
Lord God of Hosts, be with us yet,
Lest we forget, lest we forget!

Far-call'd our navies melt away —
　　On dune and headland sinks the fire —
Lo, all our pomp of yesterday
　　Is one with Nineveh and Tyre!
Judge of the Nations, spare us yet,
Lest we forget, lest we forget!

If, drunk with sight of power, we loose
　　Wild tongues that have not Thee in awe —
Such boasting as the Gentiles use
　　Or lesser breeds without the Law —
Lord God of Hosts, be with us yet,
Lest we forget, lest we forget!

For heathen heart that puts her trust
　　In reeking tube and iron shard —
All valiant dust that builds on dust,
　　And guarding calls not Thee to guard —
For frantic boast and foolish word,
Thy Mercy on Thy People, Lord!

— *Rudyard Kipling*

THE BALLAD OF EAST AND WEST

1889

*Oh, East is East, and West is West. and never the twain
    shall meet,*
*Till Earth and Sky stand presently at God's great Judgment
    Seat;*
*But there is neither East nor West, Border, nor Breed, nor
    Birth,*
*When two strong men stand face to face, though they come from
    the ends of the earth !*

Kamal is out with twenty men to raise the Border side,
And he has lifted the Colonel's mare that is the Colonel's
    pride.
He has lifted her out of the stable-door between the dawn
    and the day,
And turned the calkins upon her feet, and ridden her far
    away,
Then up and spoke the Colonel's son that led a troop of the
    Guides:
"Is there never a man of all my men can say where Kamal
    hides?"
Then up and spoke Mohammed Khan, the son of the
    Ressaldar:
"If ye know the track of the morning-mist, ye know where
    his pickets are.
"At dusk he harries the Abazai — at dawn he is into Bonair,
"But he must go by Fort Bukloh to his own place to fare.
"So if ye gallop to Fort Bukloh as fast as a bird can fly,
"By the favour of God ye may cut him off ere he win to the
    Tongue of Jagai.

"But if he be past the Tongue of Jagai, right swiftly turn ye
then,

"For the length and breadth of that grisly plain is sown
with Kamal's men.

"There is rock to the left, and rock to the right, and low lean
thorn between,

"And ye may hear a breech-bolt snick where never a man is
seen."

The Colonel's son has taken a horse, and a raw rough dun
was he.

With the mouth of a bell and the heart of Hell and the head
of a gallows-tree.

The Colonel's son to the Fort has won, they bid him stay to
eat —

Who rides at the tail of a Border thief, he sits not long at
his meat.

He's up and away from Fort Bukloh as fast as he can fly,

Till he was aware of his father's mare in the gut of the Tongue
of Jagai,

Till he was aware of his father's mare with Kamal upon her
back,

And when he could spy the white of her eye, he made the
pistol crack.

He has fired once, he has fired twice, but the whistling ball
went wide.

"Ye shoot like a soldier," Kamal said. "Show now if ye
can ride!"

It's up and over the Tongue of Jagai, as blown dust-devils go,

The dun he fled like a stag of ten, but the mare like a barren
doe.

The dun he leaned against the bit and slugged his head
above,

But the red mare played with the snaffle-bars, as a maiden
    plays with a glove.

There was rock to the left and rock to the right, and low lean
    thorn between,

And thrice he heard a breech-bolt snick tho' never a man was
    seen.

They have ridden the low moon out of the sky, their hoofs
    drum up the dawn,

The dun he went like a wounded bull, but the mare like a
    new-roused fawn.

The dun he fell at a water-course — in a woeful heap fell he,

And Kamal has turned the red mare back, and pulled the
    rider free.

He has knocked the pistol out of his hand — small room was
    there to strive,

"'T was only by favour of mine," quoth he, "ye rode so long
    alive:

"There was not a rock for twenty mile, there was not a
    clump of tree,

"But covered a man of my own men with his rifle cocked on
    his knee.

"If I had raised my bridle-hand, as I have held it low,

"The little jackals that flee so fast were feasting all in a
    row.

"If I had bowed my head on my breast, as I have held it
    high,

"The kite that whistles above us now were gorged till she
    could not fly."

Lightly answered the Colonel's son: "Do good to bird and
    beast,

"But count who comes for the broken meats before thou
    makest a feast.

"If there should follow a thousand swords to carry my bones
away,

"Belike the price of a jackal's meal were more than a thief
could pay.

"They will feed their horse on the standing crop, their men
on the garnered grain,

"The thatch of the byres will serve their fires when all the
cattle are slain.

"But if thou thinkest the price be fair, — thy brethren wait
to sup,

"The hound is kin to the jackal-spawn, — howl, dog, and call
them up!

"And if thou thinkest the price be high, in steer and gear
and stack,

"Give me my father's mare again, and I'll fight my own way
back!"

Kamal has gripped him by the hand and set him upon his
feet,

"No talk shall be of dogs," said he, "when wolf and grey
wolf meet.

"May I eat dirt if thou hast hurt of me in deed or
breath;

"What dam of lances brought thee forth to jest at the dawn
with Death?"

Lightly answered the Colonel's son: "I hold by the blood of
my clan;

"Take up the mare for my father's gift — by God, she has
carried a man!"

The red mare ran to the Colonel's son, and nuzzled against
his breast;

"We be two strong men," said Kamal then, "but she loveth
the younger best.

"So she shall go with a lifter's dower, my turquoise-studded rein,

"My 'broidered saddle and saddle-cloth, and silver stirrups twain."

The Colonel's son a pistol drew, and held it muzzle-end,

"Ye have taken the one from a foe," said he; "will ye take the mate from a friend?"

"A gift for a gift," said Kamal straight; "a limb for the risk of a limb.

"Thy father hath sent his son to me, I'll send my son to him!"

With that he whistled his only son, that dropped from a mountain-crest —

He trod the ling like a buck in spring, and he looked like a lance in rest.

"Now here is thy master," Kamal said, "who leads a troop of the Guides,

"And thou must ride at his left side as shield on shoulder rides.

"Till Death or I cut loose the tie, at camp and board and bed,

"Thy life is his — thy fate is to guard him with they head.

"So, thou must eat the White Queen's meat, and all her foes are thine,

"And thou must harry thy father's hold for the peace of the Border-line.

"And thou must make a trooper tough and hack thy way to power —

"Belike they will raise thee to Ressaldar when I am hanged in Peshawur."

They have looked each other between the eyes, and there
they found no fault,
They have taken the Oath of the Brother-in-Blood on
leavened bread and salt:
They have taken the oath of the Brother-in-Blood on fire
and fresh-cut sod,
On the hilt and the haft of the Khyber knife, and the Won-
drous Names of God.
The Colonel's son he rides the mare and Kamal's boy the dun,
And two have come back to Fort Bukloh where there went
forth but one.
And when they drew to the Quarter-Guard, full twenty
swords flew clear —
There was not a man but carried his feud with the blood of
the mountaineer.
"Ha' done! ha' done!" said the Colonel's son.   "Put up the
steel at your sides!
"Last night ye had struck at a Border thief — to-night 'tis
a man of the Guides!"
*Oh, East is East, and West is West, and never the twain shall
meet,*
*Till Earth and Sky stand presently at God's great Judgment
Seat;*
*But there is neither East nor West, Border, nor Breed, nor
Birth,*
*When two strong men stand face to face, though they come from
the ends of the earth!*

— Rudyard Kipling

WILLIAM BUTLER YEATS

William Butler Yeats was born in 1865 in Sligo, the wildest part of western Ireland. He was educated at the Godolphin School, Hammersmith (England) and at Erasmus Smith School, Dublin, Ireland. He was one of the initiators of the Irish Renaissance, working with Lady Gregory, Douglas Hyde, Edward Martyn, George Moore, "A. E.," and John M. Synge to revive the literature of the ancient Irish language. For their work in English they all sought a subtler form and rhythm than their predecessors. With Lady Gregory, Mr. Yeats founded the Irish National Theatre, which developed later into the Abbey Theatre. Mr. Yeats has written many admirable poetic dramas, *The Countess Kathleen, The Shadowy Waters, The Land of Heart's Desire, Kathleen Ni Hoolihan, At the King's Threshold,* and others. But he is even more likely to be remembered in years to come as one of the few greatest lyrists of this period.

The *Collected Edition* of his works in eight volumes (1908) contains the revised versions of his most important poems. Since then we have had *Responsibilities* in 1916, and *The Wild Swans at Coole* in 1919. Many influences have made his work what it is. Celtic mysticism and foreign magic, the influence of Blake, the study of folklore, a wide knowledge of the world and the things that are in it, all contribute to an individuality that is not overcome by any of them. It is now twenty-five years or so since William Butler Yeats began to preach the doctrine of simple words — the diction of the best human speech — as the language of poetry. Since that time his doctrine has been accepted by the best poets on both sides of the Atlantic, with the result that many literary artificialities and much purposeless and superficial ornamentation has been utterly purged away from the poetry of the period. Mr. Yeats is not only a great poet himself, but has been a strong and beneficent influence on the work of many other poets.

Mr. Yeats' lyrics are austere and exquisite, remarkable for a noble simplicity of style and for a discriminating candor of emotional utterance. "The Wild Swans at Coole" is one of his later lyrics, full of suggestive overtones that move with the swans — almost out of reach above our heads. It has a calm and certain music. "The Song of Wandering Aengus" is a more popular poem and was written much earlier. It shows what a beautiful language English can be when it is used by a master.

THE WILD SWANS AT COOLE

The trees are in their autumn beauty,
The woodland paths are dry,
Under the October twilight the water
Mirrors a still sky;
Upon the brimming water among the stones
Are nine and fifty swans.

The nineteenth Autumn has come upon me
Since I first made my count;
I saw, before I had well finished,
All suddenly mount
And scatter wheeling in great broken rings
Upon their clamorous wings.

I have looked upon those brilliant creatures,
And now my heart is sore.
All's changed since I, hearing at twilight,
The first time on this shore,
The bell-beat of their wings above my head,
Trod with a lighter tread.

Unwearied still, lover by lover,
They paddle in the cold,
Companionable streams or climb the air;

Their hearts have not grown old;
Passion or conquest, wander where they will,
Attend upon them still.

But now they drift on the still water
Mysterious, beautiful;
Among what rushes will they build,
By what lake's edge or pool
Delight men's eyes, when I awake some day
To find they have flown away?

— William Butler Yeats

THE SONG OF WANDERING AENGUS

I went out to the hazel wood
Because a fire was in my head,
And cut and peeled a hazel wand,
And hooked a berry to a thread;
And when white moths were on the wing,
And moth-like stars were flickering out,
I dropped the berry in a stream,
And caught a little silver trout.

When I had laid it on the floor,
I went to blow the fire a-flame,
But something rustled on the floor,
And some one called me by my name:
It had become a glimmering girl,
With apple-blossom in her hair,
Who called me by my name and ran
And faded through the brightening air.

Though I am old with wandering
Through hollow lands and hilly lands,
I will find out where she has gone,
And kiss her lips and take her hands;
And walk among long dappled grass,
And pluck till time and times are done
The silver apples of the moon,
The golden apples of the sun.

— *William Butler Yeats*

TO A FRIEND WHOSE WORK HAS COME TO NOTHING

Now all the truth is out,
Be secret and take defeat
From any brazen throat,
For how can you compete,
Being honour bred, with one
Who, were it proved he lies,
Were neither shamed in his own
Nor in his neighbor's eyes?
Bred to a harder thing
Than Triumph, turn away
And like a laughing string
Whereon mad fingers play
Amid a place of stone,
Be secret and exult,
Because of all things known
That is most difficult.

— *William Butler Yeats*

LYRIC FROM "THE LAND OF HEART'S DESIRE"

The wind blows out of the gates of day,
The wind blows over the lonely of heart,
And the lonely of heart is withered away,
While the færies dance in a place apart,
Shaking their milk-white feet in a ring,
Shaking their milk-white arms in the air;
For they hear the wind laugh, and murmur and sing
Of a land where even the old are fair,
And even the wise are merry of tongue;
But I heard a reed of Coolaney say,
"When the wind has laughed and murmured and sung,
The lonely of heart is withered away."

— *William Butler Yeats*

RICHARD LE GALLIENNE

Richard Le Gallienne was born at Liverpool, England, in 1866. He was educated at Liverpool College. He was in business for seven years, but abandoned it for literature. He has written sane and kindly criticism and essays that have a charming prose style as well as poetry. He lives in New York.

His most important books of verse are *The Lonely Dancer* (1913) and *The Junkman and Other Poems* (1921). His verse is graceful and musical and, at its best, enables us to share the poet's delicate perceptions of people and things.

A BALLADE-CATALOGUE OF LOVELY THINGS

I would make a list against the evil days
   Of lovely things to hold in memory;
First I set down my lady's lovely face,
   For earth has no such lovely thing as she;
   And next I add, to bear her company,
The great-eyed virgin star that morning brings;
   Then the wild-rose upon its little tree —
So runs my catalogue of lovely things.

The enchanted dogwood, with its ivory trays,
   The water-lily in its sanctuary
Of reeded pools, and dew-drenched lilac sprays,
   For these, of all fair flowers, the fairest be;
   ' Next write I down the great name of the sea,
Lonely in greatness as the names of kings;
   Then the young moon that hath us all in fee —
So runs my catalogue of lovely things.

272

Imperial sunsets that in crimson blaze
   Along the hills, and, fairer still to me,
The fireflies dancing in a netted maze
   Woven of twilight and tranquillity;
   Shakespeare and Virgil, their high poesy;
Then a great ship, splendid with snowy wings,
   Voyaging on into eternity —
So runs my catalogue of lovely things.

ENVOI

Prince, not the gold bars of thy treasury,
   Not all thy jewelled sceptres, crowns and rings,
Are worth the honeycomb of the wild bee —
   So runs my catalogue of lovely things.

— Richard Le Gallienne

LAURENCE BINYON

Laurence Binyon was born at Lancaster, England, in 1869. He was educated at St. Paul's School and at Oxford. He worked for a while in the Department of Printed Books in the British Museum and is now Assistant Keeper of Oriental Prints and Drawings.

He is the author of *London Visions* (1896), *Odes* (1901), *The Four Years* (1919), *The Secret* (1920), and *Selected Poems* (1922).

His war poem "To Women" needs no explanation. "A Song" should be compared with "A Talisman" by Louise Imogen Guiney. We may agree with both poets, although they seem to be contradicting each other, if we will only stop to consider what things they are for which Mr. Binyon recommends excess, and what things Miss Guiney had in mind when she recommended temperance.

TO WOMEN

Your hearts are lifted up, your hearts
That have foreknown the utter price,
Your hearts burn upward like a flame
Of splendour and of sacrifice.

For you, you too, to battle go,
Not with the marching drums and cheers,
But in the watch of solitude
And through the boundless night of fears.

Swift, swifter than those hawks of war,
Those threatening wings that pulse the air,
Far as the vanward ranks are set
You are gone before them, you are there!

274

And not a shot comes blind with death
And not a stab of steel is pressed
Home, but invisibly it tore
And entered first a woman's breast.

Amid the thunder of the guns,
The lightnings of the lance and sword,
Your hope, your dread, your throbbing pride,
Your infinite passion is outpoured.

From hearts that are as one high heart
Withholding nought from doom and bale,
Burningly offered up, — to bleed,
To bear, to break, but not to fail!

— Laurence Binyon

A SONG

For Mercy, Courage, Kindness, Mirth,
    There is no measure upon earth.
Nay, they wither, root and stem,
    If an end be set to them.

Overbrim and overflow,
    If your own heart you would know;
For the spirit born to bless
    Lives but in its own excess.

— Laurence Binyon

KATHARINE TYNAN

Katharine Tynan was one of the leaders of the Irish **Renaissance**. She reviews Irish literature for the London *Bookman*.

Her books are *Irish Love Songs* (1892), *Irish Poems* (1914), *Flower of Youth* (1915), and *Herb o' Grace* (1918).

"The Choice," given below, is a lovable, domestic lyric.

THE CHOICE

When skies are blue and days are bright
A kitchen-garden's my delight,
Set round with rows of decent box
And blowsy girls of hollyhocks.

Before the lark his Lauds hath done
And ere the corncrake's southward gone;
Before the thrush good-night hath said
And the young Summer's put to bed.

The currant-bushes' spicy smell,
Homely and honest, likes me well,
The while on strawberries I feast,
And raspberries the sun hath kissed.

Beans all a-blowing by a row
Of hives that great with honey go,
With mignonette and heaths to yield
The plundering bee his honey-field.

Sweet herbs in plenty, blue borage
And the delicious mint and sage,

Rosemary, marjoram, and rue,
And thyme to scent the winter through.

Here are small apples growing round,
And apricots all golden-gowned,
And plums that presently will flush
And show their bush a Burning Bush.

Cherries in nets against the wall,
Where Master Thrush his madrigal
Sings, and makes oath a churl is he
Who grudges cherries for a fee.

Lavender, sweet-briar, orris.   Here
Shall Beauty make her pomander,
Her sweet-balls for to lay in clothes
That wrap her as the leaves the rose.

Take roses red and lilies white,
A kitchen-garden's my delight;
Its gillyflowers and phlox and cloves,
And its tall cote of irised doves.

— *Katharine Tynan*

WILLIAM H. DAVIES

William H. Davies was born at Newport, Wales, in 1870. He ran away from home as a boy and tramped the wide world over, finding what work he could and going hungry when he could not find any. He lost a foot trying to board a moving train in Canada. He crossed the Atlantic a number of times by working on cattle boats. He inherited money that brought him a small income of about ten shillings a week (in normal times about two dollars and a half), and decided to begin to write poetry. When he had collected a number of his nature lyrics he had them printed, but nobody would buy them. He sent them, with a letter, to Bernard Shaw, who recognized his talent and helped him to get them before the public. He had no education except the education that can be had by studying nature in the open and human nature wherever it is to be found.

His *Collected Poems* were published in 1916. *Forty New Poems* appeared in 1918 and *The Song of Life* in 1920.

As would be expected, Mr. Davies' best poems are lyrics of nature, and they owe their beauty to his power of minute and accurate observation. Many another man might have tramped the highways of the open world without becoming a poet, without ever learning to see in that world the things Mr. Davies has seen and made known to us in his poetry. "Nature's Friend," quoted here, is a delightful song of the friendliness that may exist between man and the dumb animals who share his life on this planet. It makes one think of St. Francis and of his friendship with the birds.

NATURE'S FRIEND

Say what you like,
  All things love me!
I pick no flowers —
  That wins the Bee.

278

The Summer's Moths
   Think my hand one —
To touch their wings —
   With Wind and Sun.

The garden Mouse
   Comes near to play;
Indeed, he turns
   His eyes away.

The Wren knows well
   I rob no nest;
When I look in,
   She still will rest.

The hedge stops Cows,
   Or they would come
After my voice
   Right to my home.

The Horse can tell,
   Straight from my lip,
My hand could not
   Hold any whip.

Say what you like,
   All things love me!
Horse, Cow, and Mouse,
   Bird, Moth and Bee.

— *William H. Davies*

JOHN McCRAE

John McCrae was born in Scotland in 1872, but was taken to Canada as a very young child and grew up a Canadian. In the great war he was a Lieutenant-Colonel in the Medical Corps. His poem, "In Flanders Fields," was one of the most popular lyrics of the war and made him famous the world over. He died in 1918 and the book which contained the poem was posthumously published in 1919 with an appreciative essay on John McCrae by Sir Andrew MacPhail.

IN FLANDERS FIELDS

In Flanders fields the poppies blow
Between the crosses, row on row,
 That mark our place, and in the sky,
 The larks, still bravely singing, fly,
Scarce heard amid the guns below.

We are the dead; short days ago
 We lived, felt dawn, saw sunset glow,
Loved and were loved, and now we lie
 In Flanders fields.

Take up our quarrel with the foe!
To you from failing hands we throw
 The torch: be yours to hold it high!
 If ye break faith with us who die,
We shall not sleep, though poppies grow
 In Flanders fields.

— John McCrae

From *In Flanders Fields* by Lieutenant-Colonel John McCrae.

RALPH HODGSON

Ralph Hodgson was born in Yorkshire in 1872. He has lived in America. He has worked as a pressman in Fleet Street, and as a draughtsman, and as an editor. He is the leading English authority on bull terriers. Many of his poems show an unusual sympathy with animals.

He is the author of *The Last Blackbird* (1907) and *Poems* (1917). From the second book is taken "The Song of Honour," a rarely beautiful hymn of praise for all the wonders of creation. Mr. Hodgson hears

> the universal choir,
> The Sons of Light exalt their Sire
> With universal song.

Through life in all its forms and ways of manifestation, in flowers, birds, beasts, fighters, lovers, and sages, he hears the great "song of being" rise to God —

> Earth's lowliest and loudest notes,
> Her million times ten million throats
> Exalt Him loud and long.

The climax at the end of the poem is exceedingly fine — the silence, the reiterated "Amen" and the lines —

> My eyes were blind with stars and still
> I stared into the sky.

THE SONG OF HONOUR

I climbed a hill as light fell short,
And rooks came home in scramble sort,
And filled the trees and flapped and fought
And sang themselves to sleep;

An owl from nowhere with no sound
Swung by and soon was nowhere found,
I heard him calling half-way round,
Holloing loud and deep;
A pair of stars, faint pins of light,
Then many a star, sailed into sight,
And all the stars, the flower of night,
Were round me at a leap;
To tell how still the valleys lay
I heard a watchdog miles away, —
And bells of distant sheep.

I heard no more of bird or bell,
The mastiff in a slumber fell,
I stared into the sky,
As wondering men have always done
Since beauty and the stars were one
Though none so hard as I.

It seemed, so still the valleys were,
As if the whole world knelt at prayer,
Save me and me alone;
So pure and wide that silence was
I feared to bend a blade of grass,
And there I stood like stone.

There, sharp and sudden, there I heard —
  Ah ! some wild lovesick singing bird
  Woke singing in the trees?
  The nightingale and babble-wren
  Were in the English greenwood then,
  And you heard one of these?
The babble-wren and nightingale

Sang in the Abyssinian vale
That season of the year!
Yet, true enough, I heard them plain
I heard them both again, again,
As sharp and sweet and clear
As if the Abyssinian tree
Had thrust a bough across the sea,
Had thrust a bough across to me
With music for my ear!

I heard them both, and oh! I heard
The song of every singing bird
That sings beneath the sky,
And with the song of lark and wren
The song of mountains, moths and men
And seas and rainbows vie!

I heard the universal choir,
The Sons of Light exalt their Sire
With universal song,
Earth's lowliest and loudest notes,
Her million times ten million throats
Exalt Him loud and long,
And lips and lungs and tongues of Grace
From every part and every place
Within the shining of His face,
The universal throng.

I heard the hymn of being sound
From every well of honour found
In human sense and soul:

The song of poets when they write
The testament of Beauty sprite
Upon a flying scroll,
The song of painters, when they take
A burning brush for Beauty's sake
And limn her features whole —

The song of men divinely wise
Who look and see in starry skies
Not stars so much as robins' eyes,
And when these pale away
Hear flocks of shiny Pleiades
Among the plums and apple trees
Sing in the summer day —

The song of all both high and low
To some blest vision true,
The song of beggars when they throw
The crust of pity all men owe
To hungry sparrows in the snow,
Old beggars hungry too —
The song of kings of kingdoms when
They rise above their fortune Men,
And crown themselves anew —

The song of courage, heart and will
And gladness in a fight,
Of men who face a hopeless hill
With sparking and delight,
The bells and bells of song that ring
Round banners of a cause or king
From armies bleeding white —

The song of sailors every one
When monstrous tide and tempest run
At ships like bulls at red,
When stately ships are twirled and spun
Like whipping tops and help there's none
And mighty ships ten thousand ton
Go down like lumps of lead —

And song of fighters stern as they
At odds with fortune night and day,
Crammed up in cities grim and grey
As thick as bees in hives,
Hosannas of a lowly throng
Who sing unconscious of their song,
Whose lips are in their lives —

And song of some at holy war
With spells and ghouls more dread by far
Than deadly seas and cities are
Or hordes of quarrelling kings —
The song of fighters great and small,
The song of pretty fighters all
And high heroic things —

The song of lovers — who knows how
Twitched up from place and time
Upon a sigh, a blush, a vow,
A curve or hue of cheek, or brow,
Borne up and off from here and now
Into the void sublime!

And crying loves and passions still
In every key from soft to shrill

And numbers never done,
Dog-loyalties to faith and friend,
And loves like Ruth's of old no end,
And intermission none —

And burst on burst for beauty and
For numbers not behind,
From men whose love of motherland
Is like a dog's for one dear hand,
Sole, selfless, boundless, blind —
And song of some with hearts beside
For men and sorrows far and wide,
Who watch the world with pity and pride
And warm to all mankind —

And endless joyous music rise
From children at their play,
And endless soaring lullabies
From happy, happy mothers' eyes,
And answering crows and baby-cries,
How many who shall say!
And many a song as wondrous well
With pangs and sweets intolerable
From lonely hearths too grey to tell,
God knows how utter grey!
And song from many a house of care
When pain has forced a footing there
And there's a Darkness on the stair
Will not be turned away —

And song — that song whose singers come
With old kind tales of pity from
The Great Compassion's lips,

That make the bells of Heaven to peal
Round pillows frosty with the feel
Of Death's cold finger tips —
The song of men all sorts and kinds,
As many tempers, moods and minds
As leaves are on a tree,
As many faiths and castes and creeds,
As many human bloods and breeds
As in the world may be;

The song of each and all who gaze
On Beauty in her naked blaze,
Or see her dimly in a haze,
Or get her light in fitful rays
And tiniest needles even,
The song of all not wholly dark,
Not wholly sunk in stupor stark
Too deep for groping Heaven —

And alleluias sweet and clear
And wild with beauty men mishear,
From choirs of song as near and dear
To Paradise as they,
The everlasting pipe and flute
Of wind and sea and bird and brute,
And lips deaf men imagine mute
In wood and stone and clay,
The music of a lion strong
That shakes a hill a whole night long,
A hill as loud as he,
The twitter of a mouse among
Melodious greenery,
The ruby's and the rainbow's song,

The nightingale's — all three,
The song of life that wells and flows
From every leopard, lark and rose
And everything that gleams or goes
Lack-lustre in the sea.

I heard it all, each, every note
Of every lung and tongue and throat,
Ay, every rhythm and rhyme
Of everything that lives and loves
And upward, ever upward moves·
From lowly to sublime!
Earth's multitudinous Sons of Light,
I heard them lift their lyric might
With each and every chanting sprite
That lit the sky that wondrous night
As far as eye could climb!

I heard it all, I heard the whole
Harmonious hymn of being roll
Up through the chapel of my soul
And at the altar die,
And in the awful quiet then
Myself I heard, Amen, Amen,
Amen I heard me cry!
I heard it all and then although
I caught my flying senses, Oh,
A dizzy man was I!
I stood and stared; the sky was lit,
The sky was stars all over it,
I stood, I knew not why,
Without a wish, without a will,

I stood upon that silent hill
And stared into the sky until
My eyes were blind with stars and still
I stared into the sky.

— *Ralph Hodgson*

WALTER DE LA MARE

Walter de la Mare was born at Charlton, in Kent, England, in 1873. He was educated in London, at St. Paul's Cathedral Choir School. For nearly twenty years he worked in the English branch of the Standard Oil Company of America.

He is the author of *Songs of Childhood* (1902), *Poems* (1906), *The Return*, a novel which won the first Edmond de Polignac Prize, the gift of the Royal Society of Literature, in 1910, *The Listeners* (1912 in England and 1916 in the United States), *Peacock Pie* (1917), *Motley and Other Poems* (1918), and *The Veil and Other Poems* (1922). His *Collected Poems*, 1901-1918, appeared in 1918. Of these books, probably *Peacock Pie* and *The Listeners* are the most important (the same poems are given in *Collected Poems*, of course) and the most interesting single volumes of his work. *Peacock Pie* is the finest book of poems ever written for children in our language, finer even than Stevenson's *Child's Garden of Verses*.

Mr. de la Mare is a poet of delicate lights and shadows and of subtle and exquisite suggestions and overtones. His presentation of personality in his short character sketches never lacks distinction. His presentation of fairies and of the spirits that haunt the border-lines of his consciousness never lacks an element of seriousness. He observes nature and life gravely and records his observations faithfully, but there is also a quiet, shy, quaint humor in many of his lyrics. His rhythms are fluent and admirably adjusted to the moods and meanings that move with them. His images are just and right.

"Silver" is a nocturne and a color-study, an exquisite picture-poem, sharing all that can be seen in the barnyard by night. "Wanderers" is another lovely little song of the night, picturing the heavens. The first lines of it may be compared with Longfellow's

Silently, one by one, in the infinite meadows of Heaven,
Blossomed the lovely stars, the forget-me-nots of the angels.

"Tartary" is a poem of more robust type — a rich, delicious, blustering song of self-glorification, telling how one feels in a lofty and hilarious mood, what one would do as overlord of a vast domain! It must not be taken too seriously. We must remember that lyrics are for the expression of human emotion and that many of them have no "message" or philosophy. They are written for the pleasure of people who enjoy sharing them. And many of them, like "Tartary," are a delightful "make-believe" whose chief use is to quicken and train the imagination.

WANDERERS

Wide are the meadows of night,
　　And daisies are shining there,
Tossing their lovely dews,
　　Lustrous and fair;
And through these sweet fields go,
　　Wanderers amid the stars —
Venus, Mercury, Uranus, Neptune,
　　Saturn, Jupiter, Mars.

Attired in their silver, they move,
　　And circling, whisper and say,
Fair are the blossoming meads of delight
　　Through which we stray.

— Walter de la Mare

TARTARY

If I were Lord of Tartary,
　　Myself and me alone,
My bed should be of ivory,
　　Of beaten gold my throne;

And in my court should peacocks flaunt,
And in my forests tigers haunt,
And in my pools great fishes slant
   Their fins athwart the sun.

If I were Lord of Tartary,
   Trumpeters every day
To every meal should summon me,
   And in my courtyard bray;
And in the evening lamps would shine,
Yellow as honey, red as wine,
While harp, and flute, and mandoline,
   Made music sweet and gay.

If I were Lord of Tartary,
   I'd wear a robe of beads,
White, and gold, and green they'd be —
   And clustered thick as seeds;
And ere should wane the morning-star,
I'd don my robe and scimitar,
And zebras seven should draw my car
   Through Tartary's dark glades.

Lord of the fruits of Tartary,
   Her rivers silver-pale!
Lord of the hills of Tartary,
   Glen, thicket, wood, and dale!
Her flashing stars, her scented breeze,
Her trembling lakes, like foamless seas,
Her bird-delighting citron-trees
   In every purple vale!

               — *Walter de la Mare*

SILVER

Slowly, silently, now the moon
Walks the night in her silver shoon;
This way, and that, she peers and sees
Silver fruit upon silver trees;
One by one the casements catch
Her beams beneath the silvery thatch;
Couched in his kennel, like a log,
With paws of silver sleeps the dog;
From their shadowy cote the white breasts peep
Of doves in a silver-feathered sleep;
A harvest mouse goes scampering by,
With silver claws, and a silver eye;
And moveless fish in the water gleam,
By silver reeds in a silver stream.

— Walter de la Mare

GORDON BOTTOMLEY

Gordon Bottomley was born in 1874 and is the author of *The Mickle Drede* (1896), *Poems at White Nights* (1899), *The Gate of Smaragdus* (1904), *Chambers of Imagery* (1907), *Chambers of Imagery* (second series) (1912), and *King Lear's Wife and Other Plays* (1920).

Mr. Bottomley's work always has distinction and the tang of a decided personality. "Eager Spring" is no exception. It gives freshness and spontaneous grace to a mood that nearly everybody has to know at one time or another, sooner or later.

EAGER SPRING

Whirl, snow, on the blackbird's chatter;
You will not hinder his song to come.
East wind, Sleepless, you cannot scatter
Quince-bud, almond-bud,
Clustering brood,
Nor unfurl the tips of the plum.
No half born stalk of a lily stops;
There is sap in the storm-torn bush;
And, ruffled by gusts in a snow-blurred copse,
"Pity to wait," sings a thrush.

Love, there are few Springs left for us;
They go, and the count of them as they go
Makes surer the count that is left for us.
More than the East wind, more than the snow,
I would put back these hours that bring
Buds and bees and are lost;
I would hold the night and the frost,
To save for us one more Spring.

— *Gordon Bottomley*

294

JOHN MASEFIELD

John Masefield was born in Shropshire, England, in 1874. In his boyhood he was indentured to a sea captain and sent to sea where he worked before the mast as a common sailor for a number of years. In 1902 he came to America almost destitute and did all kinds of work, including manual labor and odd jobs. It was while he was employed in a restaurant in Yonkers that he bought a volume of Chaucer's poems and made the acquaintance of the father of English poetry. So enthusiastic did he become that, at twenty-eight years of age, he decided to be a poet. When he could, he returned to England and began to write. He owes his start to John Yeats, the artist, brother of William Butler Yeats, the poet. At first he was a hack writer. He won world fame with the publication of *The Everlasting Mercy and The Widow in the Bye Street* (1911-12).

He has written plays and prose books as well as poetry, but will be remembered chiefly for his poetry. His most important books in verse are *Saltwater Ballads* (1902), *Ballads* (1903), *Poems and Ballads* (1910), *The Everlasting Mercy and The Widow in the Bye Street* (1912), *Dauber* (probably his greatest poem) (1913), *Sonnets and Poems* (1916), *Lollingdon Downs* (1917), *Collected Poems and Plays* (1919), *Reynard the Fox* (1920), and *Right Royal* (1921). Just as William Butler Yeats is master of the lyric, John Masefield is a master of narrative. He has something of Chaucer's gift of sharing the flavor of persons and circumstances, much of the delicate perception of beauty that was in Keats, much of the color of Coleridge and the plain earth-wisdom of Burns, much even of the sap and savor of life that are in Shakespeare.

He has, moreover, a music of his own, and a sense of the significance of life which, because it is modern, is more searching than any philosophy of earlier days. The world has lived and died many times since the period of Chaucer and has known many resurrections. John Masefield has shared the life and death and the rising again into light.

Since Chaucer's day the love and fear of potentates has been a dying cult. To-day nobody seems splendid because he wears purple robes and a crown. A belief in the heroism and beauty of the common people has lightened perceptibly the blear darkness of our modern world. This growing faith in mankind has been choked off again and again by greed and violence, but it can never be held by death. Always it breaks free of the dark bondage and comes back stronger than ever. In the poetry of John Masefield the light of this belief shines proudly. Over and over again, in words as clean as silver, firm as bronze, and ruddy as gold, he tells his times the value of that which was once considered valueless. He is the spokesman of all defeats that have been spiritual victories, of all good losers who have been a gain to the race, of the poor, and the weak, and the humble, whose bodies and souls have built stairs by which our race may climb. It is in this spirit that "A Consecration" is written, a strong hymn of democracy.

"Cargoes" is a poem made out of a single symbol — the cargo. In terms of that symbol, and in three short stanzas, Mr. Masefield describes commerce in three great periods of the world's history. "Ships" tells the story of an Englishman's love of ships and of the sea as only a man who had been a sailor would tell it. "Night is on the Downland" is a lovely picture of the English moorland.

A CONSECRATION

Not of the princes and prelates with periwigged charioteers
Riding triumphantly laurelled to lap the fat of the years,
Rather the scorned — the rejected — the men hemmed in
    with the spears;

The men of the tattered battalion which fights till it dies,
Dazed with the dust of the battle, the din and the cries,
The men with the broken heads and the blood running into
    their eyes.

Not the be-medalled Commander, beloved of the throne,
Riding cock-horse to parade when the bugles are blown,
But the lads who carried the koppie and cannot be known.

Not the ruler for me, but the ranker, the tramp of the road,
The slave with the sack on his shoulders pricked on with the
    goad,
The man with too weighty a burden, too weary a load.

The sailor, the stoker of steamers, the man with the clout,
The chanty man bent on the halliards putting a tune to the
    shout,
The drowsy man at the wheel and the tired lookout.

Others may sing of the wine and the wealth and the mirth,
The portly presence of potentates goodly in girth; —
Mine be the dirt and the dross, the dust and scum of the
    earth!

Theirs be the music, the color, the glory, the gold;
Mine be a handful of ashes, a mouthful of mould.
Of the maimed, of the halt and the blind in the rain and the
    cold —

Of these shall my songs be fashioned, my tale be told.   Amen.

— John Masefield

SHIPS

I cannot tell their wonder nor make known
Magic that once thrilled through me to the bone,
But all men praise some beauty, tell some tale,
Vent a high mood which makes the rest seem pale,

Pour their heart's blood to flourish one green leaf,
Follow some Helen for her gift of grief,
And fail in what they mean, whate'er they do:
You should have seen, man cannot tell to you
The beauty of the ships of that my city.
That beauty now is spoiled by the sea's pity;
For one may haunt the pier a score of times,
Hearing St. Nicholas bells ring out the chimes,
Yet never see those proud ones swaying home
With mainyards backed and bows a cream of foam,
Those bows so lovely-curving, cut so fine,
Those coulters of the many-bubbled brine,
As once, long since, when all the docks were filled
With that sea-beauty man has ceased to build.

Yet, though their splendor may have ceased to be
Each played her sovereign part in making me;
Now I return my thanks with heart and lips
For the great queenliness of all those ships.

And first the first bright memory, still so clear,
An autumn evening in a golden year,
When in the last lit moments before dark
The *Chepica*, a steel-gray lovely barque,
Came to an anchor near us on the flood,
Her trucks aloft in sun-glow red as blood.

Then come so many ships that I could fill
Three docks with their fair hulls remembered still,
Each with her special memory's special grace,
Riding the sea, making the waves give place
To delicate high beauty; man's best strength,
Noble in every line in all their length.

Ailsa, Genista, ships, with long jibbooms,
The *Wanderer* with great beauty and strange dooms,
Liverpool (mightiest then) superb, sublime,
The *California* huge, as slow as time.
The *Copley* swift, the perfect *J. T. North*,
The loveliest barque my city has sent forth,
Dainty *John Lockett* well remembered yet,
The splendid *Argus* with her skysail set,
Stalwart *Drumcliff*, white-blocked, majestic *Sierras*,
Divine bright ships, the water's standard-bearers;

Melpomene, Euphrosyne, and their sweet
Sea-troubling sisters of the Fernie fleet;
Corunna (in whom my friend died) and the old
Long since loved *Esmeralda* long since sold.
Centurion passed in Rio, *Glaucus* spoken,
Aladdin burnt, the *Bidston* water-broken,
Yola, in whom my friend sailed, *Dawpool* trim,
Fierce-bowed *Egeria* plunging to the swim,
Stanmore wide-sterned, sweet *Cupica*, tall *Bard*,
Queen in all harbors with her moon-sail yard.

Though I tell many, there must still be others,
McVickar Marshall's ships and Fernie Brother's,
Lochs, Counties, Shires, Drums, the countless lines
Whose house-flags all were once familiar signs
At high main-trucks on Mersey's windy ways
When sunlight made the wind-white water blaze.
Their names bring back old mornings, when the docks
Shone with their house-flags and their painted blocks,
Their raking masts below the Custom House
And all the marvellous beauty of their bows.

Familiar steamers, too, majestic steamers,
Shearing Atlantic roller-tops to streamers,
Umbria, *Etruria*, noble, still at sea,
The grandest, then, that man had brought to be.
Majestic, *City of Paris*, *City of Rome*,
Forever jealous racers, out and home.
The *Alfred Holt's* blue smoke-stacks down the stream,
The fair *Loanda* with her bows a-cream.
Booth liners, Anchor liners, Red Star liners,
The marks and styles of countless ship-designers,
The *Magdalena*, *Puno*, *Potosi*,
Lost *Cotopaxi*, all well known to me.

These splendid ships, each with her grace, her glory,
Her memory of old song or comrade's story,
Still in my mind the image of life's need,
Beauty in hardest action, beauty indeed.
"They built great ships and sailed them," sounds most brave,
Whatever arts we have or fail to have.
I touch my country's mind, I come to grips
With half her purpose, thinking of these ships:
That art untouched by softness, all that line
Drawn ringing hard to stand the test of brine;
That nobleness and grandeur, all that beauty
Born of a manly life and bitter duty,
That splendor of fine bows which yet could stand
The shock of rollers never checked by land;
That art of masts, sail-crowded, fit to break,
Yet stayed to strength and backstayed into rake;
The life demanded by that art, the keen
Eye-puckered, hard-case seamen, silent, lean.
They are grander things than all the art of towns;

Their tests are tempests and the sea that drowns.
They are my country's line, her great art done
By strong brains laboring on the thought unwon
They mark our passage as a race of men —
Earth will not see such ships as those again.

— *John Masefield*

CARGOES

Quinquireme of Nineveh from distant Ophir,
Rowing home to haven in sunny Palestine,
   With a cargo of ivory
   And apes and peacocks,
Sandalwood, cedarwood, and sweet, white wine.

Stately Spanish galleon coming from the Isthmus,
Dipping through the Tropics by the palm-green shores
   With a cargo of diamonds,
   Emeralds, amethysts,
Topazes, and cinnamon, and gold moidores.

Dirty British coaster with a salt-caked smoke stack,
Butting through the channel in the mad March days
   With a cargo of Tyne coal
   Road rails, pig lead,
Firewood, ironware, and cheap tin trays.

— *John Masefield*

"NIGHT IS ON THE DOWNLAND"

Night is on the downland, on the lonely moorland,
On the hills where the wind goes over sheep-bitten turf,

Where the bent grass beats upon the unploughed poorland
And the pine woods roar like the surf.

Here the Roman lived on the wind-barren lonely,
Dark now and haunted by the moorland fowl;
None comes here now but the peewit only,
And moth-like death in the owl.

Beauty was here, on this beetle-droning downland;
The thought of a Cæsar in the purple came
From the palace by the Tiber in the Roman townland
To this wind-swept hill with no name.

Lonely beauty came here and was here in sadness,
Brave as a thought on the frontier of the mind,
In the camp of the wild upon the march of madness,
The bright-eyed Queen of the blind.

Now where Beauty was are the wind-withered gorses
Moaning like old men in the hill-wind's blast,
The flying sky is dark with running horses
And the night is full of the past.

— John Masefield

G. K. CHESTERTON

Gilbert Keith Chesterton was born at London in 1874 and was educated at St. Paul's School and at the Slade School of Art. He began his career as a reviewer of art books. He has written many essays and indulged in controversy. His two books, *Heretics* and *Orthodoxy* are witty and eloquent in support of Christianity as opposed to materialism. In his social and political thought he is something of a radical.

His *Poems* were published in 1915 and many critics believe that they are the soundest and strongest part of his work. He is a master of rhythm. He has true poetic energy and passion. And whereas his thoughts are often more witty than wise, his feelings are magnificent; they cannot be gainsaid and it is difficult not to share them.

"Lepanto" is a superb ballad. No poem of modern times rings with a richer music of the martial type. It tells the story of the Battle of Lepanto (the Gulf of Corinth or Lepanto) fought October 7th, 1571, between the Turks and the Holy League of Christian nations. The conquest of Cyprus by the Turks had frightened the Christian powers into forming this league for defense. Pope Pius V was the main promoter, but the bulk of the forces were supplied by the Republic of Venice and by Philip II of Spain. As a compliment to King Philip, the general command of the fleet of the Christians was given to his kinsman, Don John of Austria. The Christian fleet collected at Messina. The Turkish fleet anchored in the Gulf of Patras. On October seventh the Christian fleet advanced to the neighborhood of Cape Scropha and south of the Cape the two fleets met. The Turks, with greater numbers, tried to outflank the Christians, but the latter had better boats and better discipline and were able to withstand them. The Turks lost about twenty thousand men, the Christians about eight thousand and the naval power of the Turks never recovered from the blow. The battle is interesting because it was the last encounter of galleys on a large scale and also the last of the crusades or holy wars. It saved the Christian kingdoms of Europe from being conquered. Many of Europe's great men took part in the battle.

LEPANTO

White founts falling in the Courts of the sun,
And the Soldan of Byzantium is smiling as they run;
There is laughter like the fountains in that face of all men
    feared,
It stirs the forest darkness, the darkness of his beard,
It curls the blood-red crescent, the crescent of his lips,
For the inmost sea of all the earth is shaken with his ships.
They have dared the white republics up the capes of Italy,
They have dashed the Adriatic round the Lion of the Sea,
And the Pope has cast his arms abroad for agony and loss,
And called the kings of Christendom for swords about the
    Cross.
The cold queen of England is looking in the glass;
The shadow of the Valois is yawning at the Mass;
From evening isles fantastical rings faint the Spanish gun,
And the Lord upon the Golden Horn is laughing in the sun.
Dim drums throbbing, in the hills half heard,
Where only on a nameless throne a crownless prince has stirred,
Where, risen from a doubtful seat and half attainted stall,
The last knight of Europe takes weapons from the wall,
The last and lingering troubadour to whom the bird has sung,
That once went singing southward when all the world was
    young.
In that enormous silence, tiny and unafraid,
Comes up along a winding road the noise of the Crusade.
Strong gongs groaning as the guns boom far,
Don John of Austria is going to the war,

Stiff flags straining in the night-blasts cold
In the gloom black-purple, in the glint old-gold,
Torchlight crimson on the copper kettle-drums,
Then the tuckets, then the trumpets, then the cannon, and
    he comes.
Don John laughing in the brave beard curled,
Spurning of his stirrups like the thrones of all the world,
Holding his head up for a flag of all the free.
Love-light of Spain — hurrah!
Death-light of Africa!
Don John of Austria
Is riding to the sea.

Mahound is in his paradise above the evening star,
(*Don John of Austria is going to the war.*)
He moves a mighty turban on the timeless houri's knees,
His turban that is woven of the sunsets and the seas.
He shakes the peacock gardens as he rises from his ease,
And he strides among the tree-tops and is taller than the trees,
And his voice through all the garden is a thunder sent to bring
Black Azrael and Ariel and Ammon on the wing.
Giants and the Genii,
Multiplex of wing and eye,
Whose strong obedience broke the sky
When Solomon was king.

They rush in red and purple from the red clouds of the morn,
From temples where the yellow gods shut up their eyes in
    scorn;
They rise in green robes roaring from the green hells of the
    sea
Where fallen skies and evil hues and eyeless creatures be;

On them the sea-valves cluster and the grey sea-forests curl,
Splashed with a splendid sickness, the sickness of the pearl;
They swell in sapphire smoke out of the blue cracks of the
    ground, —
They gather and they wonder and give worship to Mahound.
And he saith, "Break up the mountains where the hermit-
    folk can hide,
And sift the red and silver sands lest bone of saint abide,
And chase the Giaours flying night and day, not giving rest,
For that which was our trouble comes again out of the west.
We have set the seal of Solomon on all things under sun,
Of knowledge and of sorrow and endurance of things done,
But a noise is in the mountains, in the mountains, and I know
The voice that shook our palaces — four hundred years ago:
It is he that saith not 'Kismet'; it is he that knows not Fate;
It is Richard, it is Raymond, it is Godfrey in the gate!
It is he whose loss is laughter when he counts the wager worth,
Put down your feet upon him, that our peace be on the
    earth."
For he heard drums groaning and he heard guns jar,
(*Don John of Austria is going to the war.*)
Sudden and still — hurrah!
Bolt from Iberia!
Don John of Austria
Is gone by Alcalar.

St. Michael's on his Mountain in the sea-roads of the north
(*Don John of Austria is girt and going forth.*)
Where the grey seas glitter and the sharp tides shift
And the sea-folk labor and the red sails lift.
He shakes his lance of iron and he claps his wings of stone;
The noise is gone through Normandy; the noise is gone alone;

The North is full of tangled things and texts and aching eyes
And dead is all the innocence of anger and surprise,
And Christian killeth Christian in a narrow dusty room,
And Christian dreadeth Christ that hath a newer face of
    doom,
And Christian hateth Mary that God kissed in Galilee,
But Don John of Austria is riding to the sea.
Don John calling through the blast and the eclipse
Crying with the trumpet, with the trumpet of his lips,
Trumpet that sayeth ha!
    Domino gloria!
Don John of Austria
Is shouting to the ships.

King Philip's in his closet with the Fleece about his neck
(*Don John of Austria is armed upon the deck.*)
The walls are hung with velvet that is black and soft as sin,
And little dwarfs creep out of it and little dwarfs creep in.
He holds a crystal phial that has colours like the moon,
He touches, and it tingles, and he trembles very soon,
And his face is as a fungus of a leprous white and grey
Like plants in the high houses that are shuttered from the day
And death is in the phial and the end of noble work,
But Don John of Austria has fired upon the Turk.
Don John's hunting, and his hounds have bayed —
Booms away past Italy the rumor of his raid.
Gun upon gun, ha! ha !
Gun upon gun, hurrah!
Don John of Austria
Has loosed the cannonade.

The Pope was in his chapel before day or battle broke,
(*Don John of Austria is hidden in the smoke.*) .

The hidden room in man's house where God sits all the year,
The secret window whence the world looks small and very
dear.
He sees as in a mirror on the monstrous twilight sea
The crescent of his cruel ships whose name is mystery;
They fling great shadows foe-wards, making Cross and Castle
dark,
They veil the plumèd lions on the galleys of St. Mark;
And above the ships are palaces of brown, black-bearded
chiefs,
And below the ships are prisons where with multitudinous
griefs,
Christian captives sick and sunless, all a laboring race repines
Like a race in sunken cities, like a nation in the mines.
They are lost like slaves that swaet, and in the skies of
morning hung
The stairways of the tallest gods when tyranny was young.
They are countless, voiceless, hopeless as those fallen or
fleeing on
Before the high Kings' horses in the granite of Babylon.
And many a one grows witless in his quiet room in hell
Where a yellow face looks inward through the lattice of his
cell,
And he finds his God forgotten, and he seeks no more a sign —
(*But Don John of Austria has burst the battle line!*)
Don John pounding from the slaughter-painted poop.
Purpling all the ocean like a bloody pirate's sloop,
Scarlet running over on the silvers and the golds,
Breaking of the hatches up and bursting of the holds,
Thronging of the thousands up that labor under sea
White for bliss and blind for sun and stunned for liberty.
Vivat Hispania!

Domino Gloria!
Don John of Austria
Has set his people free!

Cervantes on his galley sets the sword back in the sheath
(*Don John of Austria rides homeward with a wreath.*)
And he sees across a weary land a straggling road in Spain,
Up which a lean and foolish knight forever rides in vain,
And he smiles, but not as Sultans smile, and settles back the
  blade. . .
(*But Don John of Austria rides home from the Crusade.*)

— *G. K. Chesterton*

EVELYN UNDERHILL

Evelyn Underhill was born in 1875. She is the author of a number of books on mysticism and is considered a leader in the world of religious thought.

Her first book of verse, *Immanence*, appeared in 1914 and was followed by *Theophanies* in 1917. "The Lady Poverty" quoted here is very well known and has been reprinted many times.

THE LADY POVERTY

I met her on the Umbrian hills:
   Her hair unbound, her feet unshod.
As one whom secret glory fills
   She walked, alone with God.

I met her in the city street:
   Oh, changed was her aspect then!
With heavy eyes and weary feet
   She walked alone, with men.

— Evelyn Underhill

Eva (Selina) Gore-Booth is a sister of Countess Markievicz **and** has written many plays. Her *Unseen Kings*, a book of verse, appeared in 1904 and her *Egyptian Pillars* in 1907.

"Harvest" is a quiet, restrained, thoughtful lyric of the immanence of God in His world. "The Little Waves of Breffny" tells the personal love of an individual human being for a particular place. The charming music of it is due in part to the choice of a winning rhythm, but even more, perhaps, to the adroit repetition of words, phrases, cadences, and their accompanying ideas.

THE LITTLE WAVES OF BREFFNY

The grand road from the mountain goes shining to the sea,
    And there is traffic in it, and many a horse and cart;
But the little roads of Cloonagh are dearer far to me,
    And the little roads of Cloonagh go rambling through my
      heart.

A great storm from the ocean goes shouting o'er the hill,
    And there is glory in it, and terror on the wind;
But the haunted air of twilight is very strange and still,
    And the little winds of twilight are dearer to my mind.

The great waves of the Atlantic sweep storming on their way,
    Shining green and silver with the hidden herring shoal;
But the little waves of Breffny have drenched my heart in
     spray,
    And the little waves of Breffny go stumbling through my
     soul.

                        — *Eva Gore-Booth*

HARVEST

Though the long seasons seem to separate
Sower and reaper or deeds dreamed and done,
Yet when a man reaches the Ivory Gate
Labour and life and seed and corn are one.

Because thou art the doer and the deed
Because thou art the thinker and the thought,
Because thou art the helper and the need,
And the cold doubt that brings all things to nought.

Therefore in every gracious form and shape
The world's dear open secret shalt thou find,
From the One Beauty there is no escape
Nor from the sunshine of the Eternal mind.

The patient labourer, with guesses dim,
Follows this wisdom to its secret goal.
He knows all deeds and dreams exist in him,
And all men's God in every human soul.

— *Eva Gore-Booth*

From *The Agate Lamp*

EDWARD THOMAS

Edward Thomas ("Edward Eastaway") was born in 1878. He was educated at St. Paul's School, London, and at Oxford University. He was early associated with G. K. Chesterton and Hilaire Belloc and gave his time to criticism and biography. He served in the great war and was killed in action.

A very small volume of his excellent poems was published in the United States in 1917 and dedicated to Robert Frost. Some of the poems included had been previously published in periodicals under the pen name, "Edward Eastaway." In England he had long been well known for his prose. In our country he is known almost exclusively by his poetry, and known only to the few who care for good poetry.

The two lyrics given here are by far the best known of his poems. An easy, natural rhythm, almost nonchalant in its grace, a whimsical turn of the thought, and a delightful use of the quaint names of places give these lyrics their hold upon the mind. This way of using the names of places in typically English. Walter de la Mare makes fine poetry out of names in his tale of the old woman who went

> blackberry picking
> Half way over from Weep to Wicking

and also in his tale of the three jolly farmers ("Berries" and "Off the Ground" in *Peacock Pie*). John Drinkwater has written a little lyric called "Mamble," which does nothing much but play with that odd name. Americans have never learned this knack of using names to give music, atmosphere, and flavor to poetry, although we have numbers of Indian names of places that could be beautifully used.

Both of these lyrics given below are delightfully natural and close to life and they are founded on a sane and ancient philosophy of poverty that puts modern materialism to shame.

IF I SHOULD EVER BY CHANCE

If I should ever by chance grow rich
I'll buy Codham, Cockridden, and Childerditch,
Roses, Pyrgo, and Lapwater,
And let them all to my elder daughter.
The rent I shall ask of her will be only
Each year's first violets, white and lonely,
The first primroses and orchises —
She must find them before I do, that is.
But if she finds a blossom on furze
Without rent they shall all for ever be hers,
Codham, Cockridden, and Childerditch,
Roses, Pyrgo, and Lapwater, —
I shall give them all to my elder daughter.

— *Edward Thomas*

WHAT SHALL I GIVE?

What shall I give my daughter the younger
More than will keep her from cold and hunger?
I shall not give her anything.
If she shared South Weald and Havering,
Their acres, the two brooks running between
Paine's Brook and Weald Brook,
With peewit, woodpecker, swan, and rook,
She would be no richer than the queen
Who once on a time sat in Havering Bower
Alone, with the shadows, pleasure and power.
She could do no more with Samarcand,
Or the mountains of a mountain land,
And its far white house above cottages,
Like Venus above the Pleiades.

Her small hands I would not cumber
With so many acres and their lumber,
But leave her Steep and her own world
And her spectacled self with hair uncurled,
Wanting a thousand little things
That time without contentment brings.

— *Edward Thomas*

THOMAS MACDONAGH

Thomas MacDonagh was born near Tipperary in 1878, the son of a schoolmaster. He was educated at the National University and soon became a contributor to *The Irish Review*. He was executed for taking part in the Irish Rebellion of 1916. With Padraic Pearse, Joseph Mary Plunkett, and Sir Roger Casement he is represented in the book of *Poems of the Irish Revolutionary Brotherhood* edited by Padraic Colum and Edward O'Brien.

His *Poetical Works* appeared in book form posthumously in 1917. The prayer for his little son which is quoted here shows a beautiful and impassioned idealism which we must respect for its own sake, no matter what our political opinions may be, no matter what we may think of the wisdom or folly of the Irish Revolution.

WISHES FOR MY SON

(Born on St. Cecilia's Day, 1912)

Now, my son, is life for you,
And I wish you joy of it, —
Joy of power in all you do,
Deeper passion, better wit
Than I had who had enough,
Quicker life and length thereof,
More of every gift but love.

Love I have beyond all men,
Love that now you share with me —
What have I to wish you then
But that you be good and free,
And that God to you may give
Grace in stronger days to live?

316

For I wish you more than I
Ever knew of glorious deed,
Though no rapture passed me by
That an eager heart could heed,
Though I followed heights and sought
Things the sequel never brougat:

Wild and perilous holy things
Flaming with a martyr's blood,
And the joy that laughs and sings
Where a foe must be withstood,
Joy of headlong happy chance
Leading on the battle dance.

But I found no enemy,
No man in a world of wrong,
That Christ's word of Charity
Did not render clean and strong —
Who was I to judge my kind,
Blindest groper of the blind?

God to you may give the sight
And the clear undoubting strength
Wars to knit for single right,
Freedom's war to knit at length,
And to win, through wrath and strife,
To the sequel of my life,

But for you, so small and young,
Born on Saint Cecilia's Day,
I in more harmonious song
Now for nearer joys should pray —

Simple joys: the natural growth
Of your childhood and your youth.
Courage, innocence, and truth:

Tnese for you, so small and young,
In your hand and heart and tongue.

— *Thomas MacDonagh*

HAROLD MONRO

Harold Monro was born at Brussels in 1879. In 1912 he founded the well-known Poetry Bookshop in London. It has become an important literary center. Mr. Monro is also a critic of considerable acumen.

His first volume of verse, *Children of Love*, was published in 1914, followed by *Strange Meetings* in 1917, and *Real Property* in 1922.

The poems quoted here are four of the "Week-end" group taken from *Strange Meetings*. They are chiefly remarkable for a certain homely quaintness of style. The bread "longs for butter." The "torpid stair" "will grumble at our feet." "Words become princes that were slaves before." Such phrasing makes veritable poetry out of plain things.

WEEK-END SONNETS

I

The train! The twelve o'clock for paradise.
　Hurry, or it will try to creep away.
Out in the country everyone is wise:
　We can be only wise on Saturday.
There you are waiting, little friendly house:
　Those are your chimney-stacks with you between,
Surrounded by old trees and strolling cows,
　Staring through all your windows at the green.
Your homely floor is creaking for our tread;
　The smiling tea-pot with contented spout
Thinks of the boiling water, and the bread
　Longs for the butter. All their hands are out
　　To greet us, and the gentle blankets seem
　　Purring and crooning: "Lie in us and dream."

II

The key will stammer, and the door reply,
   The hall wake, yawn, and smile; the torpid stair
Will grumble at our feet, the table cry:
   "Fetch my belongings for me; I am bare."
A clatter! Something in the attic falls.
   A ghost has lifted up his robes and fled.
The loitering shadows move along the walls;
   Then silence very slowly lifts his head.
The starling with impatient screech has flown
   The chimney, and is watching from the tree.
They thought us gone forever: mouse alone
   Stops in the middle of the floor to see.
     Now all you idle things resume your toil.
     Hearth, put your flames on. Sulky kettle, boil.

III

Contented evening; comfortable joys;
   The snoozing fire, and all the fields are still:
Tranquil delight, no purpose, and no noise —
   Unless the slow wind flowing round the hill.
"Murry" (the kettle) dozes; little mouse
   Is rambling prudently about the floor.
There's lovely conversation in this house:
   Words become princes that were slaves before.
What a sweet atmosphere for you and me
   The people that have been here left behind. . .
Oh, but I fear it may turn out to be
   Built of a dream, erected in the mind:
     So if we speak too loud we may awaken
     To find it vanished and ourselves mistaken.

VI

Morning! Wake up! Awaken! All the boughs
    Are rippling on the air across the green.
The youngest birds are singing to the house.
    Blood of the world! — and is the country clean?
Disturb the precinct.   Cool it with a shout.
    Sing as you trundle down to light the fire.
Turn the encumbering shadows tumbling out,
    And fill the chambers with a new desire.
Life is no good unless the morning brings
    White happiness and quick delight of day.
These half-inanimate domestic things
    Must all be useful, or must go away.
      Coffee, be fragrant.   Porridge in my plate,
      Increase the vigor to fulfil my fate.

— Harold Monro

WILFRID WILSON GIBSON

Wilfrid Wilson Gibson was born at Hexham, Northumberland, in 1880 and now lives in Gloucestershire. His life has been quiet, domestic, and uneventful.

He is the author of *Stonefolds* (1906), *Daily Bread* (1908), *Womenkind* (1909), *Fires* (1910-11), *Thoroughfares and Borderlands*, *Battle* (1914-15), and *Livelihood*. His *Collected Poems*, including all these, were published in 1917. Since then *Neighbors* has appeared in 1920.

It is difficult to select from Mr. Gibson's work any one or two poems that will be thoroughly characteristic. The best of them are rather long stories in dramatic form, and quite tragic. They tell how the poor must struggle for a living and what life brings them of suffering and want. They show the dignity and strength in the lives of plain, honest working people. "The Operation" is a tale of patient, heroic suffering which ought to be unnecessary. "The Orphans" is a bit of English humor which Americans can see and understand. "On Broadway" is a homesick lyric. "To the Memory of Rupert Brooke" is a picture of a last good-bye.

THE OPERATION

Persons:

WILLIAM LOWRY, *a printer.*
HESTER LOWRY, *his wife.*
LETTY LOWRY, *their daughter.*

Scene: A room in tenements, late at night. WILLIAM LOWRY *sits with his coat off, in an armchair, smoking, and reading a newspaper. The door opens, and* HESTER LOWRY *enters. Over her arm is a basket, laden with purchases, which she lays on the table with a sigh.*

WILLIAM. You're late to-night.
You should have let me come with you:
That basket's heavy, wife.

HESTER. 'Twas not the basket, William:
I was kept.

WILLIAM. What kept you, wife?
The shops would not be thronged, to-night.

HESTER. I finished with the shops, three hours ago.
I had to wait my turn.

WILLIAM. Your turn?
Who kept you waiting?

HESTER. The doctors, husband.

WILLIAM. Doctors, wife?

HESTER. I thought 'twas time to have the thing
away; And so I went to see.
The doctors shook their heads;
And said, next week, it might have been too late. . .

WILLIAM. Too late? What ails you, wife? I never
knew . . .

HESTER. They say it's cancer.
They were very kind;
And wanted me to stay, to-night,
And have it done, at once.
They'd hardly let me leave.
I said, I must come home to see you first.
They'll take me in to-morrow.

WILLIAM. To-morrow, wife! And I . . . I
never knew.
You must have guessed, before you went . . .

HESTER. Yes, lad; I knew: and 'twas no shock to me;
I've known so long.

WILLIAM. So long! . . . and never told me!

But, lass, the pain   .   .   .

HESTER.   Ay; it was bad to bear.
At first I scarce could keep from crying out;
But, as the years went by   .   .   .

WILLIAM.   The years!   You've had the pain for
     years?

HESTER.   Ay, off and on.
It's full eleven years, since first I felt it.

WILLIAM.   And, from the first, you knew   .   .   .

HESTER.   I knew.
My father died of it.

WILLIAM.   Eleven years!   And never breathed a
     word,
Nor murmured once, but patiently   .   .   .

HESTER.   I come of fisherfolk, who live on patience.
It's little use for any man
To be impatient with the sea.

WILLIAM.   And I   .   .   .   I never guessed.
I've seen you, day by day,
And slept, each night, beside you in the bed;
And yet, you never breathed a word   .   .   .

HESTER.   Nay, lad; I've kept the thing from you:
'Twould not have eased the pain to share it.
You slept the sounder, knowing nothing;
Though, there were times the gnawing was so bad,
I could have torn   .   .   .

WILLIAM.   And I slept on unknowing!
You never even wakened me.
And every little ache I've had,
I've made a pretty song about it!

HESTER.   You've made a song!
And what about the time your arm was caught   .   .   .

Was caught in the machine, and you were hanging . .
Were hanging by the flesh, a mortal hour!
  WILLIAM. Nay; Michael held me up upon his back.
  HESTER. But, all that time your arm was in the
    wheels;
And you . . . you never murmured, once, they say;
But, only laughed, and jested;
Although they had to take a chisel,
And cut each cog out separately,
Before the flesh was freed.
How you could bear the strain and jar,
And never once lose heart,
I cannot think; and your poor arm . . .
Your poor, poor arm, with all the sinews torn . . .
  WILLIAM. I've never really played the fiddle since:
I've got to make the notes, that used to come.
But you, wife, all these years . . .
And I slept on . . . .
  HESTER. 'Twould not have eased . . .
  WILLIAM. But, if I'd known.
You should have had the doctor at the first.
  HESTER. I knew you could not spare me then:
Those were not easy times!
You, laid off idle through your accident,
And Letty, but a baby:
And we had both enough to do,
To keep the home together.
I hoped, at least, to keep things going;
Till I should be past doing things.
The time has come . . .
But I . . . I've saved a bit:
And Letty's thirteen past,

And finished schooling,
And old enough to manage for you.
Is she in bed?

WILLIAM. She went an hour ago.
She wanted sorely to wait up for you;
But she was sleepy, so I wouldn't let her.

HESTER. Ay, she's been at it all day long;
And she's a handy lass,
And will do well enough for you,
Until . . . until . . .

WILLIAM. Does Letty know?

HESTER. Nay, she knows nothing, William;
And I'll not tell her now till morning.
I would not spoil her sleep.
Poor child, she little dreams!
But she's a plucky girl,
And I have taught her everything:
And she can cook, and scrub, and wash,
As well as any woman.
You'll scarcely miss me . . .

WILLIAM. Wife!

HESTER. I've seen to all your clothes,
And there are shirts and stockings
To last for many weeks,
To last until . . .
I mayn't be long away.

WILLIAM. O, wife, it's terrible . . . I cannot
think . . .
It seems so strange that all these years . . .

HESTER. You never saw my father.
He suffered long, poor fellow,
But never rightly knew that it was cancer,

Till very nigh the end.
It laid him low at last,
When he was far from home,
After the herring in the Western seas.
The doctor said he must return by train,
But he'd not leave his boat;
And so his mates set sail,
(The season just begun,
And catches heavier than they'd been for years)
And brought him home.
And, when the *Ella* neared the harbour,
He left his bunk, and took the tiller,
And brought her in himself.
Though, in his heart, he knew it was the last time,
Yet he'd a smile for us;
And when the boat was berthed,
He looked my mother bravely in the eyes,
And clasped her hand, and they went home together.
He never rose again:
The doctors could do nothing:
But he was brave and gay until the end;
And always smiled, and said it did not hurt,
Although his teeth were clenched,
And his strong fingers clutched the bedclothes tightly.

    WILLIAM.   And you're his daughter, wife!

    HESTER.   But I've cried out before I'm hurt too
      sorely.

Next week, the doctors said, it might have been   .   .   .
It's taken in the nick of time,
And I will soon be well again.
Folk go through such, and worse, each day:
It's naught to make a fuss about.

I've only one more night to bear the pain   .   .   .
And then   .   .   .
    WILLIAM.   Ay, wife, you'll soon be well again,
With such a heart in you.
And yet, if you had gone too long   .   .   .
You should have told me at the first,
And let us fend   .   .   .
    HESTER.   My father brought his boat in.

[*The inner door opens, and* LETTY *stands in the door-
    way, in her night-dress.*]

    LETTY.   Is mother not home yet?
Oh, there you are!
You stayed so long to-night,
I've been asleep and dreaming!
Oh, such a dreadful dream!
I dreamt that you   .   .   .
But you are safe and sound!
You are not ailing, mother?
    HESTER.   Lass, I'm as well as I have been for
        years.
But you'll catch cold:
You'd better get to bed again.
    LETTY.   But, I shall dream.
    HESTER.   Nay, you'll sleep sound, to-night.

[LETTY *kisses her father and mother good-night and
    goes back to the bedroom.*]

—*Wilfrid Wilson Gibson*

TO THE MEMORY OF RUPERT BROOKE

He's gone.
I do not understand.
I only know
That as he turned to go
And waved his hand
In his young eyes a sudden glory shone:
And I was dazzled by a sunset glow,
And he was gone.

— *Wilfrid Wilson Gibson*

ON BROADWAY

Daffodils dancing by moonlight in English meadows,
Moon-pale daffodils under the April moon —
Here in the throng and clangour and hustle of Broadway,
Broadway brawling and loud in the glare of the noon,
Comes to me now as a half-remembered tune
The silence and wonder of daffodils dancing by moonlight,
Dreamily dancing in dew-sprinkled moonshiny meadows,
Ghostly daffodils under a ghostly moon.

— *Wilfrid Wilson Gibson*

THE ORPHANS

At five o'clock one April morn
I met them making tracks,
Young Benjamin and Abel Horn,
With bundles on their backs.

Young Benjamin is seventy-five,
Young Abel, seventy-seven —
The oldest innocents alive
Beneath that April heaven.

I asked them why they trudged about
With crabby looks and sour —
"And does your mother know you're out
At this unearthly hour?"

They stopped: and scowling up at me
Each shook a grizzled head,
And swore; and then spat bitterly,
As with one voice they said:

"Homeless, about the country-side
We never thought to roam;
But mother, she has gone and died,
And broken up the home."

— Wilfrid Wilson Gibson

ALFRED NOYES

Alfred Noyes was born in Staffordshire, England, in 1880 and was educated at Oxford. He made poetry his profession at once. He married an American and in 1914 was appointed Professor of Modern English Literature at Princeton University. He has written numerous books of poetry and is most gifted as a maker of stirring ballads.

He is the author of *The Loom of Years* (1902), *The Flower of Old Japan* (1903), *Poems* (1904), *The Forest of Wild Thyme* (1905), *Forty Singing Seamen* (1907), *Drake* (1908), *The Enchanted Island and Other Poems* (1909), *Collected Poems* (1910), *Robin Hood* (1912), *The Elfin Artist,* (1920) and *Collected Poems* (1920-volume III.)

"The Highwayman" is justly famous as a tragic ballad, full of swift action, ringing music, and the indefinable magic of atmosphere that belongs to a long time ago.

THE HIGHWAYMAN

1

The wind was a torrent of darkness among the gusty trees,
The moon was a ghostly galleon tossed upon cloudy seas,
The road was a ribbon of moonlight over the purple moor,
And the highwayman came riding —
      Riding — riding —
The highwayman came riding, up to the old inn-door.

2

He'd a French cocked-hat on his forehead, a bunch of lace at
   his chin,
A coat of the claret velvet, and breeches of brown doe-skin;

They fitted with never a wrinkle: his boots were up to the
        thigh!
And he rode with a jewelled twinkle,
          His pistol butts a-twinkle,
His rapier hilt a-twinkle, under the jewelled sky.

3

Over the cobbles he clattered and clashed in the dark inn-
        yard,
And he tapped with his whip on the shutters, but all was
        locked and barred;
He whistled a tune to the window, and who should be waiting
        there
But the landlord's black-eyed daughter,
          Bess, the landlord's daughter,
Plaiting a dark red love-knot into her long black hair.

4

And dark in the dark old inn-yard a stable-wicket creaked
Where Tim, the ostler, listened; his face was white and
        peaked;
His eyes were hollows of madness, his hair like mouldy hay,
But he loved the landlord's daughter;
          The landlord's red-lipped daughter,
Dumb as a dog he listened, and he heard the robber say —

5

"One kiss, my bonny sweetheart, I'm after a prize tonight,
But I shall be back with the yellow gold before the morning
        light;

Yet if they press me sharply, and harry me through the day,
Then look for me by moonlight,
> Watch for me by moonlight,
I'll come to thee by moonlight, though hell should bar the
> way."

6

He rose upright in the stirrups; he scarce could reach her
> hand,
But she loosened her hair i' the casement! His face burnt
> like a brand
As the black cascade of perfume came tumbling over his
> breast;
And he kissed its waves in the moonlight,
> (Oh, sweet black waves in the moonlight,)
Then he tugged at his reins in the moonlight, and galloped
> away to the West.

PART TWO

1

He did not come in the dawning; he did not come at noon;
And out of the tawny sunset, before the rise o' the moon,
When the road was a gypsy's ribbon, looping the purple moor,
A red-coat troop came marching —
> Marching — marching —
King George's men came marching, up to the old inn-door.

2

They said no word to the landlord, they drank his ale instead,
But they gagged his daughter and bound her to the foot of
> her narrow bed;

Two of them knelt at her casement, with muskets at the side!

There was death at every window;

And Hell at one dark window;

For Bess could see, through her casement, the road that *he* would ride.

3

They had tied her up to attention, with many a sniggering jest;

They had bound a musket beside her, with the barrel beneath her breast!

"Now keep good watch!" and they kissed her.

She heard the dead man say —

Look for me by moonlight;

Watch for me by moonlight;

I'll come to thee by moonlight, though hell should bar the way!

4

She twisted her hands behind her; but all the knots held good!

She writhed her hands till her fingers were wet with sweat or blood!

They stretched and strained in the darkness, and the hours crawled by like years,

Till, now, on the stroke of midnight,

Cold, on the stroke of midnight,

The tip of one finger touched it! The trigger at least was hers!

5

The tip of one finger touched it; she strove no more for the
    rest!
Up, she stood to attention, with the barrel beneath her breast,
She would not risk their hearing: she would not strive again;
For the road lay bare in the moonlight;
            Blank and bare in the moonlight;
And the blood of her veins in the moonlight throbbed to her
    love's refrain.

6

Tlot-tlot; tlot-tlot! Had they heard it? The horse-hoofs
    ringing clear —
Tlot-tlot, tlot-tlot in the distance? Were they deaf that they
    did not hear?
Down the ribbon of moonlight, over the brow of the hill,
The highwayman came riding,
            Riding, riding!
The red-coats looked to their priming! She stood up straight
    and still!

7

Tlot-tlot, in the frosty silence! *Tlot-tlot* in the echoing night!
Nearer he came and nearer! Her face was like a light!
Her eyes grew wide for a moment; she drew one last deep
    breath,
Then her finger moved in the moonlight,
            Her musket shattered the moonlight,
Shattered her breast in the moonlight and warned him —
    with her death.

8

He turned; he spurred him Westward; he did not know who
    stood
Bowed with her head o'er the musket, drenched with her own
    red blood!
Not till the dawn he heard it, and slowly blanched to hear
How Bess, the landlord's daughter,
        The landlord's black-eyed daughter,
Had watched for her love in the moonlight, and died in the
    darkness there.

9

Back, he spurred like a madman, shrieking a curse to the
    sky,
With the white road smoking behind him, and his rapier
    brandished high!
Blood-red were his spurs i' the golden noon; wine-red was
    his velvet coat;
When they shot him down on the highway,
        Down like a dog on the highway,
And he lay in his blood on the highway, with the bunch of
    lace at his throat.

   .   .   .   .   .   .

And still of a winter's night, they say, when the wind is in the
    trees,
When the moon is a ghostly galleon tossed upon cloudy seas,
When the road is a ribbon of moonlight over the purple moor,
A highwayman comes riding —
        Riding — riding —
A highwayman comes riding, up to the old inn-door.

10

Over the cobbles he clatters and clangs in the dark inn-yard;
And he taps with his whip on the shutters, but all is locked and
*   barred;*
He whistles a tune to the window, and who should be waiting
*   there*
But the landlord's black-eyed daughter,
*   Bess, the landlord's daughter,*
***Plaiting** a dark red love-knot into her long black hair.*

—*Alfred Noyes*

PADRAIC COLUM

Padraic Colum was born in Longford, Ireland, in 1881. He **was educated** at local schools. He wrote for the Abbey Theater. He came to the United States before the war and has been living here since then. He has written admirable books for children, of which *The King of Ireland's Son*, a beautiful fairy tale, is surely one of the best.

Two volumes of his lyrics have been published in this country, *Wild Earth and Other Poems* (1907) and *Dramatic Poems* (1922). Mr. Colum's lyrics are strong and dignified, concerned with human nature at its best and with the homeliness of the earth subdued to meet the needs of man. They celebrate the simple and universal needs, loves, and tragedies. The two lyrics quoted here are quite characteristic.

AN OLD WOMAN OF THE ROADS

O, to have a little house!
To own the hearth and stool and all!
The heaped up sods upon the fire,
The pile of turf against the wall!

To have a clock with weights and chains
And pendulum swinging up and down!
A dresser filled with shining delph,
Speckled and white and blue and brown!

I could be busy all the day
Clearing and sweeping hearth and floor,
And fixing on their shelf again
My white and blue and speckled store!

I could be quiet there at night
Beside the fire and by myself,
Sure of a bed and loth to leave
The ticking clock and the shining delph!

Och! but I'm weary of mist and dark,
And roads where there's never a house nor bush,
And tired I am of bog and road,
And the crying wind and the lonesome hush!

And I am praying to God on high,
And I am praying Him night and day,
For a little house — a house of my own —
Out of the wind's and the rain's way.

— Padraic Colum

THE FAIR HILLS OF EIRÉ

Bear the love of my heart to my land far away,
And the fair hills of Eiré O,
And to all of Eivir's race that in her valleys stay.
And the fair hills of Eiré O.
That land of mine beloved, where the brown thrush's song
Fills hazel glen and ivied close the summer twilight long;
Oh, how woeful swells his music for the downfall of the Strong,
On the fair hills of Eiré O.

'Tis my lone soul's long sorrow that I must still be far
From the fair hills of Eiré O,
Nor watch a maiden coming as through the mist a star,
On the fair hills of Eiré O!
Oh, the honey in her tree-tops where her oakwoods darkly
  grow

And the freshness of her cresses where her clear well-waters
  flow,
And the lushness of her meadows where her soft-eyed cattle
  low,
On the fair hills of Eiré O.

— Padraic Colum

JOSEPH CAMPBELL

Joseph Campbell was born at Belfast, Ireland, in 1881. He is an illustrator by profession.

His books are *The Mountainy Singer* (1909) and *Irishry* (1913). Since the publication of *Irishry* his verse has been appearing more frequently in American magazines. It has strongly marked individuality. "The Old Woman" presents a person and a picture of a person with perfect felicity. Every line fits into the picture which the poet has seen, felt, and presented. The symbolism is true. The melody lives. Not a word embarrasses the meaning. The poem is marvelously concise.

THE OLD WOMAN

As a white candle
   In a holy place,
So is the beauty
   Of an agèd face.

As the spent radiance
   Of the winter sun,
So is a woman
   With her travail done,

Her brood gone from her,
   And her thoughts as still
As the waters
   Under a ruined mill.

                    — Joseph Campbell

JOHN DRINKWATER

John Drinkwater was born in 1882. He spent twelve years in the insurance business and then became co-founder of the Pilgrim Players, an organization which developed into the Birmingham Repertory Theatre Company, of which he is now manager. He is well known in this country because of his play, *Abraham Lincoln*, which made a great success on the American stage.

He is the author of *Poems* (1903), *Poems* (1908-14), *Swords and Ploughshares* (1915), *The Storm* (1915), *Olton Pools* (1916), and *Poems* (1908-1919). His lyrics are quiet and restrained, somewhat deficient in the passion and abandon which gives vitality to the work of greater poets, but worth reading for their reflective charm.

"Holiness" is an exceedingly wise little poem, for it teaches what some of our Puritan ancestors needed to learn, and what the people who live on "Main Street" must yet discover and demonstrate, that beauty is holy and creates a gaiety that belongs rightly to "a spiritual land." "The Feckenham Men" is created out of a similar philosophy. The Feckenham men believed that a deed done simply for beauty's sake has value, even if it seems to be foolish in the eyes of the worldly and practical people. Poets, from the beginning of time, have been telling the world this truth in a thousand varying ways. The world still needs to be reminded. So Mr. Drinkwater takes an extreme and fanciful example and makes a brief story of it in this poem. The Feckenham men destroy a field of beans in order to have the pleasure of seeing a rick of blossoms. A "fiery-hearted thing to do" indeed! Mr. Drinkwater does not want us to do the same thing with our bean fields. But he wants us to be as fiery-hearted, so that we can recognize other and higher values than the purely practical ones even in our fields. But like all good poems, these lyrics should be enjoyed first of all and analyzed afterwards. We have no right to take poems seriously until we have taken them happily.

HOLINESS

If all the carts were painted gay,
    And all the streets swept clean,
And all the children came to play
    By hollyhocks, with green
    Grasses to grow between,

If all the houses looked as though
    Some heart were in their stones,
If all the people that we know
    Were dressed in scarlet gowns,
    With feathers in their crowns,

I think this gaiety would make
    A spiritual land.
I think that holiness would take
    This laughter by the hand,
    Till both should understand.

                                    — *John Drinkwater*

THE FECKENHAM MEN

The jolly men at Feckenham
Don't count their goods as common men,
Their heads are full of silly dreams
From half-past ten to half-past ten,
They'll tell you why the stars are bright,
And some sheep black and some sheep white.

The jolly men at Feckenham
Draw wages of the sun and rain,
And count as good as golden coin

The blossoms on the window-pane,
And Lord! they love a sinewy tale
Told over pots of foaming ale.

Now here's a tale of Feckenham
Told to me by a Feckenham man,
Who, being only eighty years,
Ran always when the red fox ran,
And looked upon the earth with eyes
As quiet as unclouded skies.

These jolly men of Feckenham
One day when summer strode in power
Went down, it seems, among their lands
And saw their bean fields all in flower —
"Wheat-ricks," they said, "be good to see;
What would a rick of blossoms be?"

So straight they brought the sickles out
And worked all day till day was done,
And builded them a good square rick
Of scented bloom beneath the sun.
And was not this I tell to you
A fiery-hearted thing to do?

— *John Drinkwater*

JAMES STEPHENS

James Stephens was born in Ireland in 1882. He was discovered by George William Russell ("A. E.") while he was working as a typist for a Dublin lawyer. He has written admirable prose and exquisite poetry. His *Irish Fairy Tales* are wild, delightful stories.

His books of verse are *The Hill of Vision* (1912), *Songs from the Clay* (1914), and *Reincarnations* (1917).

If "In the Poppy Field" has any "message" or moral, it is in the second stanza that it can be found.

> He said the devil had no hand
> In spreading flowers tall and fair
> Through corn and rye and meadow land,
>
> *   *   *
>
> The devil has not any flower,
> But only money in his power.

In other words, beauty is of God, like truth and goodness. This lyric uses an ancient literary device to avoid direct preaching. It puts the sermon in the mouth of "mad" Patsy, because, like the Court Fool, he can say many things that nobody else would be permitted to say. The poet cannot preach as gracefully himself, in his own proper person.

IN THE POPPY FIELD

> Mad Patsy said, he said to me,
> That every morning he could see
> An angel walking on the sky;
> Across the sunny skies of morn
> He threw great handfuls far and nigh
> Of poppy seed among the corn;
> And then, he said, the angels run
> To see the poppies in the sun.

A poppy is a devil weed,
I said to him — he disagreed;
He said the devil had no hand
In spreading flowers tall and fair
Through corn and rye and meadow land,
By garth and barrow everywhere:
The devil has not any flower,
But only money in his power.

And then he stretched out in the sun
And rolled upon his back for fun:
He kicked his legs and roared for joy
Because the sun was shining down,
He said he was a little boy
And would not work for any clown:
He ran and laughed behind a bee,
And danced for very ecstasy.

— *James Stephens*

JAMES ELROY FLECKER

James Elroy Flecker was born in 1884. He was educated at Oxford and by travel in France and Italy. He was in the British Consular Service in Constantinople, Smyrna, and Beirut. He died of consumption, at Davos Platz in 1915.

His *Ninety-six Poems* were published in 1910, *Forty-two Poems* in 1911, *The Golden Journey to Samarkand* in 1913 and 1915, and his *Collected Poems* (introduced by J. C. Squire) in 1916.

"The Golden Journey to Samarkand" appears to be simply a picture of a caravan "in olden times," leaving Bagdad to go to Samarkand. But more and more as we read line after line of the poem we are made to feel that Samarkand is also a name for the goal that all men are seeking and that the golden journey is the hurried journey that all men try to make toward their dreams and desires.

THE GOLDEN JOURNEY TO SAMARKAND

At the Gate of the Sun, Bagdad, in olden time.

THE MERCHANTS (*together*)

Away, for we are ready to a man!
    Our camels sniff the evening and are glad.
Lead on, O master of the Caravan:
    Lead on the Merchant-Princes of Bagdad.

THE CHIEF DRAPER

Have we not Indian carpets dark as wine,
    Turbans and sashes, gowns and bows and veils,
And broideries of intricate design,
    And printed hangings in enormous bales?

THE CHIEF GROCER

We have rose-candy, we have spikenard,
  Mastic and terebinth and oil and spice,
And such sweet jams meticulously jarred
  As God's own Prophet eats in Paradise.

THE PRINCIPAL JEWS

And we have manuscripts in peacock styles
  By Ali of Damascus; we have swords
Engraved with storks and apes and crocodiles,
  And heavy beaten necklaces, for Lords.

THE MASTER OF THE CARAVAN

But you are nothing but a lot of Jews.

THE PRINCIPAL JEWS

Sir, even dogs have daylight, and we pay.

THE MASTER OF THE CARAVAN

But who are ye in rags and rotten shoes,
  You dirty-bearded, blocking up the way?

THE PILGRIMS

We are the Pilgrims, master; we shall go
  Always a little further: it may be
Beyond that last blue mountain barred with snow,
  Across that angry or that glimmering sea,

White on a throne or guarded in a cave
  There lives a prophet who can understand
Why men were born, but surely we are brave,
  Who make the golden journey to Samarkand.

THE CHIEF MERCHANT

We gnaw the nail of hurry.   Master, away!

ONE OF THE WOMEN

O turn your eyes to where your children stand.
Is not Bagdad the beautiful?   O stay!

THE MERCHANTS (*in chorus*)

We take the Golden Road to Samarkand.

AN OLD MAN

Have you not girls and garlands in your homes,
    Eunuchs and Syrian boys at your command?
Seek not excess: God hateth him who roams!

THE MERCHANTS (*in chorus*)

We make the golden journey to Samarkand.

A PILGRIM WITH A BEAUTIFUL VOICE

Sweet to ride forth at evening from the wells
    When shadows pass gigantic on the sand,
And softly through the silence beat the bells
    Along the golden road to Samarkand.

A MERCHANT

We travel not for trafficking alone:
    By hotter winds our fiery hearts are fanned:
For lust of knowing what should not be known
    We make the golden journey to Samarkand.

THE MASTER OF THE CARAVAN

Open the gate, O watchman of the night!

THE WATCHMAN

Ho, travellers, I open.   For what land
Leave you the dim-moon city of delight?

THE MERCHANTS (*with a shout*)

We make the golden journey to Samarkand.
    (*The Caravan passes through the gate.*)

THE WATCHMAN (*consoling the women*)

What would ye, ladies?   It was ever thus.
Men are unwise and curiously planned.

A WOMAN

They have their dreams, and do not think of us.

VOICES OF THE CARAVAN (*in the distance, singing*)

We make the golden journey to Samarkand.

— *James Elroy Flecker*

SIEGFRIED SASSOON

Siegfried (Loraine) Sassoon was born in 1886 and educated at Marlborough College and at Cambridge. He won the Military Cross for service in France and Palestine, but since the end of the war has been writing against the iniquity of warfare and urging mankind to work for peace.

His best known books are *The Old Huntsman* (1917), *Counter-attack* (1918), and *Picture-show* (1920). Many of the poems in them are bitter and ironical, but quite truthful and sincere pictures of what war does to men. "A Mystic as a Soldier" is a subjective lyric, an outcry for the loveliness of life which war despoils. "Everyone Sang" is a lyrical expression of the great thankfulness that came with the Armistice.

A MYSTIC AS SOLDIER

I lived my days apart,
Dreaming fair songs for God,
By the glory in my heart
Covered and crowned and shod.

Now God is in the strife,
And I must seek Him there,
Where death outnumbers life,
And fury smites the air.

I walk the secret way
With anger in my brain.
O music through my clay,
When will you sound again?

— *Siegfried Sassoon*

EVERYONE SANG

Everyone suddenly burst out singing;
And I was filled with such delight
As prisoned birds must find in freedom,
Winging wildly across the white
Orchards and dark-green fields; on — on — and out of sight.

Everyone's voice was suddenly lifted;
And beauty came like the setting sun:
My heart was shaken with tears; and horror
Drifted away . . . O, but Everyone
Was a bird; and the song was wordless; the singing will never
    be done.

— *Siegfried Sassoon*

F. S. FLINT

F. S. Flint was born and lives in London. He is an Imagist (for a discussion of Imagism see Introduction) and a clever radical critic.

He is the author of *In the Net of the Stars* (1909), *Cadences* (1915), and *Otherworld* (1920). His themes are somewhat closer to common humanity than the themes of the other Imagists and many of his poems are about London. This nearness of common humanity is easily felt in his "Prayer."

PRAYER

As I walk through the streets.
I think of the things
That are given to my friends:
Myths of old Greece and Egypt,
Greek flowers, Greek thoughts,
And all that incandescence,
All that grace,
Which I refuse.

If even the orchards of England,
Its garden and its woods,
Its fields and its hills,
Its rivers and its seas,
Were mine;
But they are not.

But these are nothing.
Give me the flame, O Gods,
To light these people with,

These pavements, this motor traffic,
These houses, this medley.

Give me the vision,
And they may live.

— *F. S. Flint*

RUPERT BROOKE

Rupert Brooke was born at Rugby, England, in 1887, and educated at Rugby School, where his father was a master, and at King's College, Cambridge. In 1913 he was elected a Fellow of King's College, and travelled for a year in America, Samoa, and Tahiti.

In September, 1914, he enlisted in the navy for the Great War.

He died of blood poisoning on board a hospital ship at Lemnos in 1915.

His first volume of poems was published in 1911. A second, called *1914 and Other Poems*, appeared in 1915, shortly after his death. All of Rupert Brooke's work had a native and undeniable distinction of manner. He died before he had settled on any clearly defined philosophy of life. He had not had time, perhaps, to make a synthesis of the thoughts that grew out of his multiform and varicolored experience. His poems must be regarded as reflections of that experience, and if they contradict each other, we must realize the naturalness of the contradiction. We ourselves do not have the same experiences every day and year, nor are we possessed always of the same thoughts and emotions. The reflections of the light that was in Rupert Brooke's personality give us poems full of color and vitality, for which we should be thankful.

The two sonnets quoted here are from the group called *1914*. They are full of the unselfish ardor and exaltation with which young men entered the great war in 1914. In Rupert Brooke's war poetry we find none of the bitterness of disillusionment that marks the later poetry of the war, the poetry of the men who, like Siegfried Sassoon, lived long enough to "see it through."

THE SOLDIER

If I should die, think only this of me:
That there's some corner of a foreign field

That is forever England. There shall be
In that rich earth a richer dust concealed;
A dust whom England bore, shaped, made aware,
Gave, once, her flowers to love, her ways to roam;
A body of England's, breathing English air,
Washed by the rivers, blest by suns of home.
And think, this heart, all evil shed away,
A pulse in the eternal mind, no less
Gives somewhere back the thoughts by England given;
Her sights and sounds; dreams happy as her day;
And laughter, learnt of friends; and gentleness,
In hearts at peace, under an English heaven.

— *Rupert Brooke*

II — THE DEAD

These hearts were woven of human joys and cares,
  Washed marvellously with sorrow, swift to mirth.
The years had given them kindness. Dawn was theirs,
  And sunset, and the colors of the earth.
These had seen movement, and heard music; known
  Slumber and waking; loved; gone proudly friended;
Felt the quick stir of wonder; sat alone;
  Touched flowers and furs and cheeks. All this is ended.

There are waters blown by changing winds to laughter
And lit by the rich skies, all day. And after,
  Frost, with a gesture, stays the waves that dance
And wandering loveliness. He leaves a white
  Unbroken glory, a gathered radiance,
A width, a shining peace, under the night.

— *Rupert Brooke*

FRANCIS LEDWIDGE

Francis Ledwidge was born in Ireland in 1891. He was educated by life and labor, working, even in his boyhood, as a miner, a grocer's clerk, a farmer's boy. In 1912 he sent a copy book full of his verse to Lord Dunsany who, be it said in his honor, recognized the young man's talent and became his friend and adviser. Francis Ledwidge went into the Great War and was killed in Flanders in 1917.

His books are *Songs of the Fields* (1914), *Songs of Peace* (1916), *Last Songs* (1917), and *Complete Poems* (1920). Nobody now writing of nature has observed more carefully or recorded more accurately the minute events of life and death in the open world. The poems offered here come from the heart of a peasant, but also from the genius of a poet.

JUNE

Broom out the floor now, lay the fender by,
And plant this bee-sucked bough of woodbine there,
And let the window down. The butterfly
Floats in upon the sunbeam, and the fair
Tanned face of June, the nomad gipsy, laughs
Above her widespread wares, the while she tells
The farmers' fortunes in the fields, and quaffs
The water from the spider-peopled wells.

The hedges are all drowned in green grass seas,
And bobbing poppies flare like Elmo's light,
While siren-like the pollen-stainèd bees
Drone in the clover depths. And up the height
The cuckoo's voice is hoarse and broke with joy.

And on the lowland crops the crows make raid,
Nor fear the clappers of the farmer's boy
Who sleeps, like drunken Noah, in the shade.

And loop this red rose in that hazel ring
That snares your little ear, for June is short
And we must joy in it and dance and sing.
And from her bounty draw her rosy worth.
Ay, soon the swallows will be flying south,
The wind wheel north to gather in the snow,
Even the roses spilt on youth's red mouth
Will soon blow down the road all roses go.

— *Francis Ledwidge*

DESIRE IN SPRING

I love the cradle songs the mothers sing
In lonely places when the twilight drops,
The slow endearing melodies that bring
Sleep to the weeping lids; and, when she stops,
I love the roadside birds upon the tops
Of dusty hedges in a world of Spring.

And when the sunny rain drips from the edge
Of midday wind, and meadows lean one way,
And a long whisper passes thro' the sedge,
Beside the broken water let me stay,
While these old airs upon my memory play,
And silent changes color.up the hedge.

— *Francis Ledwidge*

RICHARD ALDINGTON

Richard Aldington was born in 1892 and was educated at London University. He is Assistant Editor of *The Egoist* and one of the leaders of the group of Imagist poets (for the Imagists see Introduction). He translates classical poetry admirably.

His books are *Images Old and New* (1915), *War and Love* (1915-18) (1919), *Images of War* (1919), and *Images of Desire* (1920). The lyric quoted here is not so typical of Mr. Aldington's work as others that might have been chosen, but is is a favorite everywhere with the reading public, probably because of the Elizabethan atmosphere which clings to it as if created in the manner of long ago.

AFTER TWO YEARS

She is all so slight
And tender and white
  As a May morning.
She walks without hood
At dusk.   It is good
  To hear her sing.

It is God's will
That I shall love her still
  As He loves Mary.
And night and day
I will go forth to pray
  That she love me.

She is as gold
Lovely, and far more cold.

Do thou pray with me,
For if I win grace
To kiss twice her face
God has done well to me.

— *Richard Aldington*

IRENE RUTHERFORD McLEOD

Irene Rutherford McLeod (Mrs. A. de Selincourt) is one of the younger English poets.

Her books are *Songs to Save a Soul* (1915), *Swords for Life* (1916), and *Before Dawn* (1918). The Song from "April" is not a lyric of revolt like many of her others, but a gay, fresh, spontaneous, and very young-hearted song of nature.

SONG FROM "APRIL"

I know
　　Where the wind flowers blow!
I know,
　　I have been
Where the wild honey bees
　　Gather honey for their queen!

I would be
　　A wild flower,
Blue sky over me,
　　For an hour . . . an hour!
So the wild bees
　　Should seek and discover me,
And kiss me . . . kiss me . . . kiss me!
　　Not one of the dusky dears should miss me!

I know
　　Where the wind flowers blow!
I know,
　　I have been
Where the little rabbits run
In the warm, yellow sun!

Oh, to be a wild flower
For an hour . . . an hour . . .
   In the heather!
A bright flower, a wild flower,
   Blown by the weather!

I know,
   I have been
Where the wild honey bees
   Gather Honey for their queen!

—Irene Rutherford McLeod

MOIRA O'NEILL

Moira O'Neill (Mrs. Skinner) lives in County Wexford, Ireland. Her *Songs from the Glens of Antrim* were first published on the other side of the Atlantic in 1900, and reissued with *More Songs of The Glens of Antrim* in the United States in 1922. The poems are simple, spontaneous, and exquisitely musical.

THE BOY FROM BALLYTEARIM

He was born in Ballytearim, where there's little work to do,
An' the longer he was livin' there the poorer still he grew;
Says he till all belongin' him, "Now happy may ye be!
But I'm off to find me fortune," sure he says, says he.

"All the gold in Ballytearim is what's stickin' to the whin;
All the crows in Ballytearim has a way o' gettin' thin."
So the people did be praisin' him the year he wint away, —
"Troth, I'll hould ye can do it," sure they says, says they.

Och, the boy ud still be thinkin' long, an' he across the foam,
An' the two ould hearts be thinkin' long that waited for him
    home:
But a girl that sat her lone an' whiles, her head upon her knee,
Would be sighin' low for sorra, not a word says she.

He won home to Ballytearim, an' the two were livin' yet,
When he heard where she was lyin' now the eyes of him were
    wet;
"Faith, here's me two fists full o' gold, an' little good to me
When I'll never meet an' kiss her," sure he says, says he.

363

Then the boy from Ballytearim set his face another road,
An' whatever luck has followed him was never rightly
knowed:
But still it's truth I'm tellin' ye — or may I never sin! —
All the gold in Ballytearim is what's stickin' to the whin.

— *Moira O'Neill*

GRACE FOR LIGHT

When we were little childer we had a quare wee house,
Away up in the heather by the head o' Brabla' Burn;
The hares we'd see them scootin', an' we'd hear the crowin'
grouse,
An' when we'd all be in at night ye'd not get room to turn.

The youngest two She'd put to bed, their faces to the wall,
An' the lave of us could sit aroun', just anywhere we might;
Herself 'ud take the rush dip an' light it for us all,
An' "*God be thanked!*" she would say, — "*now we have a
light.*"

Then we be to quet the laughin' an' pushin' on the floor,
An' think on One who called us to come and be forgiven;
Himself 'ud put his pipe down, an' say the good word more,
"*May the Lamb o' God lead us all to the Light o' Heaven!*"

There' a wheen things that used to be an' now has had their
day,
The nine Glens of Antrim can show ye many a sight;
But not the quare wee house where we lived up Brabla' way,
Nor a child in all the nine Glens that knows the grace for
light.

— *Moira O'Neill*